FRACTURED MILITANCY

D1248388

FRACTURED MILITANCY

Precarious Resistance in South Africa after Racial Inclusion

Marcel Paret

ILR PRESS

AN IMPRINT OF CORNELL UNIVERSITY PRESS   ITHACA AND LONDON

Copyright © 2022 by Cornell University

All rights reserved. Except for brief quotations in a review, this book, or parts thereof, must not be reproduced in any form without permission in writing from the publisher. For information, address Cornell University Press, Sage House, 512 East State Street, Ithaca, New York 14850. Visit our website at cornellpress.cornell.edu.

First published 2022 by Cornell University Press

Library of Congress Cataloging-in-Publication Data

Names: Paret, Marcel, author.
Title: Fractured militancy : precarious resistance in South Africa after racial inclusion / Marcel Paret.
Description: Ithaca [New York] : ILR Press, an imprint of Cornell University Press, 2022. | Includes bibliographical references and index.
Identifiers: LCCN 2021039535 (print) | LCCN 2021039536 (ebook) | ISBN 9781501761782 (hardcover) | ISBN 9781501761799 (paperback) | ISBN 9781501761812 (pdf) | ISBN 9781501761805 (epub)
Subjects: LCSH: Political culture—South Africa. | Post-apartheid era—South Africa. | Blacks—Political activity—South Africa. | Social classes—Economic aspects—South Africa. | Blacks—South Africa—Social conditions— 20th century. | Blacks—South Africa—Social conditions—21st century.
Classification: LCC JQ1981 .P37 2022 (print) | LCC JQ1981 (ebook) | DDC 306.20968—dc23
LC record available at https://lccn.loc.gov/2021039535
LC ebook record available at https://lccn.loc.gov/2021039536

For Jessie
For Dan and Vic
For revolutionaries everywhere

Contents

List of Figures and Tables   ix
Preface   xi
Acknowledgments   xvii

Introduction   1

Part 1 **MOBILIZATION**

    1. National Liberation   27

    2. Betrayal   49

Part 2 **FRAGMENTATION**

    3. Community   71

    4. Nationalism   93

    5. Class Politics   112

Conclusion   138

Methodological Appendix   151
Notes   161
Index   197

Figures

1. Local protests in South Africa, 2005–2020   7
2. Official and expanded unemployment rate, South Africa, 2000–2020   15
3. Map of the four case study areas and the Johannesburg, Ekurheleni, and West Rand municipalities   23
4. ANC support in national government elections, by municipality, 1994–2019   76
5. ANC electoral performance in the four case study areas, 2004–2019   116
6. EFF electoral performance in the four case study areas, 2014–2019   117

Tables

1. Municipal-level background characteristics   24
2. Percentage of Black residents indicating discontent, overall and shack dwellers, South Africa, 2015   53
3. Politics of local community organizing   114
4. Interview summary   153

Preface

Black liberation implies a world where Black people can live in peace, without the constant threat of the social, economic, and political woes of a society that places almost no value on the vast majority of Black lives.

—Keeanga-Yamahtta Taylor, *#BlackLivesMatter to Black Liberation*

So you've come to see our horrible lives. This horrible place. This dirty place. It's a pigsty.

—Passerby in Motsoaledi informal shack settlement, Soweto, Johannesburg, South Africa, 2013

South Africa is a hotbed of protest. In April 2013, residents of the Elias Motsoaledi informal shack settlement—situated in the heart of Soweto, a previous epicenter of antiapartheid resistance—took to the streets. They demanded the provision of a formal housing development, which government officials had promised but failed to deliver. Later that year, residents of Bekkersdal, a township on the West Rand, followed with their own protests. Here the upsurge was a response to various grievances, including high grave tariffs, poor sewer infrastructure, and infrequent waste collection. The following April, residents of Tsakane Extension 10 (Tsakane10)—an informal shack settlement located on the East Rand—protested as well. They wanted the government to develop the area, and especially to relieve severe overcrowding. Three months later, back in the south of Johannesburg not far from Motsoaledi, residents of the Thembelihle informal shack settlement barricaded roads after the state removed their illegal electricity connections, which they relied on to cook, watch television, and light their shacks.

All four episodes took place along the historic Witwatersrand, a fifty-six-kilometer rock scarp where prospectors discovered gold in the late nineteenth century. The gold mining industry laid the foundation for what eventually became a massive metropolitan area of more than eight million residents, including the city of Johannesburg.[1] Stemming from the colonial and apartheid legacy, extreme and racialized inequality define the area. It is marked by a contrast between rapidly diversifying affluent neighborhoods on the one hand and almost exclusively Black poor neighborhoods on the other.[2] Each of the episodes described above revolved around slightly different specific grievances, but they shared one fundamental similarity: they all emanated from predominantly Black urban residential areas ravaged by poverty and unemployment.

Far from aberrations, the protests reflected a much broader surge of popular resistance throughout South Africa. Local protests accelerated dramatically in the wake of the 2008–2009 global economic recession. Media outlets reported an average of close to one local protest per day, and police incident reports suggest that the true numbers were much higher.[3] The dramatic increase in South African protest resembled the rise in protest globally between 2009 and 2014. Following the Arab Spring, which included revolutions in Tunisia and Egypt and uprisings throughout the Middle East and North Africa, the global protest wave spawned antiausterity protests in Greece, Spain, and Portugal; the Occupy movement in the United States; and popular revolts in Ukraine, Brazil, and Turkey. Some scholars likened the global protest wave to previous surges in 1848, 1905, and 1968.[4] In 2011, *Time* magazine declared "The Protester" its Person of the Year.

There were important parallels between South Africa's protests and those taking place elsewhere.[5] Unemployment and economic insecurity loomed large, as did frustration with government institutions that protected elites at the expense of ordinary people. Further, in South Africa as elsewhere, traditional organizational vehicles, such as trade unions and political parties, often played only peripheral roles. Beyond these similarities, however, a comparison is more of a stretch. One clear difference was their class basis. Scholars often traced the global protest wave to the declining fortunes and frustrations of middle classes and educated youth. Conversely, in South Africa the protesters were more economically insecure. They often scraped by through survivalist activities, small government cash transfers, and sharing through kinship networks. In South Africa, as well, the historical legacy of apartheid and national liberation shaped protests in a way that did not have a clear parallel in the iconic examples of the new global protests.[6]

Protests by Black residents in Ferguson and Baltimore, which shook the United States in 2014–2015, represented a closer parallel to South Africa's local protests. Police killings of Black men—Michael Brown in Ferguson, Freddie Gray in Baltimore—provided the immediate triggers for resistance. The killings activated long-standing resentment, frustration, and anger. Like local protests in South Africa, the Ferguson and Baltimore protests emanated from Black residential areas marked by concentrated poverty and disproportionate levels of unemployment. The Ferguson and Baltimore protests also reflected a parallel history of racial inclusion, marked by the abolition of legalized and state-sanctioned racial exclusion. The shared images and memes that circulated through the networks of Egyptian revolutionaries, Spanish *indignados*, and American Occupy protesters hardly penetrated the townships and informal

shack settlements surrounding Johannesburg. Neither were they major reference points in Ferguson and Baltimore. What mattered more in Johannesburg,
Ferguson, and Baltimore was the failure of racial inclusion to deliver liberation.

Scholars have long emphasized parallels between the United States and South
Africa with respect to racial domination and resistance.[7] In both places, the state
implemented explicit and overt systems of legalized racial exclusion in the twentieth century, which in turn spawned vibrant Black movements for racial inclusion. In the United States, the civil rights movement challenged the legalized
racism of Jim Crow, while in South Africa popular struggles challenged the racist apartheid state. The civil rights and antiapartheid movements were, of
course, very different, as were their targets and their eventual consequences. In
South Africa, where Black residents represent approximately 80 percent of the
total population, racial inclusion led to a major racial transformation of the
state. The predominantly Black African National Congress (ANC) assumed
power in 1994 and remains in power today. Conversely, Black residents in the
United States, who only account for about 13 percent of the total population,
never achieved the same measure of political power. Despite these contrasts,
however, the parallels are instructive.

During the civil rights movement, Martin Luther King famously dreamed of
liberation from racial oppression in his 1963 "I Have a Dream" speech in Washington, DC. Half a century later, in places such as Ferguson and Baltimore, the
daily realities of unemployment, economic insecurity, police surveillance, and
mass incarceration demonstrated the gap between the ideal of liberation and the
realities of everyday life. As Keeanga-Yamahtta Taylor puts it, "The young people
of Ferguson had great reverence and respect for the memory of the civil rights
movement, but the reality is that its legacy meant little in their everyday lives."[8] In
his classic poem "Harlem," published in 1951, Langston Hughes famously posed
the question: "What happens to the dream deferred?" In Ferguson and Baltimore,
the deferred dream of liberation exploded in protest, as Hughes prophetically anticipates: "Maybe it just sags like a heavy load? *Or does it explode?*"[9]

In South Africa, the transition from apartheid to democracy brought a new
constitution that abolished legalized racism and treated Black residents as full
citizens with equal rights. On top of these legal changes, the ANC's promise to
provide a "better life for all" encapsulated the dream of Black liberation. As inequality and economic insecurity deepened, however, the better life proved
elusive for many Black residents. With apartheid-era restrictions on movement lifted, the Black poor increasingly concentrated in peripheral urban areas
where unemployment, poverty, informal housing, and limited access to water
and electricity marked everyday life. For these residents, racial inclusion had severe limits. In the South African case, deferred liberation proved even more

explosive. Widespread local protests became a staple of the postapartheid landscape, and they show little sign of disappearing. The struggle for liberation continues, just as it did in Ferguson and Baltimore.

A further parallel revolves around the role of previous movement heroes. In the Ferguson protests, and later in the Black Lives Matter (BLM) movement that they helped to spawn, young Black activists sometimes clashed with such established Black American leaders as Al Sharpton, Jesse Jackson, and representatives of the Congressional Black Caucus. Some BLM activists felt that the older generation had sold them out and had little understanding of their everyday struggles. This dynamic loomed even larger in South Africa, where former heroes of the antiapartheid movement led the government. A deep sense of betrayal permeated the impoverished Black townships and informal settlements. Many resented that politicians appeared to pursue their own narrow interests, while the Black poor continued to await the promised better life. In South Africa, feelings of betrayal and resentment underpinned the consistent surge of local protests.

Police surveillance and mass incarceration did not define life in South Africa's impoverished Black urban areas in the same way that they did in the United States. Issues of police brutality certainly arose in South Africa's local protests, most often in response to police repression, but they were less central. Whereas the protests in Ferguson and Baltimore emerged through opposition to state violence, local protests in South Africa called on the state to provide resources, such as housing and electricity—what residents called "service delivery." Race represented another crucial difference. Protests in Ferguson and Baltimore thrust racial disparity to the forefront. They highlighted how law enforcement disproportionately targeted and attacked Black residents and communities. Race did not figure as prominently in South Africa's local protests, even if it always lurked just beneath the surface. Protesters referenced class identities as often as racial ones. References to "the poor" were prominent.[10] To be sure, racial inequality remains extreme in democratic South Africa. The urban poor are well aware that poverty remains concentrated among Black residents. In a situation, however, where Black politicians dominate the state, and where the Black middle class outnumbers the white middle class, race does not illuminate the challenge at hand in quite the same way.

The differences between the struggles for Black liberation in the two places came into focus in 2020, as the coronavirus crisis swept across the globe. In the United States, the police killing of George Floyd in Minneapolis reignited the BLM movement. Following the local uprising in Minneapolis, in which protesters burned down a police station, protests quickly spread across the country. Marking possibly the greatest mobilization in US history to date, the BLM protests of summer 2020 were remarkable for the wide geographic scope, the extension of protests beyond major cities and into small conservative towns, the widespread participation of fifteen to twenty-six million people, and the racial diversity among protesters.[11] Indeed, white participation in the protests surpassed what it had been during the civil rights movement of the 1960s. Each protest had its own inflections, and specific demands varied. Still, the resistance suggested a shared national opposition to police killings of Black residents and to what those killings implied about the unfinished character of Black liberation in the United States.

Meanwhile, in South Africa, local protests proceeded to proliferate. By one estimate, there were more than six hundred local protests in 2020.[12] In contrast to the American case, however, they remained highly localized and isolated from each other. There was no evidence of converging national resistance around a project of Black liberation. The following chapters attempt to explain the fragmentation of resistance in South Africa and, in turn, the lack of a broader social movement to address unfinished Black liberation. In South Africa, where the transition from apartheid to democracy was so dramatic and where economic inequality is so extreme, it is impossible to understand popular struggles separately from capitalism and the legacy of struggles for national liberation. My account emphasizes the importance of capitalism and its articulations, or entanglements, with the politics of national liberation and racial inclusion. I place specific emphasis on political dimensions of class struggle, from the compromises and maneuvers of elites to the collective formations of the economically marginalized. Three decades into the democratic period, these class struggles have continued to operate on the terrain of racial inclusion.

This book is about the ongoing quest for liberation, after racial inclusion. The quest for Black liberation in South Africa began long before apartheid and continued in its wake. Local protests for service delivery carry on the legacy of Black liberation struggle by asserting that Black lives matter and have value, even if protesters do not frame their struggles in racial terms. I tell this story through the lens of the four residential areas that feature in the opening paragraph—Motsoaledi, Bekkersdal, Tsakane10, and Thembelihle. My account is not celebratory. It is as much about the challenges that confront Black movements in South Africa as it is about their valiant resistance. History is crucial. The ways in which South Africa resolved—only partially—the contradictions of apartheid capitalism help us to understand why current struggles remain so fragmented. I draw a comparison to the United States not to suggest South Africa's essential similarity. My aim, rather, is to highlight the historical dimension of racial inclusion. The advances and limits associated with racial inclusion shape Black movements today, from Ferguson to Johannesburg. They often do so in contradictory, and not necessarily fruitful, ways. Nonetheless, the struggle for liberation persists, seeking to realize dreams deferred.

Acknowledgments

This book has been a long time in the making. I took my first trip to Johannesburg in 2007, began writing this book in 2015, and conducted fieldwork for the book through 2019. Over this period of more than a decade, I incurred many debts. I am grateful to all who have provided me with encouragement, practical support, constructive criticism, and guidance. Thank you.

Above all, I am grateful to my interviewees, who gave their energy, thoughtfulness, and time—often hours—despite limited direct benefits. To everybody who spoke with me, I hope the following pages do some justice to the wisdom that you imparted. While I use pseudonyms throughout the book, I want to acknowledge a few individuals who gave me written permission to use their names: Simphiwe Zwane, Nhlakanipo Masheshisa Lukhele, Mhleli Soyiko, Collen Mthabela, Elvis Lewele, Wonder Modise, and Bongani Jonas. I am also grateful to all those who participated in the October 2017 workshop in Johannesburg.

It is difficult to imagine this book without Nhlakanipo Masheshisa Lukhele, who assisted with fieldwork in Bekkersdal and Tsakane and taught me a great deal about Thembelihle. The Bekkersdal and Tsakane case studies would not exist without him. He very effectively built rapport with residents, recruited interviewees, and helped me to conduct interviews. Equally important were the many hours that we spent debating and discussing politics while traversing Gauteng Province. Comrade Nhlakanipo: I hope you got at least a fraction of the joy and benefit from these experiences that I did.

Moving into the academy, I am grateful for the comfort of knowing that I could always count on Michael Burawoy. He was extremely generous with his time, always encouraging and supportive, and never failed to provide critical and productive feedback. This book is a testament to Michael's incredible mentorship. I hope to honor him by carrying forward his unwavering devotion to students.

I owe special thanks to Kate Alexander, who provided crucial insight and guidance and, perhaps most importantly, welcomed me into the South African Research Chair in Social Change (and the closely linked Center for Social Change) at the University of Johannesburg. I am grateful to everybody within this vibrant and activist-oriented intellectual community for helping to cultivate my book—from the students, postdocs, and affiliated researchers to the foundation provided by Lucinda Becorny and Craig Solomon. I am especially grateful for Carin Runciman, who taught me so much and provided consistent support. Trevor Ngwane, Luke Sinwell, Claire Ceruti, and Francesco Pontarelli deserve special mention for their support, guidance, and critical feedback, as does the dependable assistance of Uyanda Siyotula, who transcribed most of my interviews and assisted with a few fieldwork visits. Thank you all for enabling this book to emerge and grow. At Wits, Eddie Webster has been a consistent and inspiring mentor from my first trip to Johannesburg to the present. Michelle Williams, Vishwas Satgar, and Loren Landau provided essential support during my early trips, without which this book may have never been born. Karl von Holdt, Noor Nieftagodien, Ben Scully, Bridget Kenny, Claire Benit-Gbaffou, and Roger Southall offered valuable feedback and support.

Beyond the university, activists from across Gauteng provided crucial support. I owe special thanks to my good friend Sifiso Mlambo, for teaching me about Motsoaledi and helping me to navigate the area. Mhleli Soyiko and Lucky Ngobeni also provided welcoming support. In Thembelihle, the activists surrounding the Thembelihle Crisis Committee were a consistent bedrock of support and inspiration, including Nhlakanipo Masheshisa Lukhele, Siphiwe Mbatha, Simphiwe Zwane, Bhayiza Miya, Edwin Lefutswane, Sello, and Siphiwe Segodi, among quite a few others. In Tsakane, Bekkersdal, Ivory Park, and around Johannesburg, I am grateful to Tebza Mokgope, Refilwe, Wonder Modise, Lebo Masenya, Zimkitha, Paseka Ndevu, Zola, Oupa, Cleopatra Shezi, Bobo Makhoba, Amos Magadla, and Jan Bhutane. I owe special thanks to Athish Kirun Satgoor, who welcomed me as a roommate and helped introduce me to South Africa. I am eternally grateful to Liz Kading and Ben Scully, who welcomed me into their home and sustained me through many trips to Johannesburg with logistical support, delicious meals, and, above all, friendship. Special thanks as well to Gina Snyman, Njogu Morgan, Jo Veary, Alex Wafer, and Amy Watson for community and friendship.

At the University of California, Berkeley, I am thankful for all of the faculty and graduate students who supported and guided me, laying a foundation for this book. Sandra Smith and Peter Evans were consistently generous and supportive mentors. Mike Levien and Abigail Andrews read full drafts of the manuscript and helped to steer it toward this final version. Shannon Gleeson guided me like a mentor, always there to lift me up and provide direction. Jennifer Jones, Tianna Paschel, Fidan Elcioglu, Eli Friedman, Kate Maich, and Edwin Ackerman provided friendship and valuable feedback. Zachary Levenson became my most important interlocutor on issues related to South Africa. At the University of Utah, I am grateful to my colleagues and students in sociology and beyond, as well as to the wonderful sociology office staff, for providing the support and stimulation I needed to complete this book. I owe special thanks to Brett Clark, Sarita Gaytan, Ella Myers, and Rudiger von Arnim for critical feedback and guidance. Beyond Berkeley and Utah, Jennifer Chun, Chris Tilly, Patrick Heller, Gay Seidman, Ruth Milkman, Steve McKay, and Erin Hatton offered sage wisdom and support. Matt Barreto and James Mahoney were gracious to read and comment on parts of the book. At Cornell University Press, Frances Benson and Ellen Labbate were a joy to work with and provided consistent support. Thank you for ushering this book into print.

Institutional support and funding from various places made this book possible: the Center for African Studies, Sociology Department, Graduate Division, and Boalt Law School at the University of California, Berkeley; the South African Research Chair in Social Change and the Center for Social Change at the University of Johannesburg; the Sociology Department at the University of the Witwatersrand; and the Sociology Department, College of Social and Behavioral Sciences, and University Research Committee at the University of Utah. I received valuable feedback on parts of the manuscript at various meetings of the American Sociological Association (ASA) and the International Sociological Association (ISA); conferences sponsored by the Labor and Labor Movements, Sociology of Development, Political Sociology, and Comparative Historical Sociology sections of ASA; the Economic and Social Research Council seminar series in the United Kingdom, organized by Davide Pero; the Center for Indian Studies in Africa (CISA) at Wits University; the Center for Social Change at the University of Johannesburg; and seminars/conferences at Pennsylvania State University, Cornell University, the University of California, Los Angeles, and the University of California, Santa Cruz.

I am thankful for permission to include previously published material from the following, which appears in pieces throughout the book: Marcel Paret, "Violence and Democracy in South Africa's Community Protests," *Review of African Political Economy* 42, no. 143 (2015): 107–123; Marcel Paret, "Precarious Class Formations in the United States and South Africa," *International Labor and Working-Class History* 89 (2016): 84–106; Marcel Paret, "Working Class Fragmentation, Party Politics, and the Complexities of Solidarity in South Africa's United Front," *Sociological Review* 65, no. 2 (2017): 267–284; Marcel Paret, "Postcolonial Politics: Theorizing Protest from Spaces of Exclusion," in *Southern Resistance in Critical Perspective: The Politics of Protest in South Africa's Contentious Democracy*, edited by Marcel Paret, Carin Runciman, and Luke Sinwell (New York: Routledge, 2017), 55–70; Marcel Paret, "Migration Politics: Mobilizing Against Economic Insecurity in the United States and South Africa," *International Journal of Comparative Sociology* 59, no. 1 (2018): 3–24; Marcel Paret, "The Politics of Local Resistance in Urban South Africa: Evidence from Three Informal Settlements," *International Sociology* 33, no. 3 (2018): 337–356; Marcel Paret, "Critical Nostalgias in Democratic South Africa," *Sociological Quarterly*

59, no. 4 (2018): 678–696; Marcel Paret, "The Community Strike: From Precarity to Militant Organizing," *International Journal of Comparative Sociology* 61, no. 2–3 (2020): 159–177; Marcel Paret, "The Persistent Protest Cycle: A Case Study of Contained Political Incorporation," *Current Sociology*, published online, https://journals.sagepub.com/doi/abs/10.1177/0011392120932936; Marcel Paret, "Resistance within South Africa's Passive Revolution: From Racial Inclusion to Fractured Militancy," *International Journal of Politics, Culture, and Society*.

Writing this book would have been much less enjoyable, and maybe impossible, without family and friends. I feel fortunate for the community of friends that radiated out from the Bay Area, sustaining me with good music and lovely dinners. In Salt Lake City, I am grateful to Josh, Erin, Leslie, and Kerry for surrounding me with such a wonderful and supportive community and to Ella, Mark, Todd, Susannah, Sarah, Chris, and Paula for friendship and consistent encouragement. The Mandles (and Chen/Lai) graciously welcomed me in as the book was taking flight. Dan and Vic, I consider this the culmination of a long journey that began in Cambridge—thank you for everything! To Neve, Frankie, and Jessie, thank you for sustaining me with such joy and love. It has been a wonderful ride, and I am so happy that we took it together. You inspire me.

There is a special place in my heart for Jessie Mandle, who nurtured this book from its very beginning and helped me to navigate its many stages and forms. From Oakland to Johannesburg to Salt Lake City, in the kitchen or on the phone or on the trail, Jessie was there alongside me with love, support, and guidance. It might be only a slight exaggeration to say that this book is our third child! Dear Jessie: thank you for talking with me for hours about ideas, for matching my doubt with encouragement, and for believing in me and in my work. I love you.

FRACTURED MILITANCY

INTRODUCTION

On a sunny morning in May 2017, Nhlakanipo and I joined a meeting of about two hundred residents on an all-dirt soccer field in Tsakane Extension 10 (hereafter Tsakane10). A sea of tin shacks surrounded the meeting. Off in the distance, however, it was easy to see an array of formal housing settlements. This included housing that the postapartheid state built and delivered to residents at no cost. Under apartheid, Tsakane and the surrounding areas—known popularly as the East Rand—represented the heart of South Africa's booming manufacturing sector. Two decades after the collapse of apartheid, however, many Tsakane residents were unemployed. Deindustrialization hollowed out much of the urban manufacturing sector, while rapid urbanization continued to fuel population growth within the area. As in most of South Africa's urban areas, many Tsakane residents lived in informal settlements or "squatter camps," composed of tin shacks and dirt roads. Tsakane10 was one of these informal settlements.

The meeting was a regular gathering of the Kwatsaduza Community and Workers Forum (KCWF), a local activist group that many referred to simply as Kwatsaduza or KCWF.[1] Forming a circle, the exclusively Black crowd was a mixture of men and women, young and old.[2] The discussion revolved around everyday grievances associated with life in the shacks: problems of overcrowding; what to do about vacant shacks; nonworking streetlights, which the municipality disconnected due to their frequent usage for illegal connections; the possible relocation of residents to state-subsidized RDP housing; and allegations of government corruption around housing allocation. The grievances were familiar. Issues of housing, electricity, and corruption loomed large in informal settlements across the country.

Residents also discussed a protest planned for the following day by members of the Economic Freedom Fighters (EFF), a new political party that recently broke away from the ruling African National Congress (ANC). Local EFF activists wanted to contest the proposed municipal budget. They claimed that it did not allocate any funds for Ward 84, which included Tsakane10 and other nearby areas. One resident asked whether they should attend the planned protest. The mood shifted slightly, growing tense. Another resident offered an impassioned warning about outsiders using the community for their own narrow interests. He complained, "The community, Extension 10, it seems we are vulnerable." Loud applause followed. It was the most energetic response of the entire ninety-minute meeting. The moderator was especially unhappy. He criticized the EFF activists, who were not at the meeting, for failing to properly consult the community and for fomenting division by bringing political parties into the community struggle. He suggested that residents could support the protest if they wanted but that they should not barricade the roads—a common practice during local protests in South Africa—because "the community" had not endorsed the protest.

When we returned the following morning at nine o'clock, stones of varying sizes lay scattered along the main road into Tsakane10. Four EFF activists had woken up early in the morning, about five o'clock, to block the road. Without broader support within the area, however, the blockade did not last. By the time we arrived, somebody—most likely minibus taxi drivers, the primary source of transportation in the area—had removed enough stones for vehicles to pass. We met three of the EFF activists at the very same sports ground where twenty-four hours previously we had attended the Kwatsaduza meeting. This time, however, the field was empty. One of the activists blew a whistle several times to call residents to join the protest. Nobody came. This did not reflect an opposition to protesting. In fact, residents of Tsakane10 had taken to the streets several times in previous months. Clouded by the fog of political party politics, the attempted mobilization failed.

Tsakane10, however, was only part of the story. The EFF activists planned to unite two different areas, Extensions 10 and 17, in a march to local municipal offices. In Extension 17, the protest was underway. A huge cement block stood in the intersection, and a group of about three hundred people gathered while others mingled. Tires were burning, and youth stoked the flames with garbage from a nearby field. A staple of collective resistance in South Africa, burning tires produce a funnel of smoke that shoots into the air, announcing the emergence of protest action and calling the attention of the state.[3] Activists in Extension 17 also woke up early to block the roads, prompting rubber bullets and tear gas from the police. With help from the local ward councilor, an ANC member, the police identified and arrested three protest leaders, who were all EFF members. The police charged the leaders with committing public violence.

By the time we arrived at Extension 17, residents were trying to figure out how to proceed. One group began marching to the police station and then quickly retreated. Shortly afterward a large, armored police vehicle—what South Africans refer to as a Hippo—rounded the corner. A sense of fear engulfed the area as residents ran and scattered. A sense of calm returned, like a deflating balloon, after the Hippo passed. The same cycle repeated a few minutes later. Deterred by the police, residents decided to abandon their mass march and instead send a delegation of fifteen women to the police station. As the women sat outside awaiting details about the arrested activists, they fell captive to an enthusiastic EFF activist, who asked if they were members of EFF. The women affirmed that they were not, and indeed, one woman wore an ANC shirt. They identified instead as ordinary community members. Unlike their counterparts in Tsakane10, EFF activists in Extension 17 successfully connected to a broader community interest. In the end, though, solidarity between the two areas never materialized.

Taking place over a period of thirty hours, these events illustrated the complexity of popular politics in postapartheid South Africa. They reflected prominent patterns that were evident well beyond Tsakane: militant and disruptive protests, police repression, political divisions, the opposition of community and political parties, and the localization of popular resistance. The events also highlighted the difficulties that activists confronted in their attempts to organize, build solidarity, and sustain social movements. Resistance was rampant but also shot through with divisions. This book is about that duality—the simultaneous proliferation and fragmentation of resistance—which I refer to as *fractured militancy*.

Fractured Militancy

In the late 1990s and early 2000s, shortly after the transition from apartheid to democracy, rosy images of South Africa as a progressive beacon and harmonious "rainbow nation" predominated. Nearly three decades after the democratic transition, however, such optimistic images are long out of favor. Through the 2010s, extreme and racialized inequality, rampant unemployment and poverty, reoccurring xenophobic attacks against foreign-born residents, and government corruption scandals tarnished the country's image. Two alternative narratives began to predominate. One narrative paints the democratic transition as a failure. According to this narrative, the state caters to the narrow interests of either capital or political elites, at the expense of the predominantly Black poor and working class.[4]

A second narrative highlights widespread struggles from below and the emergence of new social movements. In this narrative, the agency of the Black poor and working class offers hope for further transformation and social justice.[5] While affirming these narratives in my account, I aim to move beyond the opposition between flawed elites and a virtuous Black working class. I do so by showing how the logics and practices of the former infiltrate the latter. Rather than glorify struggles from below, I aim to demonstrate their political complexity as well as their limitations.

To explain the simultaneous reemergence of popular mobilization and its fragmentation, I emphasize the dynamic interaction between class struggles from above and class struggles from below *within* the process of democratization and racial inclusion. My central argument is that the elite-led reorganization of South African capitalism, secured through racial inclusion and the transition from apartheid to democracy, both animated popular frustration and sowed the seeds of division. The reorganization failed to bring about fundamental changes to the distribution of wealth and income. For most Black residents, economic insecurity persisted into the postapartheid period. Feelings of betrayal provided a common foundation for the explosion of local protests. At the same time, though, the politics of capitalist reorganization encouraged narrow and competitive struggles over access to state resources. Residents isolated themselves from each other, antagonized workers and migrants within their own neighborhoods, and pursued divergent political projects. Rather than a coherent left movement, the reorganization of capitalism through racial inclusion produced *fractured militancy*.

In developing this argument, I draw on Antonio Gramsci's theory of *passive revolution*, which refers to an elite-led reorganization of society that preserves the existing order through demobilization and limited reform. In South Africa, passive revolution took place through the process of racial inclusion. Scholars have increasingly deployed the concept of passive revolution to understand how elites absorb and thwart radical challenges. Rather than focus primarily on elites, however, I show how passive revolution represented both an elite response to popular mobilization under apartheid, and a source of fractured militancy in the postapartheid period. On the one hand, passive revolution produced resistance by dangling the possibility of deeper change and then preserving economic inequality and insecurity. On the other hand, passive revolution fragmented resistance by demobilizing popular organizations and redirecting popular aspirations toward the government delivery of public resources.

Emphasizing a view from below, this is a story about precarious resistance after racial inclusion. The notion of *precarious resistance* has a double meaning. Against pessimistic accounts, I show that economically insecure groups do have the capacity for autonomous collective action. Their struggles, however, are often weak, localized, or fragmented, and they may waver between inclusionary and exclusionary positions. In short, if agency may emerge from precarious living conditions, that agency itself often remains precarious. Like most subjects, the urban poor are complex and diverse. Their resistance deserves a comparative political sociology that respects their agency, however constrained it may be.[6] This requires not uncritical celebration but, rather, taking seriously the politics of precarity, with attention to its substantive content as well as its limits and possibilities.

In South Africa, it is crucial to situate the politics of precarity as taking place *after racial inclusion*. By racial inclusion, I mean the dismantling of state-approved racial exclusion and the formal inclusion of previously excluded racial groups as citizens with equal rights. The consequences of such legal-bureaucratic moves may radiate throughout society, shaping popular consciousness, mainstream politics, and the development of social movements. In South Africa, racial inclusion defined the terrain upon which popular resistance unfolded. Racial inclusion facilitated passive revolution, encouraged strong feelings of betrayal, and ultimately helped to both generate and fragment popular resistance. The dynamic interaction between race and mobilization thus represents an important point of departure for this study.

From Racial Inclusion to Remobilization: Two Puzzles

It is impossible to understand contemporary South African protest independently of the dramatic process of racial inclusion and democratization that unfolded in the 1980s and 1990s. The anti-apartheid struggle was more complex than a broad-stroke narrative of unified Black opposition to a white supremacist state implies. Popular resistance refracted through local political dynamics and a multitude of social and political divisions. Nonetheless, the brutality and blunt racism of apartheid did help to unify oppositional forces. The impressive solidarities forged through common opposition to apartheid—between different categories of workers, between unions and community groups, between different ethnicities and nationalities, and between different political tendencies— propelled the national liberation movement and distinguished South Africa as a land of radical possibility.

South Africa's democratic transition carried this hope. In 1994, the world watched in awe as Black residents voted for the first time and elected Nelson Mandela, the icon of national liberation, as president. From Mandela's public appearances with the last apartheid president F. W. De Klerk, to the airing of past human rights violations during the celebrated Truth and Reconciliation Commission, South Africa appeared to symbolize how a country may effectively overcome histories of racialized violence and division. Democratization brought racially inclusive elections and a new constitution that abolished legalized racial exclusion. In contrast to apartheid, Black residents may now travel freely without asking for permission, interact with employers and coworkers without the oppressive weight of official racial domination, and engage in protest as a constitutional right. This process of formal racial inclusion enabled the rise to power of the ANC, the party of Mandela and national liberation. The state underwent a rapid racial transformation, as Black residents quickly dominated government agencies at national, provincial, and local levels.[7] The "new South Africa" was born.

The history of social movements illustrates a familiar pattern of rise and decline, with mobilization eventually giving way to demobilization. In his well-known study of protest cycles, for example, Sidney Tarrow argues that a combination of state repression, satisfaction of movement demands, and exhaustion among participants leads to demobilization.[8] Some parts of the movement may radicalize and persist while the remainder of the movement becomes institutionalized, but they are merely fringe elements.[9] Narratives of racial inclusion follow a similar pattern. Howard Winant, for example, writes that twentieth-century racial inclusion ushered in a new "racial equilibrium" across the globe that undermined resistance: "Opposition was now effectively reduced: since the moderates had been effectively satisfied by reforms, only radical groups remained restive; they could be contained by a combination of marginalization and repression."[10]

In South Africa, racial inclusion facilitated widespread demobilization. Compared to the massive mobilizations against apartheid, the democratic breakthrough appeared to bring relative calm. But the calm did not last for long. By the late 1990s and early 2000s, popular resistance was already beginning to reemerge in the form of oppositional protests and social movements.[11] From the late 2000s, resistance exploded in a growing wave of local protests. The protests emanated from the country's impoverished Black townships and informal settlements and revolved around issues of public service delivery.[12] According to a database compiled by researchers from the Center for Social Change at the University of Johannesburg, by the middle of the 2010s the number of local community protests reported by media outlets hovered around an average of one protest per day (figure 1). Police incident reports suggest that the actual numbers were likely at least four times this amount.[13] Further, estimates of protests by "residents," derived from the Armed Conflict Location and Event Data (ACLED) database, suggest that the number of local protests escalated dramatically in 2019 and 2020, reaching to above six hundred protests annually. Far from fringe, local protests represented a massive remobilization of society.[14] They have come to define the postapartheid landscape.

Widespread *re*mobilization, so soon after the dismantling of apartheid, brings us to a first puzzle: Given the abolition of state-approved racism and the ANC's

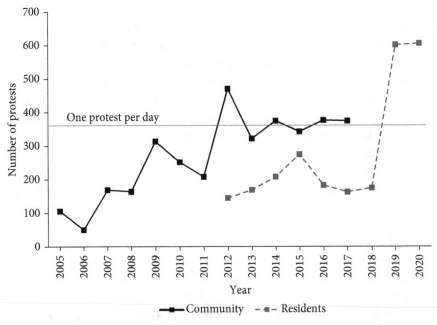

FIGURE 1. Local protests in South Africa, 2005–2020.

Sources: The *community series* (2005–2017) derives from the Center for Social Change database and refers to "protest in which collective demands are raised by a geographically defined and identified 'community' that frames its demands in support and/or defense of that community." Peter Alexander, Carin Runciman, Trevor Ngwane, Boikanyo Moloto, Kgothatso Mokgele, and Nicole van Staden, "Frequency and Turmoil: South Africa's Community Protests 2005–2017," *South Africa Crime Quarterly* 63, no. 27–42 (2018): 28, 35. The *residents series* (2012–2020) derives from the Armed Conflict Location and Event Data (ACLED) database and refers to protests in which residents were the primary actor. Kate Alexander and Lefa Lenka, "Skirmishes on the South African Battlefield," *Open Democracy*, September 11, 2020, https://www.opendemocracy.net/en/skirmishes -south-african-battlefield/. The figure uses updated estimates for the residents series, provided by Kate Alexander via personal communication in January 2021, which include counts of protests through November 2020.

rise to power, why were Black residents protesting? Scholarship on race provides important clues. On the one hand, movements against racial domination can significantly transform society. Writing about the US civil rights movement, Michael Omi and Howard Winant refer to this as the "politicization of the social: the overflow of political meaning and awareness into the arena of everyday and emotional life."[15] Once popular energy and frustrations explode into the open, they become difficult to contain. On the other hand, racial domination persists under new and less overt forms. Legalized exclusion gives way to informal practices of discrimination and the reproduction of racial inequality through purportedly egalitarian institutions. Scholars have deployed a wide range of terms to describe this reality—"systemic racism," "institutional racism," "laissez-faire racism," "colorblind racism," and "racial hegemony," just to name a few.[16]

Persistent racism helps to explain mobilization in the wake of racial inclusion. In South Africa, however, this explanation leads to a second puzzle: the faltering of social movements within a sea of mass remobilization. During the early 2000s, the resurgence of popular resistance helped to spawn a new wave of movements, such as the Anti-Privatization Forum in Johannesburg, the Concerned Citizens Forum in Durban, and the Anti-Eviction Campaign in Cape Town.[17] As local protests gained steam in the late 2000s, however, most of these movements were declining. Many left-leaning observers placed hope in subsequent movements, such as the Democratic Left Front (DLF) and the United Front (UF). These too met with limited success.[18] Abahlali baseMjondolo (AbM), one of the most internationally celebrated of South Africa's social movements, was primarily concentrated in the areas around Durban. It had only limited penetration into Gauteng, the most populous province and the focus of this study.[19] Most local protests in the country had limited connection to this second wave of postapartheid movements. Why did widespread local protests not feed into and cohere around a sustained left movement? With the persistence of racial domination, we might expect to find another movement of the kind that toppled apartheid. This has yet to materialize.

Though vitally important, on its own the dynamic interaction between race and mobilization—whether it be racial inclusion leading to demobilization or persistent racism leading to renewed mobilization—does not fully explain South Africa's fractured militancy. To develop the narrative further, I build on a long history of scholarship that emphasizes articulations of race and class, which become imbricated with and shape one another.[20] Capitalism and class are central to both processes of racial inclusion and social movements. Winant, for example, argues that racial inclusion involves two class-linked projects: the incorporation of upwardly mobile nonwhites into the elite and middle class and the ideological justification of continued deprivation for the nonwhite majority.[21] This points to the way that racial inclusion enables class differentiation within previously disadvantaged racial groups. Such differentiation is consequential for popular resistance. As Gabriel Hetland and Jeff Goodwin note, "class-divisions generated by capitalism may unevenly penetrate and fracture movements," and the "balance of class forces within movements . . . may powerfully shape movement-goals and strategies."[22] In South Africa, class divisions had important implications for antiapartheid resistance, the process of racial inclusion, and popular resistance in the postapartheid period.

Articulations of race and class have been especially prominent and crucial in South Africa, where capitalism was born on the back of harsh racial exclusion. From the migrant labor system of the late nineteenth and early twentieth centuries to the modernization of racial domination under apartheid, racism and capital accumulation frequently went hand in hand. Race and class became further entangled in the antiapartheid movement, which fused struggles for democracy, racial inclusion, and working-class liberation.[23] Far from a straightforward victory for the predominantly Black working class, however, racial inclusion and democratization failed to stem the tide of deepening inequality and economic insecurity. Like Winant suggests, racial inclusion also exacerbated class differentiation among Black residents.[24] For some scholars, democracy ushered in a shift in the character of exclusion from race to class, or as Bond puts it, from "racial apartheid" to "class apartheid."[25] Such characterizations usefully highlight widening class divisions and their increasing detachment from overt racial discrimination. Nonetheless, racial inequalities remain substantial, and racial inclusion continues to shape postapartheid politics. To make sense of the dynamic interaction between racial inclusion and class struggles, from both above and below, I turn to Gramsci's idea of passive revolution.

Passive Revolution

Antonio Gramsci used the concept of passive revolution to describe a series of political and economic transformations in nineteenth- and early twentieth-century Europe. The idea of passive revolution is especially relevant to racial inclusion in South Africa. This is because it illuminates both class struggles within processes of state formation and the ways that elites may redirect mass mobilization toward conservative projects. In this section, I begin by elaborating Gramsci's theory and then turn to the works of Partha Chatterjee and Frantz Fanon, who bring the analysis of passive revolution to the postcolonial context. The following section examines passive revolution within South Africa.

For Gramsci, passive revolution occurs when dominant classes are unable to exercise political and ideological leadership, but they are powerful enough to prevent subordinate classes from doing so.[26] Defined by "the historical fact that popular initiative is missing," this involves "the reaction of the dominant classes to the sporadic and incoherent rebelliousness of the popular masses—a reaction consisting of 'restorations' that agree to some part of the popular demands."[27] Passive revolution thus prevents fundamental transformation by skillfully managing—and partially displacing—popular demands.[28] Gramsci uses the concept of passive revolution to characterize the process of Italian unification (*Risorgimento*), which developed a "bastard" state and a "dictatorship without hegemony" defined by ineffective political leadership. This outcome stemmed from the weakness of the Action Party, which failed to connect with the peasantry and lacked the "inflexible will to become the 'leading' party."[29] He contrasts this Italian passive revolution with the proper revolution that took place in France. In the latter, the Jacobins forged an alliance between the bourgeoisie and the peasantry and established a "modern French nation" under bourgeois leadership.[30]

Three interrelated features of passive revolution merit specific attention. First, passive revolution entails the demobilization of oppositional groups. Responding to the threat of mobilization from below, dominant classes engage in deliberate moves of "disintegration, molecular transformation, absorption and incorporation" to prevent subaltern classes from having a "cathartic moment" in which they begin to develop political leadership.[31] This includes a process of *trasformismo*, which entails the "gradual but continuous absorption" of oppositional forces. In Italy, Gramsci argues, the Moderates led the passive revolution by absorbing leaders of the Action Party and eventually "entire groups of leftists," marking the "decapitation" of the opposition.[32] As Dylan Riley and Manali Desai emphasize, political parties are central to passive revolution because they facilitate the incorporation of popular forces into conservative elite projects. Passive revolution thus entails a "paradoxical combination of conservative aims and revolutionary means," in which "a mass political party rather than the state promotes economic development and national integration while leaving the pre-existing social and political order largely undisturbed."[33]

Second, passive revolution features the implementation of limited reforms that address popular demands without modifying fundamental class relations. It is a conservative form of modernization.[34] Extending the analysis of passive revolution to the broader context of nineteenth-century Europe, Gramsci argues that the "powerful shove" of the French Revolution encouraged elites to organize to prevent popular uprisings. This continent wide passive revolution entailed the incorporation of popular demands "by small doses, legally, in a reformist manner," which both prevented mobilization and preserved "the political and economic position of the old feudal classes."[35] In South Africa, as elsewhere, key reforms have included formal racial inclusion and the implementation of representative democracy and universal suffrage. Decisive for passive revolution is that such reforms do not transform but merely reorganize or modify the status quo.

Third, passive revolution produces weak political leadership and elite reliance on the state. Gramsci refers to the latter as the "Piedmont-type function," in which "a State replaces the local social groups in leading a struggle of renewal." Unable to effectively lead society, most crucially because they are unable to provide requisite material concessions, elites may instead lean on the state to reproduce their domination. The term refers to the Moderates' use of the preexisting Piedmont state in the process of Italian unification. Providing "an army and a politico-diplomatic strength," this state enabled a segment of elites to lead the formation of a ruling bloc, though one that was unable to "lead" the entire social formation.[36] Passive revolution thus reflects a situation whereby elites use the state to pursue narrow interests.

Some scholars argue that passive revolution applies primarily to capitalist development within peripheral zones of the global economy.[37] While Gramsci himself paid close attention to international forces, and to economic differences between northern and southern Italy, his analysis does not address anticolonial movements of the kind that emerged in Asia and Africa during the twentieth century.[38] Partha Chatterjee's key innovation is to link passive revolution to anticolonial nationalism, which he argues unfolds in three moments. In the first moment, the moment of departure, elites develop a national discourse, often rooted in spirituality, to contrast with Western culture.[39] The passive revolution begins to take shape with the second moment, the moment of maneuver, in which nationalist energies mobilize the masses against colonialism but also discipline them and distance them from the state.[40] In India, he argues, this moment revolved around Mohandas Gandhi, who brought peasants into the nationalist struggle through an emphasis on moral purity. Yet Gandhi's tactics of nonviolence (satyagraha and ahimsa) constituted peasants as "willing participants in a struggle wholly conceived and directed *by others*," leading to "a national state from which they are forever distanced."[41]

The third moment, the moment of arrival, consolidates passive revolution by transforming nationalist thought into a "discourse of order."[42] Unable to establish leadership within society, nationalist elites instead focus their attention on the state. In India, Nehru, leader of the Indian National Congress, proposed that national independence was a precondition for economic growth. He constituted nationalism as a theory of the "developmental state." Sidelining Gandhi and the peasantry, Nehru argued that state officials could achieve progress through technical, scientific, and expert knowledge.[43] In a separate analysis of India's passive revolution, Riley and Desai extend Chatterjee by underscoring the importance of colonial rule.[44] On the one hand, repression by the colonial regime helped to facilitate demobilization and the co-optation of popular forces into the elite-driven nationalist project. On the other hand, the simultaneity of popular and anticolonial struggles enabled elites to use nationalism to demobilize left forces and incorporate a larger section of society into their conservative project.

Fanon complements Chatterjee by highlighting the disaster of passive revolution in the postcolonial context.[45] Though he does not use the term *passive revolution*, Fanon's analysis of the "pitfalls of national consciousness" portrays a similar movement from above.[46] He argues that the aspirant "national bourgeoisie" seeks not radical transformation but rather to replace the colonizers at the helm.[47] They lack wealth and innovative energy, though, and justify their domination through national identity rather than material concessions.[48] Following the political parties of the West, Fanon argues, the emergent elites among the colonized build a nationalist party to promote their interests, ignoring the masses while becoming obsessed with organization. Once in power, they compensate for their weakness and insecurity by engaging in conspicuous consumption. They also rely heavily on the state: "It remains at the beginning and for a long time afterward a bourgeoisie of the civil service. It is the positions that it holds in the new national administration which will give it strength and serenity."[49] Finally, in some instances the national bourgeoisie becomes an intermediary, serving the interests of bourgeoisies of the West.[50]

Resembling the absence of "popular initiative" in Gramsci's account of passive revolution, Fanon expresses particular concern with how nationalist elites sideline the masses. His dream is that the masses will infuse the nationalist struggle with a deeper "social and political consciousness," leading to redistribution and radical participatory democracy.[51] Instead, nationalist leaders aim to pacify the people. The nationalist party moves quickly to silence dissent, and devolves into a repressive dictatorship that rules through "baton charges and prisons."[52] Similar to Chatterjee's account of passive revolution, Fanon thus portrays a nationalist movement that crushes civil society and increasingly centralizes power in the state.[53] While party elites may appeal to past struggles and the victory of independence, ordinary people fail to appreciate this narrative of progress: "The masses have no illusions. They are hungry. . . . They turn away from this nation in which they have been given no place and begin to lose interest in it."[54] Focusing on their own narrow interests, the national bourgeoisie squanders the national unity that emerged during the anticolonial struggle, leaving the masses demoralized and disconnected.[55] The deficiencies of passive revolution permeate society.

Passive revolution entails an elite-led response to popular mobilization that is both partial and seemingly contradictory: it modernizes while also preserving the status quo; it incorporates popular forces while also demobilizing them; and it addresses popular demands while also displacing them. Chatterjee and Fanon show how anti-colonial nationalism enables passive revolution, as nationalist elites sideline popular forces and redirect popular mobilization towards narrow political projects. They also underscore how nationalist elites rely heavily on the state to organize and pursue their interests. These accounts help to illuminate the process of racial inclusion in South Africa.

Passive Revolution through Racial Inclusion

There is an ongoing debate about passive revolution in South Africa, including both whether it applies at all and, if it does, what it entails. The debate reveals the peculiarities of South Africa's democratic transition, which resembles in some ways but deviates in others from the postcolonial transitions portrayed by Chatterjee and Fanon. A key difference is the centrality of racial inclusion, which amplified the "popular initiative" that is characteristically absent from passive revolution. Such initiative made the passive revolution in South African appear somewhat surprising. Yet the racial solidarities that lay beneath the passive revolution helped to make it both more thorough and, eventually, more explosive than the accounts of passive revolutions by Chatterjee and Fanon.

The concept of passive revolution points toward a combination of change and continuity. There is an obvious fit with South Africa's democratic transition, which combined racial inclusion in the political sphere—particularly with respect to voting and government—with the persistence of extreme and racialized inequality. But more than just a contradictory "restoration/revolution," as Gramsci sometimes calls it, passive revolution also points to dynamics of class struggle. During moments of crisis, old and new elites form alliances that thwart popular struggles from below and preserve the existing order. In South Africa, highly concentrated white capital and the political elites of the apartheid state defined the old regime, which confronted a crisis due to economic downturn, vibrant mass mobilization, and international sanctions from abroad. This compelled white capital and some political elites to push for change. A big question, however, revolved around class forces within the national liberation movement. In very broad strokes, the leading nationalist alliance around the dominant ANC included emergent political and economic elites and middle classes, a vibrant organized labor movement, and impoverished masses both urban and rural.

Vishwas Satgar makes a forceful case for the passive revolution reading.[56] He argues that ANC elites made a pact with a transnational fraction of capital. In turn, they abandoned the socialist leanings of the national liberation movement for the market-oriented policies of the World Bank. Black Economic Empowerment (BEE) programs, which focused on generating Black elites and a Black middle class, were central to the elite pact of the passive revolution: monopoly capital agreed to "deracialize" in exchange for the opportunity to "transnationalize," such that Black capitalists would reap some of the benefits of global integration.[57] Meanwhile, the corporatist incorporation of the labor movement blunted its radicalism, and participatory democratic mechanisms gave way to bureaucratic and top-down approaches. Satgar identifies the postapartheid order as a "non-hegemonic form of class rule" in which popular initiative is "constrained" and detached from policy making.[58] In a parallel formulation, Nigel Gibson argues that nationalist elites made compromises with finance and mining capital, demobilized mass movements, silenced debate and radical ideologies, and preserved racialized inequality.[59] Like Satgar, he characterizes these events as a passive revolution in which "capitalist interests, both national and multinational, helped limit the form and content of South Africa's transition."[60]

Affirming much of this analysis, Carolyn Bassett traces the evolving maneuvers of large-scale white capital.[61] At the height of popular struggles in the 1980s, she argues, capital understood apartheid as problematic because it undermined connections to the global economy. But capital also feared that majority rule would lead to redistribution and expropriation.[62] With the collapse of Soviet communism and the global ascendance of market ideology, majority rule began to appear less risky. Capital moved toward a position of collaboration with the nationalist movement and presented economic growth as good for the ANC and the Black majority.[63] Once the democratic transition restored the conditions for accumulation, such as protection of private property and integration into the global economy, capital adopted a more oppositional stance. This meant focusing on narrow economic-corporate interests, leaving the ANC to secure popular consent.[64] Echoing Satgar's claims about weak leadership, Bassett suggests that capital was in fact "too successful," failing to make the concessions needed to ensure systemic stability.[65]

These moves did facilitate the growth of a Black elite and middle class, composed of state managers and policy makers, corporate owners and managers, and professionals.[66] For many Black residents, however, postapartheid capitalism brought continued economic insecurity. The expanded unemployment rate, including discouraged work seekers who wanted a job but gave up searching for work, hovered around 35 percent (figure 2). Among those who did find work, it was often in precarious jobs that were temporary, insecure, not unionized, and offered low pay and few benefits.[67] Income inequality increased in the postapartheid period, and South Africa consistently ranked as one of, if not the, most unequal countries in the world.[68] More than three-fifths of households (63 percent) lived in poverty.[69] Despite the elimination of legalized racial discrimination, racial inequality remained prominent: 47 percent of Black households were poor, compared to less than 1 percent of white households.[70] The average annual household income of white residents was six times that of Black residents.[71] These trends underscore the ways in which passive revolution preserved and even deepened racial inequality and the economic hardships of Black residents.

These accounts of the South African transition mirror Chatterjee and Fanon. They reveal how nationalist elites accommodated the old regime, pursued their own narrow interests through the state, and abandoned the masses and broader transformation. Many observers, including critics of Satgar and Bassett, agree that racial inclusion primarily benefitted capital at the expense of the Black majority.[72] Hein Marais, for example, argues that from the mid-1990s, capital pursued their own narrow interests and the ANC illustrated an "overriding bias

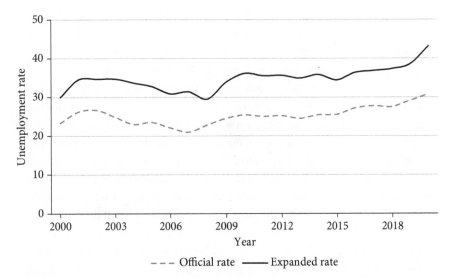

FIGURE 2. Official and expanded unemployment rate, South Africa, 2000–2020.

Source: Statistics South Africa, *Labor Force Survey: Historical Revision, September Series, 2000 to 2007* (Pretoria: Statistics South Africa, 2009); Statistics South Africa, *QLFS Trends 2008–2020Q3* (Pretoria: Statistics South Africa, 2018), tables 2 and 2.4.

towards the key desiderata of capital—particularly financial capital and conglomerates anchored in the minerals-energy complex."[73] There is little disagreement, therefore, about the preservation of capitalism, racialized inequality, and economic insecurity. Instead, disagreement revolves around the extent of ideological leadership and popular consent. Critics of Satgar and Basset underscore the crucial significance of nationalist sentiments within South Africa's passive revolution. In doing so they differ from Fanon, who shrugged off elite appeals to past struggles and progress as empty and ineffective.

Marais rejects Satgar's application of passive revolution, though his analysis does bear some resemblance to Gramsci's account of passive revolution in Italy.[74] He argues that the reorganization of civil society was a "more consensual and complicated affair" than Satgar's narrative of top-down manipulation implies, and that "popular energies and organizations" did help to shape the postapartheid order. Likewise, Marais submits, the ANC generates popular consent through social provisions, promotion of an ongoing "national democratic revolution" (NDR), and in general, the positioning of the state within the "symbolic world of national liberation and African nationalism." Gillian Hart agrees with Satgar and Bassett that South Africa represents passive revolution but criticizes them for failing to appreciate the importance of "renationalization."[75] Especially important to renationalization is the discourse of NDR, which aims to "inject selective meanings of the past into the present" through ongoing "appeals to racialized suffering, dispossession, and struggles against apartheid."[76] Hart shows how ANC elites consistently invoked the NDR and themes of national liberation. In doing so, they often leveraged and even amplified popular antagonism.[77]

These debates suggest that, despite important parallels, passive revolution in South Africa took a different form than the one described by Chatterjee and Fanon. The dynamic of racial inclusion was crucial. Brutal racial exclusion under apartheid helped to engender impressive solidarities of resistance and active participation from below, as encapsulated in popular notions of "people's power" and "workers' control." Antiapartheid resistance, therefore, was a far cry from the passive peasant resistance directed from above that Chatterjee associates with passive revolution at the "moment of maneuver." In light of this active participation and the radical possibilities that it invoked, the passive revolutionary route seemed unlikely in South Africa. As Marais implies, however, many Black residents invested in the ANC as the harbinger of freedom and thus the primary vehicle that would deliver on the hopes and dreams of national liberation. Just as anticolonial nationalism enabled passive revolution in India, such investments in the ANC provided nationalist elites with cover to prioritize capital and their own narrow interests. They also set the stage for profound feelings of betrayal as the contours and consequences of passive revolution came into focus. Crumbling support for the ANC at the polls, beginning in the second decade of democracy, underscored the weakness of the ruling party's political leadership.

Passive revolution persisted into the postapartheid period, establishing a new terrain for mobilization and the organization of oppositional forces.[78] Consistent with Chatterjee's portrayal of the Nehruvian regime under passive revolution at the "moment of arrival," ANC elites presented control of the state as the key source of transformation. Steven Friedman refers to this strategy as the "instrumentalization" of the state.[79] Popular support for the ANC helped to legitimate this approach. As both Marais and Hart suggest, symbolic appeals to the legacy of racial exclusion and the ongoing NDR, in combination with limited material concessions, enabled ANC elites to connect with popular struggles and justify their rule.[80] Significantly, though, these processes created attachments that extended beyond the ruling party. Even as disillusionment with the ANC began to set in, many residents continued to treat the state as an object of desire. This attachment stemmed from South Africa's passive revolution and its imbrications with racial inclusion, which bolstered hope in the postapartheid state.[81]

My contribution to this literature is to show how passive revolution shapes popular struggles.[82] This approach parallels that of Gibson, who briefly mentions Gramsci and passive revolution but develops a much deeper engagement with Fanon.[83] For Gibson, a Fanonian approach must complement criticism of elite-led decolonization with an emphasis on the perspectives of emergent movements from below.[84] He focuses primarily on one movement, Abahlali baseMjondolo (AbM), which he presents as impeccably pure. Radically democratic and autonomous, they reject donor funding, ethnic and national divisions, professionalization, hierarchy, and technocratic approaches that enable co-optation by the state. Though optimistic about the broader potential of AbM, Gibson admits that it is exceptional within the broader array popular struggles. The latter focus more attention on recognition and technical fixes than they do on constructing a radical democracy.[85] Like Gibson, I begin with the premise that the urban poor have the capacity to think for themselves, develop critical ideas, and exercise agency through collective action. I show, however, that popular struggles in South Africa were not nearly as pure as Gibson's picture of AbM. They were deeply entangled with the state, vulnerable to co-optation, and fragmented. These features stemmed from South Africa's passive revolution.

Precarious Resistance

For Gramsci, while the economy may set limits on possible outcomes, social change is most centrally a matter of politics. He suggests that subaltern groups must pass through three levels to undo their domination: an economic-corporate level in which narrow interests predominate; an economic-class level in which struggles exhibit a broader class unity and begin to push for legal and administrative reform; and a political or hegemonic level, where the emergent class forges "intellectual and moral unity" across society by presenting its own particular interests as equivalent to a more general or national interest.[86] This is an arduous process of class formation.[87] Gramsci argues that "the history of subaltern social groups is necessarily fragmented and episodic," not the least because they "are always subject to the activity of ruling groups, even when they rebel and rise."[88] Passive revolution denotes a certain set of movements from above that may both encourage *and* fragment struggles from below.[89] In South Africa, I argue, passive revolution through racial inclusion led to a proliferation of struggles that stalled at the economic-corporate level. This involved two interwoven dynamics: popular resistance to economic precarity and the precarity of that resistance due to fragmentation.

From Precarity to Resistance

Passive revolution is closely linked to mass mobilization, which inspires elites to organize for reforms from above.[90] In preserving the status quo, such reforms fail to resolve many of the tensions and contradictions that give rise to popular resistance in the first place. As Gramsci puts it, the crisis continues.[91] At the same time, however, the reform process affirms popular demands and raises expectations that remain unmet. Passive revolution thus manifests as an unfulfilled transformation, generating a volatile mixture of hope, frustration, and resistance. As Goodwin argues, a "newly sympathetic government" may encourage mobilization when "the statements of certain political leaders prior to their ascension to power" lead to a popular belief that authorities will "react favorably to organized pressure from below."[92] In instances of racial inclusion, elites may invite resistance by making promises that exceed what formal equality can deliver.

South Africa exemplified these processes. At the moment of the democratic transition, the ANC famously promised to deliver a "better life for all." While the ANC, once in power, did bolster certain aspects of the welfare state, public provisions provided only limited relief.[93] Despite the promise of racial inclusion, for many Black residents—especially those living in urban shack settlements—the harsh realities of economic insecurity represented continuity from apartheid. As in much of the world, so-called precarious workers and surplus populations, defined respectively by insecure employment and expulsion from the labor market, became prominent in postapartheid South Africa.[94] Levels of detachment from the economy were high but uneven. Among my interviewees, for example, some had worked only one week over the past year, others worked sporadically, others worked regularly but only once per week, while still others had never held a paid job. These precarious layers of the population, individuals without stable employment and with very low income, were the central protagonists of local protests.[95] Kate Alexander calls the protests a "rebellion of the poor."[96]

South Africa's protests resonated with one of Fanon's most important insights: the economically excluded, those with very little to lose, are often the most revolutionary. Fanon's analysis emphasizes the transformative energy of the peasantry and their urban extension, the lumpenproletariat, which bears a close resemblance to the urban poor in South Africa.[97] His view contrasts with those who emphasize the weak agency of economically insecure groups, due to their lack of workplace power, their diversity and disorganization, and their susceptibility to manipulation by outside forces.[98] Fanon aligns more clearly with those who emphasize the capacity of economically insecure groups to build solidarity and create social change.[99] He is especially critical of the organized working class, who for him represent a privileged fraction of the colonized population that becomes increasingly detached from the impoverished masses.[100] This critique points to a key aspect of South Africa's local protests, namely their detachment from workplaces. As economic precarity spreads across the globe, class struggle is beginning to shift from the workplace to cities and communities.[101] In line with this global trend, South Africa's local protests revolved around what Manuel Castells calls "demands for collective consumption": goods or services provided by the state, such as housing, water, and electricity.[102]

In recent years, scholars have turned to Karl Polanyi's theory of the "double movement" to integrate capitalism into social movement studies.[103] My emphasis here on precarity as a source of resistance fits well with Polanyi's insight that the most vulnerable layers of society, "those most immediately affected by the deleterious action of the market," will take the lead in pushing for social change.[104] Polanyi, however, fails to appreciate the deep challenges associated with building solidarity, democracy, and effective movements for social protection. He pays little attention to the actual organization of social movements, including the class dynamics within them and the ways in which they build on preexisting communities, bonds, and cultures of resistance.[105] To address these limits, it is useful to consider the ways in which passive revolution produces not just resistance but also competition and division.

The Precarity of Resistance

Drawing on continued analysis of the Indian case, Chatterjee argues that passive revolution produces a division between civil society and political society.[106] Inhabited primarily by elites and the urban middle classes, members of civil society relate to the state as citizens with equal rights. Civil society represents the "success of passive revolution." It is the terrain where capital and the imperatives of economic growth are hegemonic.[107] Excluded from civil society and its regime of citizenship, however, the vast majority of the urban and rural poor are relegated instead to what Chatterjee calls political society, which revolves around the government's obligation to secure their livelihood. As an antidote or cure for the ills of civil society and capitalist inequality, the predominant logic within political society is to reverse the negative effects of accumulation.[108] Chatterjee describes political society as a rival form of democracy. Focused on direct political negotiation with government agencies, activities within political society aim to deepen the thin representative democracy that passive revolution produces.[109] Within South Africa's passive revolution, political society aims to deepen and advance not just democracy but also racial inclusion.[110]

The distinction between civil and political society helps to illuminate popular resistance within an ongoing passive revolution and especially its fragmentation. Demobilization is central. Through the absorption and dismantling of oppositional forces, elites undermine the foundations of solidarity that activists constructed during prior waves of struggle. This is the work of Chatterjee's civil society. In South Africa, the dominant alliance around the ANC absorbed the popular organizations that fought against apartheid. While activists could draw on previous strategies and repertoires of struggle, they had to build new organizations and networks independently of those that defined resistance under apartheid. Whereas organizations that were aligned to the ANC, such as the labor federation COSATU (Congress of South African Trade Unions), developed close ties to the state, the vast majority of residents had to struggle instead to attract the attention of the state.[111] Doing so is the central task of activities within political society.

Chatterjee further contrasts political society with prior anticolonial and socialist movements, which appealed to broader notions of citizenship and social change.[112] Conversely, the strategic activities of political society focus on more narrow administrative ends. They often lack a "perspective of transition" and fail to challenge fundamental structures of power.[113] Put in Gramscian terms, they remain stuck in the economic-corporate phase. Political society is inherently competitive. Constituting themselves as deserving populations, economically marginalized groups must manipulate the state to secure access to finite public resources.[114] In South Africa, the passive revolution generated a "politics of waiting," in which residents longed for the state to deliver on the unfulfilled dreams associated with racial inclusion.[115] To the extent that the state provided such goods as free homes or cash transfers, it reinforced the dynamic. Demanding recognition and public goods from the state, local protests sought to accelerate the process and reduce the waiting time for specific groups of residents. As Chatterjee suggests, such struggles represented a somewhat narrower vision of change than the nationalist and working-class movements that propelled resistance to apartheid.[116]

Fanon anticipates how the culture of passive revolution reinforces competition within political society. He argues that the national bourgeoisie's weak leadership breeds opportunism and conflict over access to scarce state resources. Subsequent fragmentation takes two forms. One is spatial: "African unity . . . crumbles into regionalism," as rich regions look on the poor regions "with hatred" and poor regions look back with "envy and covetousness."[117] Another revolves around ethnic divisions, whether racial, tribal, religious, or national.[118] Fanon argues that elite attempts to "replace the foreigner" generate exclusion based on indigeneity among the masses. This exclusion marks a devastating return to racism: "From nationalism we have passed to ultra-nationalism, to chauvinism, and finally to racism. The foreigners are called on to leave; their shops are burned, their street stalls are wrecked."[119] As I will show, the passive revolution in South Africa produced similar forms of fragmentation.

Due to their central role in enabling conservative elite projects, political parties remain central in societies marked by passive revolution.[120] With respect to political society, parties may become important mediators between residents and the state, helping the former to develop a "viable and persuasive politics" that puts pressure in the correct places and at the right moments.[121] In South Africa, the passive revolution empowered a single political party: the ANC. The ANC has won all six national elections to date (1994–2019), but by declining margins after 2004. Along with widespread protest, this electoral decline suggests growing discontent with South Africa's passive revolution. The "articulation" and then subsequent "disarticulation" of the political bloc around the ANC helped to disorganize society.[122] The ANC loomed large within local protests, but in varied ways. Some protesters sought to use protests to communicate with,[123] restore a clientelistic relationship to,[124] or reconfigure local power within the ruling party.[125] In other instances, protesters supported opposition parties or abstained from electoral politics.[126] This fluidity stemmed from South Africa's passive revolution, which could not contain but nonetheless fractured the powerful movement for racial inclusion.

Case Studies of Resistance after Racial Inclusion

Studying popular resistance in South Africa meant confronting the spatial legacy of racial and class segregation. Despite the collapse of apartheid and some racial diversification within the affluent suburbs, the Black urban poor remained concentrated in townships and informal shack settlements on the urban periphery. It was in these predominantly Black spaces of concentrated poverty where protests erupted and where I conducted most of the research for this book. I sought to understand what the protests were about—their goals, strategies, and tactics; their political and organizational dynamics; and the lived experiences and aspirations that propelled them. I walked through residential areas, met with activists and ordinary residents, shared meals, attended meetings, joined protests, and conducted formal interviews. Overall, I completed twenty-nine months of ethnographic observation, and I collected 105 in-depth interviews and 147 brief interviews at protests. Even more important were my informal, everyday interactions with activists while in transit, at meetings, and during protests. For more than a decade, between 2007 and 2019, my research took me to townships and informal settlements across Gauteng, the most populous, urban, and economically unequal province in South Africa.

Over time, I increasingly focused on four residential areas where local protests were prominent: Motsoaledi and Thembelihle, in the Johannesburg Municipality; Tsakane10, in the Ekurhuleni Municipality; and Bekkersdal, in the Westonaria Municipality (later dissolved into Rand West City Municipality), which formed part of the larger West Rand District Municipality. All four areas were within a forty-five-minute drive of the Johannesburg city center. The map below situates the four case study areas within the broader metropolitan area, including the Johannesburg, Ekurhuleni, and West Rand municipalities (figure 3). In the postapartheid period, affluent residents and capital increasingly fled the Johannesburg city center and moved toward the northern suburbs, represented on the map by Sandton. Meanwhile, the predominantly Black urban poor concentrated in peripheral areas, from Soweto to the southern corridor along the Golden Highway and to the east, west, and north. Informal settlements, including my field sites, sprouted up within and around predominantly Black and Indian townships—such as Soweto, Lenasia, Tsakane, and Bekkersdal—established during or before apartheid.

Material deprivation permeated all four areas. Low education, unemployment, and poverty were common, and many lived without close access to water, a flush toilet, or electricity for lighting (table 1). Despite these shared living conditions, the histories and circumstances of the four areas were far from uniform. Motsoaledi and Thembelihle were both informal settlements that emerged through illegal land occupations on the eve of the democratic transition. Of the two, however, only Thembelihle faced the constant threat of eviction. Tsakane10, another informal settlement, emerged more than a decade into democracy when the state relocated residents from other areas that it deemed unsuitable for human settlement. Constructed as a formal township by the government in the 1940s, Bekkersdal was much older than the other three. It was also larger and featured a mixture of formal and informal housing. Whereas ten to twenty thousand residents lived in each of the three informal settlements, Bekkersdal included close to fifty thousand residents. These differences laid a foundation for very different politics.

South Africa's passive revolution through racial inclusion produced fractured militancy. Part 1 of the book, "Mobilization," emphasizes the militancy side of this pairing by examining two periods of mass mobilization. Using archival and secondary sources, chapter 1 traces the emergence of the passive revolution from within the antiapartheid movement. I show how the ANC and its allies, armed with the ideology of national democratic revolution (NDR), facilitated a passive revolution that undermined the radical potential of popular resistance and prioritized state politics. Chapter 2 turns to the four case studies to show how passive revolution generated widespread popular mobilization. In this moment, political society pushed forward the project of racial inclusion. Responding to elite betrayal of the promises of national liberation, protesters demanded from government officials both recognition and public service delivery. Taking part 1 as a whole, passive revolution created a bridge between two waves of militancy: antiapartheid mobilization prompted it, and postapartheid mobilization reacted to it.

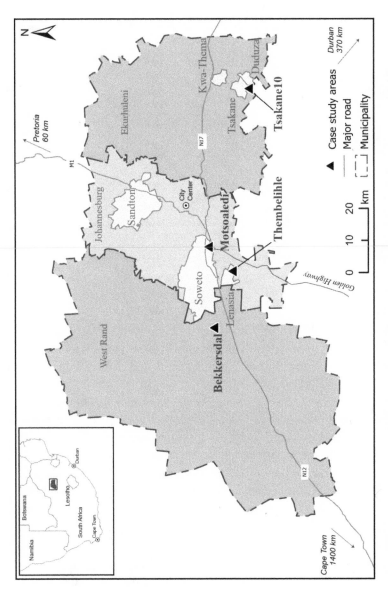

FIGURE 3. Map of the four case study areas and the Johannesburg, Ekurhuleni, and West Rand municipalities.

Credit: Phoebe B. McNeally.

TABLE 1. Municipal-level background characteristics

RELEVANT CASE STUDY	JOHANNESBURG (INFORMAL SETTLEMENTS) MOTSOALEDI, THEMBELIHLE	EKURHULENI (INFORMAL SETTLEMENTS) TSAKANE10	WESTONARIA (ALL RESIDENTS) BEKKERSDAL
Black	97.9	98.9	92.0
Secondary education	23.5	23.1	24.3
Unemployment	44.0	47.1	36.5
Poverty (FPL)	44.6	47.4	36.7
Poverty (UBPL)	65.1	65.9	50.7
Water in home/yard	42.5	29.7	70.7
Flush toilet	23.3	24.6	68.3
Electricity for lighting	38.8	17.6	69.5
Computer ownership	5.8	3.0	13.6

Source: 2011 South African Census, author's calculations.

Notes: The unemployment rate includes "discouraged" work seekers. Measured in per capita monthly household income, poverty cutoffs are R320 for the "food poverty line" (FPL) and R620 for the "upper bound poverty line" (UBPL). The focus on either informal settlements or all residents reflects the character of housing in the relevant case study. Westonaria municipality was later dissolved into the Rand West City municipality.

Part 2, "Fragmentation," digs deeper into the four case studies to reveal the fractured side of fractured militancy. Chapter 3 illuminates the limits of mobilization within political society. I show how emphasis on place-based communities and technical-bureaucratic solutions—what I call *administrative fixes*—isolated activists in different residential areas and failed to resolve crucial divisions related to employment. Chapter 4 demonstrates how competition for scarce resources spilled over into antagonism toward the foreign-born, resulting in the articulation of local protests and anti-immigrant attacks. Not only did the attacks affirm Fanon's nightmare, but as Fanon argues, they drew upon official nationalisms promoted by elites. Chapter 5 traces the divergent class politics that predominated across the four areas, reflecting their isolation from each other and the varied ways that they responded to ANC domination. Despite their weakness and fragmentation, economically precarious groups were agents rather than pawns, capable of organizing collectively and developing their own politics. The conclusion elaborates the theoretical significance of the study for scholarship on social movements and racial inclusion. I also suggest that, at least in the short term, local protests reinforce capitalist hegemony.

Part 1
MOBILIZATION

NATIONAL LIBERATION

If one had to choose a single concept to capture both ordinary South Africans' and elite actors' imaginations, aspirations, and vocabularies, as well as their historical roots, the notion of *national liberation* would be a top contender. While such terms as *democracy, service delivery*, and *corruption* may be more common in everyday language, understanding national liberation is crucial for revealing the meaning and significance of these terms. The notion of national liberation is valuable precisely because it helps to make connections between past and present. Such connections were evident in the persistent effects of colonial and apartheid rule, the ways in which popular struggles against apartheid shaped racial inclusion and democratization, and the continued references that elite politicians and ordinary residents made to these events. It is impossible to understand local protests separately from these connections. One of Fanon's most crucial insights concerns the contingency of anticolonial nationalism. This contingency is about not only the opposition between colonial and anticolonial forces but also the class struggles within the latter. Anti-colonial resistance and class struggles among the colonized shape each other reciprocally. In South Africa, forces opposed to apartheid gathered steam in the 1970s and 1980s, presenting an increasingly formidable challenge. The apartheid state's responses helped to reconfigure the opposition and shape its trajectory. That trajectory, in turn, laid a crucial foundation for politics in the postapartheid period.

This chapter traces the process of national liberation, from the beginning of the twentieth century through the first two and a half decades of postapartheid democracy. Growing opposition to apartheid contained radical possibilities and remains an important reference point in the present. Yet, similar to accounts of passive revolution in India, repression by the apartheid state helped to encourage a shift toward elite direction, state politics, and demobilization. This was the beginning of South Africa's passive revolution. The highly contested notion of a national democratic revolution (NDR) was crucial. Signaling the goal of uplifting the Black majority, the NDR concept helped to preserve an imagined connection between Black residents and the postapartheid state. It also became an important terrain of struggle between different factions and class interests. The NDR idea facilitated policies that catered to capital and an aspirant middle class, while also affirming—without necessarily delivering on—the demands of the working class and poor. It was a recipe for resurgent resistance.

Mounting Resistance

Massive resistance to apartheid built on a long legacy of popular struggles over the course of the twentieth century. Activists founded the South African Native National Congress in 1912, which became the African National Congress (ANC) in 1923. During the ANC's early years, urban elites and traditional leaders dominated the organization, which fought for inclusion within the bounds of the existing constitution. The ANC remained disconnected from the masses, including workers and trade unions.[1] Workplace resistance was prominent but racially divided, reflecting a coercive migrant labor system that subjected Black workers to the lower rungs of the labor market. In 1920, forty thousand Black mine workers went on strike for higher wages. Two years later, in 1922, white mine workers went on strike to defend their privileged position, resisting under the banner: "Workers of the world, unite and fight for a white South Africa."

Labor activity spread quickly from the 1920s as industrialization and urbanization brought growing numbers of Black workers to the cities.[2] With an explosion of worker resistance following the onset of the Second World War, Black trade unions proliferated. The Council of Non-European Trade Unions (CNETU) formed in 1941 and within three years boasted a membership of close to 150,000.[3] Rising worker militancy also featured emergent solidarities between Black, Indian, and white workers.[4] Apartheid was, at least in part, a response to these dynamics of urbanization and unrest, which threatened both capital accumulation and white dominance. After its electoral victory in 1948, the National Party (NP) established several measures to crush labor militancy. These included the Suppression of Communism Act (1950), which led to the banning of the Communist Party, and the Native Labor (Settlement of Disputes) Act (1953), which prohibited Black workers from striking or joining legally registered trade unions.[5] These were just two of the wide-ranging laws that underpinned the apartheid regime of authoritarian rule and racial exclusion.

Under apartheid, the ANC began to move toward mass struggle, even if its approach remained top-down. The organization built alliances with the South African Indian Congress (SAIC), the South African Communist Party (SACP), and the South African Congress of Trade Unions (SACTU). The first decade of apartheid saw massive protests in opposition to pass laws, which provided a basis for draconian police surveillance by restricting where Black residents could travel, live, and work. Anti-pass-law resistance included the Defiance Campaign in 1952, led by the ANC and SAIC, and the twenty-thousand-strong women's march in 1956, led by the multiracial Federation of South African Women. In 1960, the Pan Africanist Congress (PAC)—a breakaway organization from the ANC, founded in 1959—led a mass protest in Sharpeville against the pass laws. The police responded brutally, killing sixty-nine people and injuring hundreds more.

The events at Sharpeville initiated a heightening of state repression. Under the pretense of the Unlawful Organizations Act, passed just weeks after the Sharpeville massacre, the apartheid state banned both the ANC and the PAC. The labor federation SACTU also faced harsh repression and was defunct by the middle of the 1960s.[6] The ANC turned toward armed struggle, forming the military wing Umkhonto we Sizwe (MK), and the apartheid state responded with further repression.[7] The 1960s ushered in a dark period for popular resistance as repression prevailed.[8] This political climate enabled foreign direct investment and impressive economic growth, especially in urban manufacturing.[9] With a shortage of skilled white workers, Black workers increasingly entered semiskilled employment, even if apartheid policies continued to promote their exploitation and abuse at the workplace.[10] Black residents would eventually translate this combination of economic inclusion and exploitation into political power, feeding into broader resistance. The quiet of the 1960s proved to be the calm before the storm.

Popular resistance reemerged forcefully in the 1970s. Two key events, one rooted in workplaces and the other in residential areas, were especially significant. First, a massive strike wave in 1972–1973 began with dockworkers in Durban and Cape Town and later spread to textile factories and transport companies across the country.[11] Police failure to break the strikes was symbolically important, with one labor activist remarking that the experience "taught workers that the sky wouldn't fall on their head if they struck."[12] The strikes sparked resurgent union activity, with Black workers organizing into unions that operated outside of the legal industrial relations framework. By the late 1970s, the new unions claimed more than 87,000 workers.[13] In 1979, Black workers founded the Federation of South African Trade Unions (FOSATU), with an initial membership of forty-five thousand workers across twelve different unions.[14]

Second was the Soweto uprising of 1976. The apartheid government began to expand secondary education for Black residents, partially in response to employer demand, and in 1974 mandated that teachers must provide some instruction in Afrikaans, the language of the apartheid state. Students resisted, drawing inspiration from a burgeoning Black Consciousness movement (BCM). Police responded brutally to a mass march on June 16, 1976, leading to hundreds of casualties.[15] Despite ongoing repression—the state banned BCM-linked organizations and killed the iconic leader Steve Biko—youth remained active. Many joined the ANC's military wing, the MK, in exile, while others joined an outgrowth of the BCM, the Azanian People's Organization (AZAPO). The Congress of South African Students (COSAS), formed in 1979, began to organize unemployed youth and formed local youth congresses nationwide.[16]

Not only did these uprisings inspire confidence, but also deepening economic insecurity propelled resistance in both workplaces and residential areas.[17] Worker demands typically focused on wages and workplace conditions, but market-based insecurities, such as retrenchments and rising prices for food, transportation, and rent, propelled their resistance.[18] Within the urban areas, after 1971 the apartheid state discontinued subsidies from white municipalities to Black townships. Combined with rising unemployment and low wages, these conditions fueled protests around such issues as evictions, shack demolitions, and increasing rental and service charges.[19] Through the Community Councils Act of 1977 and the Black Local Authorities Act of 1982, the apartheid state sought to contain popular resistance by allowing Black township residents to elect local councils. Yet the councils were subject to the authority of the apartheid state and remained reliant on rent increases for revenue.[20] Financial instability undermined support for the councils, as did their appearance as puppets of the apartheid state.[21] They were frequent targets of protest. Radical possibilities began to emerge as the popular outbursts of the 1970s gave way to an explosion of resistance in the 1980s.

Radical Possibilities

Economic insecurities underpinned popular resistance in the 1980s, though they assumed a racialized form. The apartheid state organized markets and their attendant insecurities around explicit policies of racial domination, and common opposition to legalized racism facilitated radical political orientations. Whether in the workplace or residential areas, Black workers and residents could easily trace their hardships, economic or otherwise, to racist state policies. State racism facilitated solidarity across varied axes of difference and potential division. It also encouraged residents to imagine alternative social and political structures.

Pushed into exile, the ANC had a limited organizational presence within South Africa during the 1980s. From its base in Lusaka, Zambia, however, the liberation movement spread political messages and built unity through radio broadcasts, pamphlets, and symbolic acts of sabotage. During the middle of the 1980s, the ANC appealed to Black residents to destabilize the apartheid state by making the country ungovernable. Such calls reinforced and gave coherence to a growing wave of township revolts between 1984 and 1986.[22] The United Democratic Front (UDF), an umbrella body of resistance organizations, provided crucial organizational support. Activists founded the UDF in 1983 to oppose a variety of apartheid policies, including the Black Local Authorities Act mentioned above, new measures to restrict Black movement, and a new "tricameral" parliament that would incorporate Indian and Coloured residents while excluding their Black African counterparts.[23]

The UDF symbolized shared defiance and resistance to the apartheid state. The organization's popular slogan—"Apartheid Divides, UDF Unites"—underscored its unifying influence. Like the ANC, the UDF facilitated the promotion of popular media, propaganda, and slogans and became the convergence point for "a wide-ranging and radical ideological discourse."[24] Arguing that the UDF created "space for the proliferation of ANC imagery and discourses" and for "the strengthening of loyalties to the ANC," Jeremy Seekings concludes that "the UDF was indeed a 'front' for the ANC."[25] Nonetheless, the organization also went beyond the ANC in providing a loose structuring framework, linking together a wide range of labor, student, youth, women's, and other community-based organizations.[26] The UDF provided a bridge between local struggles, situating them as part of a broader national struggle for democracy and racial inclusion.[27]

The increasingly formidable Black trade union movement represented the other major pillar of antiapartheid resistance.[28] The Black trade unions rejected apartheid, which underpinned low wages, abusive working conditions, and the perpetual threat of dismissal. In a formal response to the minister of manpower, who invited FOSATU to a lunch meeting with an open agenda, the federation remarked that "your government is unable to open any meaningful dialogue." It thus rejected the invitation: "We are not prepared to talk to yourselves or the government that you represent. Your government is being extremely presumptuous in expecting to talk to people when it governs not by consent but by the virtual declaration of civil war on the Black people of this country."[29] Not only did unions reject apartheid, but also extraworkplace issues began to emerge within union meetings.[30] One report explained: "Workers would start raising other things that affect them, issues such as incredible water bills, unannounced rent rise, unrealistic rental accounts received by some of the people, and also Putco Bus problem i.e. shortage of School Buses, bus routes, behavior of the bus drivers and Coupon System, which was at this time changed by Putco to suit his pocket. These problems were always raised by workers as prime [concerns] demanding immediate attention."[31] Connections between workplace, community, and broader democratic struggles defined a vibrant form of labor activism. Labor scholars and activists across the globe later popularized and celebrated it as "social movement unionism."[32]

Unions bolstered antiapartheid resistance through strike action and by helping to build bridges across residential areas. A series of *stay-aways*—collective abstention from work and school, akin to a general strike—in late 1984 exemplified the growing solidarity. The uprising began with a stay-away to oppose rent increases in the Vaal townships in September 1984, a second stay-away in Soweto weeks later, and then a massive stay-away on the East Rand in October.[33] A joint committee of students and parents, including trade union activists, organized the East Rand stay-away, building on previous student support for striking workers at the Simba factory. Shortly after, the Congress of South African Students (COSAS) appealed to FOSATU for support. They noted, "Our struggle in the schools is your struggle in the factories. We fight the same bosses government, we fight the same enemy."[34] FOSATU responded positively. The joint effort resulted in a two-day stay-away across the PWV region (Pretoria-Witwatersrand-Vereeniging, later Gauteng Province) in early November, with more than eight hundred thousand workers staying away from work and four hundred thousand students staying away from school.[35]

In addition to impressive solidarities, opposition to the apartheid state also inspired radical visions of alternative futures. The notion of *people's power* exemplified this trend. Proliferating in 1985 and 1986, demands for and expressions of people's power revolved around "the assumption of administrative, judicial, welfare, and cultural functions by local civic and youth organizations."[36] The illegitimacy of the apartheid state, and especially local township administration, propelled the movement for people's power.[37] Rejecting the apartheid state, residents began to develop autonomous sources of power and governance. Street committees and other township organizations began to take over local decision making and provide services, such as street cleaning and creating parks on empty lots. So-called people's courts began to administer justice, and "people's education" efforts sought to offer new curricula and bring schools under local control.[38]

The experience of the UDF mirrored the rise of people's power. Though initially driven mostly from above, UDF activists opposed representative democracy and sought to build power within society. The organization's official launch conference decided to emphasize organization at the local and regional levels to "affect their membership in a direct way." Activists sought "to ensure that the UDF does not simply become a political protest group, but is able to build and strengthen nonracial democratic organizations as an alternative to apartheid itself."[39] With many affiliates agreeing that "leaders are at best mandated delegates," UDF functions were highly decentralized and much of the decision making rested at the local level.[40] The explosion of popular resistance in the townships reinforced these tendencies. Having difficulty keeping up with energy on the ground, UDF leaders admitted that they were "trailing behind the masses."[41]

People's power did not present a major challenge to the apartheid regime, in the sense of seriously threatening to replace the government with an alternative. The coercive apparatus of the apartheid state remained exceptionally stronger than emergent township organization.[42] Still, the idea of people's power signaled an emphasis on popular democratic participation and local decision making.[43] Activists dared to envision alternative structures, even if they remained quite a long distance away. Zwelakhe Sisulu of the National Education Crisis Committee noted, "We are not poised for the immediate transfer of power to the people. . . . We are, however, poised to enter a phase which could lead to the transfer of power."[44] For many activists, community struggles laid a foundation for participatory democracy after apartheid.[45] As the UDF leader Murphy Morobe put it: "The creation of a democratic South Africa can only become a reality with the participation of millions of South Africans in the process—a process which has already begun in the townships, factories and schools. . . . Our democratic aim therefore is control over every aspect of our lives, and not just the right (important as it is) to vote for a central government every four to five years."[46]

Mirroring the demand for people's power, the unions demanded *worker control* in the workplace.[47] For some unions, such as MAWU (Metal and Allied Workers' Union), shop floor organizing and worker control composed part of a broader socialist strategy.[48] At a national congress in 1986, held in Soweto, MAWU delegates resolved that organized workers should "bring together as many groups in society as possible . . . to build correct alliances and true socialism and democracy."[49] Socialism and worker control were not fringe ideas. The ANC's well-known "Strategy and Tactics" document of 1969, for example, affirmed the central role of the working class in the national democratic struggle, as well as the importance of nationalizing economic resources and achieving "economic emancipation."[50] ANC activists worked closely with the SACP through the 1970s and 1980s and consistently called for wealth redistribution and radical socioeconomic restructuring. In a 1971 address to the Communist Party of the Soviet Union, ANC president Oliver Tambo noted that they were leading the masses toward a revolution that would overthrow apartheid, seize state power, and build a socialist society.[51]

Along with the impressive solidarities inspired by shared resistance to apartheid, notions and practices of people's power, worker control, economic emancipation, and socialism hinted at the possibility of radical transformation. History took a different path. While ideas about national liberation remained prominent, radical ambitions faded as elites assimilated the nationalist project to liberal capitalism and representative democracy. These were defining features of passive revolution through racial inclusion, which hinged on the demobilization of society.

Demobilization and State Politics

Antiapartheid struggles persisted into the late 1980s and early 1990s, inching the country closer to a democratic transition. As Michael Neocosmos underscores, the political character of resistance shifted from a popular nationalism, based on the politicization of civil society from below, to a state nationalism, based on the politicization of civil society from above. He explains: "While the former stressed popular democracy and control, accountability and direct mandating of leaders, the latter stressed the independence of leadership, top-down prescriptions and statist arguments of various kinds."[52] This was the beginning of passive revolution. The shape of the passive revolution began to emerge as popular struggles gave way to elite control and demobilization. Each pattern reflected a shift toward state politics, at the expense of solidarities and alternatives that were rooted within society. Repression by the apartheid state played a key role.[53] Most importantly, it weakened popular participation and facilitated a shift toward top-down decision making, with national leaders directing the masses rather than taking direction from them.[54]

While continuing to promote mass mobilization and people's power, in the late 1980s the ANC also began to prepare for state power. This included formation of a Constitution Committee in 1986, which over the course of four years began to outline a vision for a future state. Reflecting an isolation from the broader liberation movement, the committee dropped commitments to people's power and socialism and emphasized a more liberal pathway organized around multiparty competition and individual rights. These formulations would inform the ANC's positions in later negotiations over the new constitution.[55] Senior ANC leaders also began to meet with Afrikaner elites, state officials, and business leaders.[56] This included a meeting in Dakar led by Frederik van Zyl Slabbert, a white leader of the official opposition to the National Party, and a series of meetings in the United Kingdom sponsored by the British gold mining company Consolidated Goldfields. Meanwhile, during his imprisonment, Nelson Mandela began to meet privately with representatives of the apartheid state. Mandela's decision to launch into these talks is revealing: "I chose to tell no one of what I was about to do. . . . I knew that my colleagues upstairs [i.e., other ANC-affiliated political prisoners] would condemn my proposal, and that would kill my initiative even before it was born. There are times when a leader must move out ahead of the flock, go off in a new direction, confident that he is leading his people the right way."[57] Not only did elite engagements lay a foundation for the elite-led negotiations of the early 1990s, but they signaled a privileging of elite politics over consultation with the mass movement. By the time the apartheid state released Mandela from jail in February 1990, the elite-led passive revolution was already well underway.

There was always a tension between different understandings of people's power. For many UDF activists, it represented a form of bottom-up decision making and prefigured a future state based on radical participatory democracy. Conversely, however, many ANC activists understood people's power in instrumental terms, as a form of insurrection that would undermine the apartheid regime and enable the ANC to seize state power. Within some local structures of popular power, demands for revolutionary unity and loyalty to the ANC, as the vanguard of national liberation, undermined the pluralism needed for radical democracy.[58] After the ANC's unbanning, this opposition played out when activists who became prominent in the 1980s began to accuse previously jailed and exiled leaders of not respecting democratic principles.[59] Nonetheless, the elitist position won the day. The ANC continued to view itself as the vanguard of social transformation and treated popular participation as an extension of its own dominance and leadership.[60]

The formal negotiations that dismantled apartheid were crucial because they elevated and formalized the dominant status of the ANC. While negotiations did eventually include a range of political organizations, several years of bilateral talks between the ANC and the apartheid state / National Party laid the foundation for these negotiations, and it remained clear throughout that the ANC and the NP were the two key players. The negotiations thus affirmed the ANC's view of itself as the sole representative of the Black majority. In so doing, they legitimated a top-down politics. Even during the height of popular resistance during the 1980s, the ANC did not prioritize popular organization, treating it instead as a way to give force to elite decisions. This created a "resistance politics in which the gap between the elite and those it sought to represent was inordinately high." It also established a pattern of disregarding popular participation that became prevalent after the transition to democracy.[61] In turn, the exclusion of the poor from the centers of power and decision making, both during and after racial inclusion, enabled the ANC's abandonment of redistribution and capitulation to capitalist interests.[62] Explaining the ANC's shift away from a social democratic agenda, Vishnu Padayachee and Robert van Niekerk argue that a "failure to subject economic policy to democratic debate within the move-ment" was "one of the greatest mistakes that occurred during the transition to democracy."[63]

Through the consolidation of representative democracy in the early 1990s, the ANC moved quickly to demobilize society. This process occurred rather "consensually and 'naturally,'" Marais suggests, as the ANC had successfully po-sitioned itself as the leading representative of "the people" and the "mother ship of liberation."[64] After the apartheid government unbanned the ANC in 1990, popular organizations conceded political space to the emergent ruling party. The idea that the ANC would disband or merge itself with other popular organ-izations was never seriously on the table.[65] The disbanding of the UDF, in 1991, was the clearest example, with one leader arguing that "the purpose for which we were set up was achieved."[66] Similarly, the ANC absorbed women's and youth organizations into its own structures, leading to the formation of the ANC Youth League and the ANC Women's League. The ANC also turned township-based "civics"—residential organizations that addressed bread-and-butter issues—into appendages of itself. In 1992, civic organizations across the country joined as the South African National Civic Organisation (SANCO), which be-came a formal partner of the ANC and followed its direction.[67]

The trade union movement represented a potential alternative. Unions' im-pressive shop floor organization and their economic centrality enabled them to better withstand increasing state repression.[68] The emergent Black unions be-came especially powerful after 1985, when they joined as the Congress of South African Trade Unions (COSATU).[69] Within COSATU, however, bureaucratic and top-down decision making began to replace emphasis on local structures and worker control.[70] Equally important was COSATU's alignment with the ANC. Within three months of forming, COSATU signed a joint statement with the ANC that identified the ANC as "regarded by the majority of the people of South Africa as the overall leader and genuine representative."[71] After 1990, CO-SATU and the SACP joined the ANC as official partners in the Tripartite Alli-ance (hereafter, the Alliance). All three organizations recognized the ANC as the "leader of the Alliance" and the NDR as their key goal.[72] COSATU's subor-dination to the ANC undermined worker leadership.[73]

Having successfully absorbed oppositional forces, the ANC presented itself, and especially its control of the state, as the key vehicle of social transforma-tion. In the lead-up to the first democratic elections in 1994, the ANC cam-paigned on the promise to provide "A Better Life for All," a slogan that the party retained two decades later. Reflecting this goal, the ANC's key macroeco-nomic policy was the Reconstruction and Development Program (RDP), which COSATU had initially drafted. The RDP represented "a form of shorthand for the values and principles that had animated the anti-apartheid struggle and which the ANC pledges still to be upholding."[74] It promised a wide range of material improvements with respect to land, housing, water, electricity, toilets, garbage removal, telephones, food, transportation, health care, and social security.[75] To achieve these ends, the RDP prioritized transformation of the public sector to better reflect the racial and gender composition of society and to "make consultation, action and *delivery* easier and more efficient."[76] In short, the ANC promised to deliver a better life for Black residents, positioning the Black poor as passive recipients of government delivery.[77]

The democratic transition of the late 1980s and early 1990s thus marked an important shift, from a society-driven politics based on oppositional solidarities to a state-driven politics based on ANC governance. The ANC assumed power after an overwhelming victory in the historic 1994 elections. From the perspective of many within the new ruling party, the oppressed masses had fulfilled their historic role in undoing apartheid. It was now time for the ANC-led state to deliver. National liberation thus became synonymous with the ANC party-state. The transition to ANC power helped to cement a particular version of national liberation, encapsulated in the prominent idea of a national democratic revolution, which elites increasingly deployed to justify postapartheid capitalism.

NDR Capitalism

The ANC officially adopted the goal of an NDR in 1969, at its first conference in exile in Morogoro, Tanzania.[78] Not only did the idea help to unify forces opposed to apartheid, but it persisted into the democratic period as an important point of reference. At a national conference in 1997, the ANC affirmed that the democratic transition laid a foundation for furthering the NDR, which it understood as "the creation of a united, non-racial, non-sexist and democratic society. This, in essence, means the liberation of Africans in particular and black people in general from political and economic bondage. It means uplifting the quality of life of all South Africans, especially the poor, the majority of whom are African and female."[79] NDR discourse enabled politicians to leverage the past by appealing to notions of racialized oppression and the need for redress. As the mixture of references to race, class, and nation suggest, its vagueness and flexibility facilitated ideological contestation and struggles for power.[80]

The prominence of NDR discourse reflected the ANC's blossoming partnership with the SACP under apartheid, when both organizations were in exile. Assimilating a Marxist class project to anticolonial nationalism, it combined goals of national independence, popular mobilization, democracy, and economic development.[81] The origins of South Africa's NDR lay in the 1927–1928 Communist International (Comintern), which declared that South Africa needed to establish an "independent native republic" before it could reach socialism. This declaration helped to pull together previously divided struggles against racial and class oppression. The ANC's adoption in 1955 of the Freedom Charter—written by Rusty Bernstein, of the Communist Party, with emphasis on "the people" rather than class hierarchy—began to represent this shift. In 1962, the SACP published *The Road to South African Freedom*, which famously characterized South Africa as "Colonialism of a Special Type" (CST): a situation of settler colonialism defined by the total merger of capitalist exploitation and racial domination into an inseparable amalgam.[82] Proponents of this theory called for a two-stage transition, first to a national democratic society and second to socialism. Within the first stage, the SACP's immediate goal was "to unite all sections and classes of oppressed and democratic people for a national democratic revolution to destroy White domination."[83]

The South African Left under apartheid was vibrant and diverse.[84] While Left intellectuals had little choice but to engage with the CST thesis, due to the prominence of the ANC and the SACP, many rejected the idea of a two-stage transition that underpinned the justification of an NDR. Some preferred instead an immediate transition to socialism. Outside of the ANC/SACP ambit, this criticism found expression in such groups as AZAPO and the New Unity Movement. Integrating Marxism into the Black Consciousness tradition, AZAPO theorized South African society as "racial capitalism" and called for Black working-class struggle to achieve a socialist state. The organization refused to participate in the formal negotiations to end apartheid and boycotted the first democratic elections in 1994. Within the ANC, a group that became the Marxist Workers Tendency (MWT) accepted the CST thesis, but not the idea of a two-stage transition or the ANC's emphasis on armed struggle. Prioritizing politics and organization, they called instead for the ANC to promote a permanent revolution in which working-class struggle would lead, simultaneously, to national liberation and socialism. Promotion of these ideas eventually led to the group's expulsion from the ANC.[85]

Arguably the most important political divide, however, was that which manifested between so-called populists and workerists. These were derogatory labels that became shorthand for disagreement about how unions should engage in the national liberation struggle. Following in the footsteps of SACTU, labor activists on the populist side wanted to fuse the labor movement with the struggle for national democracy. In contrast, the FOSATU unions prioritized worker leadership and opposition to capital. They argued that fusion with the national democratic movement would divide workers politically and compromise their socialist orientation.[86] While not opposed to involvement in extraworkplace struggles, FOSATU activists wanted to preserve a strong "worker identity" and prevent middle class and "petty bourgeois" interests from swallowing worker struggles.[87] In 1983, FOSATU declined affiliation to the UDF "because of the different class interests."[88]

The formation of COSATU represented a "strategic compromise" between the two sides, though it weakened workerism as COSATU assimilated unions to the NDR and the ANC.[89] Jeremy Baskin, a COSATU activist, remarks: "To a large extent COSATU spoke for the entire democratic movement. It was seen as the voice of the ANC in a situation where the ANC could not openly speak."[90] Political divisions persisted within COSATU, and on the eve of the democratic transition, the National Union of Metalworkers of South Africa (NUMSA) made one last push for working-class leadership. At a COSATU national congress in 1993, NUMSA—the descendant of MAWU—called for breaking with the ANC to form a separate political party for workers. Congress delegates voted the proposal down, and as a COSATU affiliate, NUMSA remained aligned with the ANC through the first two decades of democracy.[91] This marked the demise of workerism and the triumph of NDR.

NDR proved entirely compatible with the preservation of a highly unequal capitalism. In the early 1990s, goals of socialism and redistribution faded quickly from the ANC's agenda.[92] On the one hand, the ANC was notoriously weak in terms of economic policy. This left the liberation movement vulnerable to influence from both South African business and forces within the increasingly market-oriented apartheid state.[93] Marais notes that corporate interests "conducted a vigorous political and ideological struggle at a nominally technical level, deploying massive resources to great effect."[94] On the other hand, key ANC leaders rejected redistribution-oriented proposals coming from within the mass movement and fully embraced a market-oriented and business-friendly approach. Increasingly concerned about attracting foreign investment to the country, Mandela played a key role in shutting down debate and antibusiness perspectives.[95] A growing convergence among elites from the ANC, the apartheid state, and the business community pulled South Africa away from a more redistributive approach.

This process took varied forms. Mandela, for example, cultivated relationships with key business leaders in South Africa and abroad, including important meetings with Harry Oppenheimer of the Anglo American Corporation. Some ANC representatives received training from Goldman Sachs, JP Morgan, and the World Bank.[96] Others participated in corporate scenario-planning exercises—supported by such business interests as Anglo American, Nedcor/ Old Mutual, Sanlam, Rand Merchant Bank, and the South African Chamber of

Business—which communicated the potentially disastrous consequences of re-distribution.[97] Padayachee and Niekerk also underscore the important role of Derek Keys, once CEO of the mining company Gencore, who became finance minister in 1992. Keys worked with business leaders, apartheid officials, and key ANC strategists, such as Alec Erwin, to promote market-oriented economic policies. Shortly after the transition to the democracy, Erwin convened a series of secret meetings at Development Bank South Africa, in which economists hashed out a new economic policy—the Growth, Employment and Redistribution (GEAR) program—to replace the more social democratic RDP. Mandela admitted that a "decision was taken at the highest level" to implement the market-oriented GEAR as a "stability pact." Adoption of GEAR, therefore, was nonnegotiable. The closing down of the RDP office and the quick rush to push GEAR through various entities—the ANC, the cabinet, the Government of National Unity, and the parliament—represented the nail in the coffin for a more thoroughgoing redis-tributive approach.[98]

Against this backdrop, understandings of NDR increasingly emphasized Black integration into capitalism. A 1998 ANC discussion paper thus argued that "the NDR has to ensure that ownership of private capital . . . is not defined in racial terms. Thus the new state . . . promotes the emergence of a black capi-talist class." Reinforcing the death of a socialist project, the same discussion pa-per stated that "the NDR is not aimed at resolving the central question of property relations: it does not seek to create a classless society."[99] Such visions reinforced the ideas and policies of the Black Economic Empowerment (BEE) programs, which focused heavily on creating Black capitalists. NDR thus pro-vided ideological glue for passive revolution. It cloaked the preservation of capi-talism and white economic power in the language of racial redress. As Fanon warned, it also enabled the formation of a new Black elite, who could use no-tions of national liberation to promote their own narrow projects.

Critics of NDR and the two-stage transition strategy presented an alterna-tive pathway based on working-class leadership of the national liberation move-ment. Fanon, of course, was notoriously skeptical of the organized working class. He identified it as a privileged fraction of the colonized that aligned with nationalist elites and eventually lost touch with the masses. COSATU's evolv-ing partnership with the ANC seemed to affirm this prediction, as did the labor federation's growing separation from the struggles of economically marginal-ized groups in residential areas. Nonetheless, despite their frequent attachments to the working class rather than Fanon's coveted peasantry, critics of the NDR under apartheid spoke to Fanon's dream of an alternative nationalism propelled from below. Like him, they imagined a radical transformation to carry forward popular notions of people's power and worker control. Such a revolutionary break was not to pass. Instead, affirming Fanon's worst fears, the NDR became a terrain for elite empowerment. In doing so, the process of national liberation and racial inclusion increasingly fed into factionalist struggles at the top.

Elite Struggles within the NDR

Under Mandela's leadership, apparent progress toward reconciliation quickly earned democratic South Africa the label of "rainbow nation." This label revolved heavily around the appearance of racial harmony, marked by dramatic spectacles, such as unified support for the 1995 world championship run of the South African rugby team. Behind this veneer of unity, though, discontent was emerging. Voices within and beyond the ANC-led Alliance—including the emergence of new social movements such as the Anti-Privatization Forum and the sometimes critical COSATU—began to challenge the ANC's policy decisions, and especially the growing emphasis on privatization.[100] The ANC responded by sharpening party discipline.[101] Thabo Mbeki, who succeeded Mandela at the helm of the ruling party, became notorious for leading an ideological assault against "ultra-leftists," who he argued threatened to derail the NDR.[102] It was under Mbeki's rule that the postapartheid state began to reveal its coercive side, such as through evictions of shack dwellers and repression of social movements.[103] This trajectory was consistent with Fanon's warning about the devolution of the nationalist party into repression and the silencing of dissent.

In their accounts of the Mbeki period, Gillian Hart and Karl von Holdt provide complementary analysis of, respectively, ideology and elite class formation. For Hart, Mbeki's attempt to "neutralize" popular antagonisms entangled with a political project centered on the construction of a patriotic Black bourgeoisie. After 2003, however, he did begin to account for marginalized groups through a shift away from privatization. This included growing emphasis on welfare provisions, state-owned enterprises, and the "developmental state."[104] Von Holdt understands these maneuvers as speaking to an often unremarked dimension of inequality: between Black and white fractions of business and the middle classes. The Mbeki regime, he suggests, aimed to correct for the fact that colonialism and apartheid undermined the emergence of Black entrepreneurs and middle classes. BEE programs, which transferred assets to Black business partners, represented the primary tool. Ultimately, though, their limits led to informal and illegal efforts, within all levels of government, to "use revenue flows from the state to sustain or establish businesses, or simply to finance self-enrichment."[105]

The limits of Mbeki's efforts, to both contain popular antagonism and promote Black upward mobility, precipitated a major power struggle with his ultimate successor, Jacob Zuma. In addition to the eruption of local protests, popular frustration began to infiltrate the ruling Alliance. The ANC's formal partners in the Alliance, COSATU and the SACP, began to criticize the way in which capital had captured the ANC and the NDR.[106] They threw their weight behind Zuma, in the hope that he would promote a more redistributive agenda. As Hart argues, however, the coalition behind Zuma included a much wider set of disgruntled figures, such as Black capitalists, those excluded from patronage networks, and former intelligence operatives that served under Zuma in exile. Equally important, Zuma presented himself as a man of the people, against Mbeki's aloof, intellectual, and disciplinary approach. To do so, he constructed a complicated and hybrid identity as a leftist, traditionalist, antielitist, respectable patriarch, militant nationalist, and hero of national liberation. Through this rearticulation of the NDR, Hart argues, Zuma sought to both leverage and contain popular antagonisms.[107]

A groundswell of support brought Zuma to the helm of the ruling party in 2007 and the state in 2009. As implied by the wide array of forces that enabled Zuma's rise to power, this was far from a clear victory for the Left. Zuma was quick to ensure capital that he would preserve the climate for investment and the "centers of global connection and neoliberal management" within the state.[108] For Von Holdt, however, the key significance of the Zuma administration was to greatly expand the informal networks of patronage and corruption, and thus direct state resources toward Black business and personal enrichment.[109] Often subverting the law, these efforts involved growing attempts to capture key state institutions: the police, National Prosecuting Authority, SARS, and Treasury. In a further rearticulation of the NDR, elites justified these measures as consistent with a process of *radical economic transformation* (RET). Zuma emphasized RET in his 2017 State of the Nation Address, and the Gupta business family—the most prominent figures of the Zuma patronage network—hired a public relations firm to promote RET as a necessary response to continued economic domination by white monopoly capital.

The ANC's 2017 National Conference featured "radical socio-economic transformation" as part of the overarching theme, making RET a central item of discussion.[110] Despite this continuity, conference delegates selected trade-union-leader-turned-business-mogul Cyril Ramaphosa as the new ANC president. Ramaphosa promised to root out corruption and restore democracy, ushering in a further rearticulation of the NDR. Just as Zuma's rise did not eradicate the market-oriented policies solidified under Mandela and Mbeki, however, so the rise of Ramaphosa did not dislodge the strong patronage networks that had emerged under Zuma.[111] The post-2017 ANC thus represented an unstable balance between two competing elite projects: one rooted in global markets and the incorporation of Black capitalists, the other rooted in direct control of state institutions and the promotion of Black wealth through patronage and corruption.[112] Both prioritized elite empowerment over the redistribution of wealth and political power.[113]

Through these leadership changes, from Mbeki to Zuma to Ramaphosa, the ANC sought to manage both internal divisions and growing frustration and dissent in the broader society.[114] Elite divisions nonetheless spilled over into oppositional politics. While the transition from Mbeki to Zuma prompted the formation of the breakaway party Congress of the People (COPE), which declined sharply after its initial showing in the 2009 elections, much more significant was the founding of the Economic Freedom Fighters (EFF) in 2013 by former leaders of the ANC Youth League (ANCYL). The EFF leader Julius Malema was initially one of Zuma's strongest supporters.[115] During his term as president of the ANCYL between 2008 and 2012, though, Malema grew increasingly critical, leading to his expulsion from the ruling party. Malema sought to reorganize power within the ANC by amplifying popular antagonisms.[116] In 2011, Malema and the ANCYL led a fifty-kilometer March for Economic Freedom, which targeted both Zuma and prominent symbols of capital, such as the Chamber of Mines and the Johannesburg Stock Exchange. Referencing the theft of land and mineral resources by white colonizers, Malema called for nationalizing the mines and expropriating white-owned land without compensation. These later became founding principles of the EFF.[117] While the EFF's vibrant rallies and championing of local protests hinted at the Left's revival, the party tended to reproduce the ANC's top-down and vanguardist politics and increasingly prioritized engagements with the state over building solidarity within society.[118]

It is difficult to fully appreciate these developments independently of the Marikana massacre of August 2012, during which police killed thirty-four striking mine workers and injured hundreds more.[119] Reminiscent of state repression under apartheid, the episode signaled the ANC's growing detachment from the Black working class. It provided a springboard for the recently expelled Malema, who gave a rousing speech to mine workers two days after the massacre. During the speech he criticized both the ANC and the COSATU-affiliated National Union of Mineworkers (NUM). Two years later, the new EFF members of parliament adopted red mine worker uniforms as their signature outfit. The Marikana massacre also prompted a major split within COSATU, the trade union federation aligned with the ANC. At a special national congress in 2013, NUMSA delegates watched Rehad Desai's video documentary *Miners Shot Down* about the massacre and subsequently raised R350,000 for the widows of the deceased miners. The congress also called for Zuma's resignation and, marking a further fracture within the ruling Alliance, officially withdrew NUMSA's support for the ANC and the SACP. The trade union declared that, "after the mowing down of 34 miners in Marikana, it can't be 'business as usual.'"[120] This move prompted NUMSA's expulsion from COSATU the following year and eventually the formation of a new trade union federation, the South African Federation of Trade Unions (SAFTU).[121]

NUMSA's break from the ANC represented the potential for a sea change in popular politics. Crucially, the union resolved to establish the United Front, which sought to unify progressive forces opposed to neoliberalism and draw together labor and community struggles.[122] It thus held the promise of uniting fragmented local protests in impoverished residential areas and linking them to collective worker organization. In contrast to the EFF, however, which grew modestly but steadily through the 2010s, the United Front failed to gather steam. One reason is that it remained an elite project. NUMSA leaders maintained a strong grip over the direction and activities of the project, and they failed to garner a strong following among either community-based activists or NUMSA members.[123] With the United Front project stalled, NUMSA turned its energy toward the formation of a socialist and worker-oriented political party. Founded in 2019, the NUMSA-backed Socialist Revolutionary Workers' Party (SRWP) also met with limited success. Despite a NUMSA membership of more than 350,000, the SRWP secured less than twenty-five thousand votes in the 2019 national election. It was not enough for even a single seat in parliament.

These struggles over the NDR reflected an ongoing passive revolution in South Africa. Elites continued to respond to popular antagonisms, but they focused on maneuvers from above rather than mass mobilization and democratic participation from below. The passive revolution thus persisted into the postapartheid period, with crucial consequences for popular resistance. Elite factionalism reinforced feelings of betrayal as well as skepticism of party politics, which increasingly appeared to serve narrow interests. This was especially true for ANC elites but also applied, to varying degrees, to the EFF and NUMSA. Because elites sought to draw energy from growing popular frustration, factionalism affirmed popular demands and aspirations. In their struggles from below, impoverished residents often followed the lead of elites in pursuing narrow struggles over state resources.

Material Bases for Class Formation

How did elite maneuvers shape state policy and patterns of redistribution? There certainly was evidence to support the Left's critique that the postapartheid settlement primarily benefitted capital. Yet the full picture was more complex. With benefits accruing to elites, middle classes, workers, and the poor, it sometimes appeared that the ANC-led government had something to offer to everybody. In addition to the ideological dynamics surrounding national liberation and racial inclusion, the resulting material conditions further propelled popular resistance.

At the key moment of racial inclusion in 1994, the top five white-controlled conglomerates accounted for 86 percent of market capitalization on the Johannesburg Stock Exchange (JSE).[124] The negotiated settlement secured private property rights and enabled white corporate capital to reconnect with the global economy. Subsequently, a combination of capital flight and financialization reduced domestic investment in productive sectors, with devastating consequences for the working class: deindustrialization, unemployment, poverty, and inequality.[125] While wealth remained concentrated in white hands, the ANC party-state facilitated the formation of a Black corporate elite.[126] BEE programs facilitated Black ownership and entry into management.[127] Beyond BEE, one study found that nearly one-third of the ANC's National Executive Committee held directorships while more than two-thirds owned shares in companies. More widespread was the "extensive practice of 'tenderpreneurship'—that is, the allocation at all levels of government of contracts to friends, relatives and associates of politicians and public officials."[128]

Despite the ANC's efforts, including the passage of legislation, white residents continued to dominate the higher levels of the private sector.[129] Whereas Black residents composed roughly four-fifths of the working-age population, within the private sector they represented only half of skilled employees, one-quarter of professional employees, and less than one-fifth of senior and top management.[130] The ruling party had much greater control over the public sector. Due to practices of ANC "deployment"—the use of party mechanisms to fill positions—access to government jobs frequently depended more on incorporation into patronage networks than it did on such factors as skills and education. While this frustrated political outsiders, the ANC managed to significantly transform the racial composition of the public sector. Within two decades of the democratic transition, Black residents accounted for at least three-fifths of top and senior management positions at all three levels of government, and at least two-thirds of professional and technical positions within national and provincial government.[131]

The Black middle class grew substantially and eventually outnumbered the white middle class. Given that Black residents accounted for about four-fifths of the total population, however, this fact disguises the persistence of dramatic racial inequalities. The overwhelming majority of white residents (85 percent) fell within the middle and upper classes, while the overwhelming majority of Black residents (87 percent) did not.[132] When assessing the material consequences of the NDR for Black residents, it is therefore essential to look beyond the elite and middle classes. Ordinary workers and low-income residents were especially important, both numerically and politically.

The promise of dignified employment animated much of the national liberation movement, and organized labor secured significant gains, such as new workplace protections and new institutions for conflict resolution and corporatist bargaining.[133] These gains had mixed consequences. Wages rose dramatically for high-skilled workers but stagnated for medium- and low-skill workers.[134] Many union members fared well. From the late 1990s, average real wages grew for union members while they declined or stagnated for nonunion members.[135] Between 1993 and 2008, the proportion of union members in the bottom three-fifths of earners declined from 45 percent to 30 percent, while the proportion of union members in the top one-fifth of earners doubled from 20 percent to 40 percent.[136] These patterns reflected, at least partially, the fact that workers with permanent, full-time jobs and skilled, supervisory, clerical, or professional occupations increasingly dominated the membership of COSATU unions.[137] The vast majority of Black residents, however, did not experience stable and high-paying employment. Many workers continued to earn low wages, and even more eked out a living in more precarious situations, from insecure and informal work to unemployment.[138] Workers in various employment statuses frequently lived in the same households, and union members often supported family members and friends.[139] The NDR thus brought unevenness for workers. While unions could point to clear gains, they also still had much to desire.

With very little wage income, many poor Black residents relied on the welfare state. Housing proved to be one of the most politically salient public provisions, due to the ANC's promises to provide housing during the democratic transition.[140] Residents continued to refer to free, state-provided homes as "RDP houses," using the name of the ruling party's initial macroeconomic program. Within two decades of the democratic transition, the state had released subsidies for nearly four million RDP houses, though it was unclear how many it had constructed.[141] Despite these successes, as urbanization proceeded rapidly the democratic government could not keep up with demand. The housing backlog hovered around two million, and informal settlements proliferated. The government's goal of "eradicating" informal settlements, to align with the United Nations' goal of "cities without slums," proved to be a pipe dream. For the many living in informal dwellings—13 percent nationally and 19 percent in the city of Johannesburg—the ANC's promise of free housing remained unfulfilled.[142]

Government cash transfers, or "social grants," represented a second pillar of the welfare state. By 2014, the state was providing grants to about 16 million residents each month, reaching close to one-third of the entire population.[143] The

Child Support Grant (CSG), for low-income residents with children, accounted for two-thirds of the total.[144] The CSG was very small. Between 2010 and 2016, the amount of the grant hovered between R250 and R350 (roughly $25–$35) per month. A third major pillar, public employment programs, provided another form of limited relief. Beginning in 2009, the Community Work Program (CWP) sought to improve on the previous Extended Public Works Program.[145] It promised two days of work every week, indefinitely, and focused on local development projects according to local and popularly defined needs. Total participation in the CWP hovered around 250,000. With close to 8 million unemployed residents, it made only a small dent in the unemployment rate.[146]

These three politically salient pillars of the welfare state were, of course, only part of the story. The postapartheid state also offered public health care, public education through secondary school, and substantial public funding for tertiary education. These systems remained extremely weak. Underfunding and understaffing, for example, plagued the public health system. Despite serving 84 percent of the population, the public health care sector only included 30 percent of the doctors in the country. Annual per capita spending was $140 in the public sector, contrasting with $1,400 in the private sector.[147] South Africa devoted more resources to public education—about 7 percent of GDP—than many other countries. Yet the public education system continued to underperform. South Africa tended to score much lower than other middle-income countries on international tests, and many students failed to complete secondary school. Only half of young people made it to twelfth grade, and only one-third successfully passed the secondary school completion or matriculation exam.[148]

The postapartheid state, therefore, did redistribute resources to the poor. It provided free homes, cash transfers, part-time jobs, health care, and education, among others. These provisions were crucial for enabling families to survive and support extended networks. They did not, however, eliminate economic insecurity. Free homes left families scrambling to pay water and electricity bills and put food on the table. Social grants were often barely enough to cover the most basic subsistence needs. Public works programs only reached a small proportion of the unemployed population. Health care and education remained extremely weak. In short, pro-poor welfare state expansion went hand in hand with persistent inequality and economic insecurity. The former affirmed the state's role as key provider, while the latter underpinned anger and frustration. It proved to be an explosive combination.

It is difficult to overestimate the significance of racial inclusion and democratization in South Africa. Critics rightly point to a lack of economic transformation and, in turn, to the persistence of extreme inequality and widespread deprivation. As during apartheid, Black residents predominated among the urban and rural poor. Despite these consistencies, however, the process of racial inclusion marked a sea change in South African politics. In addition to eliminating formal racial discrimination, it thrust the ANC into power and reoriented the priorities of the state. It also raised popular hopes and expectations. Not only did the ANC represent a long-standing movement for national liberation, but its ascendance to power occurred on the back of massive popular mobilization. Vibrant struggles against apartheid invested the public with a sense of agency and a spirit of resistance that would not disappear quietly. At the same time, though, the growing importance of elite, top-down, and state-driven politics redirected popular aspirations toward the state, undermining practices of participatory democracy.

Meeting some of the popular expectations, the ANC did manage to redistribute resources toward the poor. The ruling party provided houses, cash transfers, and public employment programs, among others. Yet the problems were deep, and these measures only went so far. They did not eliminate economic insecurity, even for the many residents who did receive benefits. Further, two decades after the first democratic elections, some poor residents still awaited public provisions, such as RDP houses. As the democratic period wore on, many residents grew impatient. That the ANC also protected white wealth and enabled the formation of a Black elite only compounded popular frustration. These historical dynamics go a long way toward explaining South Africa's local protests.

Popular resistance stemmed from the combination of racial inclusion and economic insecurity. The latter highlighted the limits of the former. Even with a clean record, it is likely that the ANC would have confronted growing resistance. Still, the growing evidence of corruption, symbolized particularly by the scandals surrounding the ANC leader Jacob Zuma, amplified popular frustration. For many, corruption reinforced frustration with the failure of elites to deliver on the ANC's promises of a better life for all. Corruption was emblematic of both a broader turn toward elitist and statist politics and the betrayal of political leaders. Local protests responded to this betrayal. They demanded that ordinary residents should be able to participate in the benefits of racial inclusion, and especially the limited resources within the public sector. Such demands became a recipe for both militant resistance and fragmentation.

2

BETRAYAL

I met Mandla in his cold tin shack on a chilly morning in Motsoaledi, shortly after a string of protests in the area. Describing how it feels "when you come from these shacks," he expressed a deep sense of shame and demoralization: "I don't know what [they] see, whether I am a big monkey or what, the way they look at us." Mandla traced his personal shame to state neglect, noting, "Our self-esteem has been taken away from us, the way our government has treated us. It's very sad."[1] He wanted the government to restore the dignity of Motsoaledi residents by treating them as people who were valuable and worthy of time, effort, and resources. All three were in short supply. Mandla compared political officials to "a girlfriend that is not faithful to you," noting how they only showed around election time: "When we want the MEC [provincial official], we make an appointment. But when he needs votes, he just comes anytime. He will knock on my door to campaign, but when I need him, he will not do that. They run away from us."[2]

This narrative reminded me of Laurence. "Now, I am a man," he proclaimed to me proudly after establishing his first email account. Laurence's masculinist assertion of self-worth had deep roots. Describing the conditions where he lived, in the quickly formalizing township of Ivory Park, he provocatively remarked, "Things are going worse now, my brother. Apartheid is coming in full force, now. There's no more information, no more development." Laurence lamented that local government officials did not share details about job opportunities. This prevented young residents from participating in the country's progress: "If you listen to the news, there are some opportunities. Government is pumping money into those big institutions . . . but [the youth] do not have that information."[3] For Laurence, detachment from the state and the benefits of racial inclusion represented the new apartheid. His email account was just one small way of counteracting it.

Zinhle, a Soweto activist who lived not far from Motsoaledi, articulated similar feelings. She remarked, "We know it's mostly ANC people who sit in these government departments. . . . We all know that. Why aren't they doing anything, now that they are in power?" Fanon's warnings about the pitfalls of national consciousness rang in my head as she spoke. Her story was a familiar one about how elites betray the original goals of revolution. "They forgot where they came from," she said, adding, "because most of them came from these same houses." When I asked her where political officials live now, she rattled off the names of affluent neighborhoods: "Phew. In Sandton. You find them even in Fourways. You find them in richer places, in places where there is less load shedding [temporary electricity shutdowns]."[4] As in Fanon's warnings, Zinhle's account described political officials who lived luxuriously while abandoning the masses and failing to uplift the nation.

These stories were not unique. Narratives of betrayal and state neglect were rampant. Residents frequently described how politicians showed up around election time, only to disappear afterward. They spoke about how government officials squandered opportunities, became embroiled in corruption, and forgot about "the people" and "the poor." Such frustrations stemmed from South Africa's passive revolution through racial inclusion, which abolished legalized racism and brought the ANC to power but also exacerbated economic insecurity. This dramatic historical process generated expectations for a better and more dignified life. In contrast to apartheid, residents expected the democratic state to represent and care for the Black majority. The harsh realities of unemployment and poverty, as well as the apparent distance of nationalist elites in government, clashed with these expectations. The fact that passive revolution rested on massive mobilization and popular investment in the ANC only exacerbated frustration, leading eventually to resurgent mobilization and assertions of entitlement.

Across the African continent, political parties that rose to power through decolonization frequently relied on "liberation discourses," which entailed appeals to their historic role in securing independence and national liberation. Such discourses proved to be quite useful in terms of shoring up political power and diminishing the claims of challengers.[5] South Africa was typical in this regard. As Hart notes, the ANC relied heavily on "articulations of the nation, liberation, and the NDR [national democratic revolution]," which "tap into and draw upon popular understandings, memories and meanings of racial oppression, racialized dispossession and struggles for freedom."[6] Nationalist expressions and appeals to racial inclusion helped the ANC to dominate elections and thus the state apparatus. At the same time, though, they also enabled expressions of opposition and critique: "While articulations of the nation and liberation are vitally important to the ANC's hegemonic power, they are simultaneously a source of weakness and instability because they are vulnerable to counter-claims of betrayal."[7] Claims of betrayal criticized elites' failure to deliver on the expectations that racial inclusion produced.

Resistance to betrayal exemplified what Javier Auyero calls "moral politics." The idea resembles what such authors as James Scott and E. P. Thompson referred to as "moral economy," but shifts the focus from market actors to state actors. Moral politics involve "shared beliefs as to what are right and wrong *political practices*, i.e. the actions of state officials and elected representatives."[8] Auyero describes how protesters in Argentina sought to challenge what they viewed as state immorality, whether due to corrupt patronage politics or the collapse of the welfare state. A similar dynamic unfolded in South Africa, where residents' perceptions of state neglect clashed with the moral universe of racial inclusion. Auyero's portrayal of protesters, who opposed state policies and practices that confined them to "a ghost-like existence," could have referred just as well to local protests around Johannesburg: "They stayed on the road to be seen and recognized at a time when the risk of collective disappearance is a common and pressing concern."[9] Against the threat of their own collective disappearance—forgotten and left behind—protesters in South Africa demanded that political officials recognize the value of the poor to the ongoing project of national liberation and racial inclusion.

Popular resistance to betrayal unfolded in two major waves. The first wave climaxed in the early 2000s and featured the formation of new social movement organizations. The second wave accelerated after the 2008 global financial crisis and featured more amorphous and politically complex local protests. After briefly tracing this trajectory, I focus here on the second wave, examining local protests in detail through the four case studies of Motsoaledi, Thembelihle, Tsakane10, and Bekkersdal. Precisely because the passive revolution elevated the importance of the state, which the ANC presented as the key mechanism of transformation, this is where residents directed their grievances and aspirations. Local protests thus took place on the strategic terrain of Chatterjee's political society, which revolves around direct negotiations with government officials to secure a basic livelihood. Rather than reject the state, residents sought to strengthen their connection to it by demanding recognition and resources—what residents called "service delivery." Disappointment with the ANC was widespread, but these dynamics extended beyond the ruling party. Residents worried about the effectiveness of the state more broadly, and especially its capacity to deliver on the promises associated with racial inclusion.

Re-activation: From Social Movements to Local Protests

> Nineteen years later in a democracy we are becoming [the] protest headquarters of the world; we call that a ticking bomb about to explode. . . . People are waiting for that day when their human dignity would be restored.
>
> —union leader Zwelinzima Vavi[10]

The combination of formal racial inclusion with persistent economic insecurity and racialized inequality generated discontent. Drawing from round 6 (2015) of the Afrobarometer Survey in South Africa, table 2 provides a brief snapshot of popular frustration with the democratic regime among all Black residents, and shack dwellers specifically, two decades after the transition from apartheid to democracy. The results show widespread disappointment in the democratic government, political leaders, and the ruling party, especially their handling of the economy, the gap between rich and poor, the living conditions of the poor, and government corruption. Two-thirds of all Black residents and three-quarters of Black residents living in shacks believed that political leaders prioritized their own ambitions over the interests of the people. Between 69 percent and 79 percent of Black residents, overall or living in shacks, believed that members of parliament and local government councilors listened to the people "never" or "only sometimes."

Notably, whereas less than one-quarter of Black residents and shack dwellers believed that race relations worsened after the democratic transition in 1994, much higher proportions highlighted deteriorating economic conditions: the economic circumstances or employment opportunities of their own family or the gap between rich and poor. These results underscore the gap between formal racial inclusion and economic transformation. The same Afrobarometer Survey also suggests that discontent fed into action, especially at the local level. Three-fifths of Black residents had attended a community meeting in the previous year. Further, one-fifth of all Black residents and one-third of shack dwellers had participated in a demonstration or protest. Many Black residents were frustrated, and many mobilized into action.

Following a brief period of relative calm after the 1994 election, popular resistance reemerged forcefully in the late 1990s and early 2000s. A wave of struggles in the impoverished Black townships—frequently in response to rising costs for public services and disconnections due to nonpayment—fed into the growth of new social movements.[11] They were "new" in that they were distinct from the increasingly demobilized organizations of antiapartheid resistance. Most prominent in Gauteng was the Anti-Privatization Forum (APF). Focusing primarily on access to such basic needs as water and electricity, the APF organized public protests as well as collective efforts to connect residents, illegally, to

TABLE 2. Percentage of Black residents indicating discontent, overall and shack dwellers, South Africa, 2015

INDICATOR	OVERALL	SHACK
Overall the country is going in the wrong direction	59.0	76.1
Present economic condition of the country is "fairly bad" / "very bad"	49.5	62.0
Your own present living condition is "fairly bad" / "very bad"	39.0	62.1
Dissatisfied with how democracy works ("not very" / "not at all" satisfied)	45.0	60.4
Leaders of political parties are more concerned with their own political ambitions than serving the interests of the people	68.0	74.9
Distrust the ruling party (trust "not at all" or "little")	50.0	51.1
"Most" / "all" of government officials are involved in corruption	44.9	64.4
The following "never" / "only sometimes" try their best to listen . . .		
Members of parliament	79.1	76.6
Local government councilors	75.9	69.2
Government is handling the following "fairly badly" / "very badly" . . .		
Improving the living conditions of the poor	64.0	82.8
Creating jobs	75.8	83.5
Narrowing gaps between rich and poor	73.7	83.9
Fighting corruption in government	77.2	86.9
The following have become "worse" / "much worse" since the democratic transition in 1994		
Race relations	18.3	22.5
Personal safety	26.8	36.3
Family economic circumstances	32.9	49.5
Family employment opportunities	48.9	59.2
Gap between rich and poor	50.0	60.2
Attended a community meeting	60.9	57.2
Participated in a demonstration or protest march	21.2	33.7

Source: Afrobarometer Round 6, author's calculations.

Note: The shack column includes Black residents living in a "temporary structure/shack."

water and electricity. The heyday of the new social movements was short-lived, and by the end of the 2000s they were mostly extinct.[12] Even so, they helped to renew a spirit of popular resistance, pushing back against elite-led demobilization. Dale McKinley, a leading APF activist, notes that the APF's "role was to (partially) fill the organizational and political/ideological vacuum that had been created, so as to offer a new avenue for the voices and struggles of the poor."[13] The new social movements also began to raise the matter of betrayal.

In my interviews, activists remembered the APF with great admiration. Three factors stood out. First, they remembered the APF as an organization that had a presence "on the ground" and allowed grassroots forces to direct its energies. This stemmed from the APF's visible commitment to collective resistance and presence within residential areas. As Thabo from Thembelihle put it simply, "APF was a born-on-struggle organization."[14] Second, the APF built bridges across local areas. Jakobo from Tsakane remarked, "The solidarity work they did was impressive."[15] Not only did the APF connect activists to each other through regular meetings, but it also helped transport activists to meetings and protests in other areas. These activities produced a strong activist network, and many of the bonds remain today. Third, activists recalled how the APF, which received funding from the UK-based War on Want, provided food at meetings, reimbursed them for transportation costs, and covered bail for arrested protesters. Against the backdrop of grinding poverty, these benefits were significant.[16] Funding enabled the APF's efforts to build solidarity and sustain a presence on the ground.[17]

At their peak, the APF and others among the new social movements unified around opposition to the ANC and its neoliberal agenda. McKinley suggests that "the APF's relevance stemmed from the reality of the ANC state's *betrayal* of the broad working class (i.e. inclusive of the underemployed and unemployed)."[18] The APF's landmark achievement was a massive protest during the World Summit on Sustainable Development (WSSD) in 2002. Seizing the international stage, protesters criticized the South African government and the ANC for supporting neoliberal policies, such as privatization.[19] The protest drew twenty-five thousand people and represented a significant convergence of oppositional forces.[20] Some activists—including residents from impoverished urban areas, middle-class activists, and international supporters—brought a clear antineoliberal and anticapitalist politics.[21] A leading APF activist, John Appolis, recounted that the WSSD march "cemented politically" a "need for unity amongst those who are opposed to the ANC government."[22] The protest also included residents from townships and informal settlements who were primarily concerned with immediate conditions of poverty and economic insecurity and possessed a more ambivalent politics.[23]

The APF's heyday, including the WSSD protest, occurred during the ascendance of ANC popularity. The ANC lay at the center of a fragile national unity, forged during the democratic transition. Popular themes of reconciliation, redemption, and reconstruction provided a sense of possibility and inspired individuals to take part in building the "new" South Africa. The simultaneity of national unity and betrayal laid a foundation for social movement organizing. The APF and allied groups highlighted contradictions between ANC claims of progress and the persistent neglect of workers and the poor. Yet, the APF's challenge to the ANC did not always resonate with rank-and-file activists within impoverished residential areas. One local APF activist remarked that they were "not anti" the ruling party "because we are watch dogs. Because they have promised, we make sure of the promises. . . . If they fail then you see us coming in consulting them, or marching, or do whatever. So we are just rectifying what they are not doing well."[24] Rather than presenting a broad challenge to the ANC and its policies, many among the urban poor sought to hold the ruling party accountable. This uneven mixture of opposition and loyalty to the ANC was a sign of the complex future ahead.

As South Africa moved into the second decade of democracy, the fragile national unity of the previous decade began to dissipate as division erupted both inside and outside of the ANC-led Alliance. Within this fractured political context, the APF's oppositional agenda began to reach its limits.[25] Political allegiances fractured as the most effective strategy for securing state resources became increasingly obscure. While some residents sought social movements, such as the APF, others engaged the ANC or, alternatively, turned toward opposition parties. Many others became disillusioned with formal organizations altogether. They either put their energy into loosely organized protests or abstained from political organizing. Fragmented local protests proliferated on this complicated terrain.

Just as the new social movements were fading in the late 2000s, a much broader wave of resistance emerged.[26] The resistance took various forms, from local protests and mob attacks against migrants, to strikes and workplace organizing, to various expressions of factionalism within political parties. Hart characterizes these various surges as "movements beyond movements," capturing their more fluid and informal character.[27] Local protests, especially, came to define the post-apartheid landscape. They resembled the APF in that they emanated from impoverished Black townships and informal settlements, revolved around issues specific to residential areas, and mostly involved unemployed and precariously employed residents. Yet, whereas the APF channeled popular energy into a formal organization with a strong ideological opposition to neoliberalism and the ANC, local protests were more amorphous and politically ambivalent.

Betrayal and Recognition

> Protest is our AK-47. . . . Government don't have respect for poor people, especially that are from the informal settlement.
>
> —Thembelihle activist[28]

South Africa's local protests resembled what Jennifer Chun refers to as "public dramas," which use "visible and dramatic struggles waged in the public arena" to achieve recognition and material concessions and to restore dignity and justice for "socially devalued and economically marginalized workers."[29] For the urban poor in South Africa, visible public displays and demands for dignity were especially relevant. As in Chun's examples from the United States and South

Korea, protesters in South Africa drew on historically constituted notions of justice—namely, the betrayed promise of national liberation and economic improvement for the Black majority. Local protests often involved disruptive tactics—such as burning tires, barricading roads, and destroying property—with escalation reflecting the failure to achieve results through formal channels.[30] Indeed, protesters commonly expressed the idea that "violence" and disruptive protests, as opposed to "peaceful" and legally permitted marches, were the only "language" that the state understood.[31]

Simultaneous frustration and identification with the state propelled local protests. The demand for recognition was central. While the specifics of each protest were different, most shared the common goal of getting the state to recognize both the existence of residents in a specific geographic area and their pressing material needs. Nancy Fraser describes "misrecognition" as a situation whereby patterns of interaction "constitute some actors as inferior, excluded, wholly other, or simply invisible."[32] This description resonated with everyday life in South Africa's impoverished Black townships and informal settlements. Many residents felt invisible or forgotten. That state neglect betrayed the promises of racial inclusion only amplified these feelings. When they became overwhelming, residents took to the streets.[33] These dynamics were evident across residential areas.

Motsoaledi

In Motsoaledi, feelings of invisibility and neglect were acute. Norma, who had lived in the informal settlement since 1994, recalled the excitement that accompanied the first democratic elections, which she identified as "our way to freedom."[34] If the democratic transition brought hope, however, two decades of persistent material deprivation and a perceived lack of development fueled disappointment: "They have forgotten. Maybe they don't even know that we exist. I don't think they know that we exist here. Because if they knew, they should have done something for the youth."[35] The idea of "not knowing" expressed residents' sense of invisibility with respect to the state. Alice, a thirty-five-year-old resident, attributed recent protests to such misrecognition: "That's why we fight [protest] that time. Because they said they didn't know us. They say, we don't know Motsoaledi."[36]

A memorandum presented to the municipality in association with a protest laid bare the empty promises of elites to uplift the Black poor:

> We [are] the poor and continuously disadvantaged people of Elias Motsoaledi Squatter Camp. . . . The black and ANC government gave them an impression **"it will improve the lives of the black and poor majority."** . . . The first democratic government in 1994 promised to

bring development. This was supported by the mass media newspapers. Again the officials and ANC from local government came with land-scape maps. Proving that **"the development is coming and no one will be re-located"** they said repeatedly. Now the 4th elections came and go still nothing has happened. . . . This making the lives of people at Elias Motsoaledi Squatter Camp to [feel] **"meaningless."**[37]

In July 2009, activists took buses to the executive capital of Pretoria to protest for electricity, and three months later they invited the local ward councilor, who lived in an adjacent community, to a "People's Inspection" of the area. They wanted her to "walk among the people of Motsoaledi [and] see for yourself how they live."[38] She never showed.

Motsoaledi residents became increasingly frustrated in the early 2010s after several years of protesting brought promises of development but few tangible changes. In April 2013, they blocked the traffic-heavy Chris Hani Road, toppled a traffic light, and burned down a nearby KFC restaurant. Mandla recounted the deep frustration and goals that underpinned the militant protest:

> You know what happened, we had nine peaceful marches. Then it's when we started to make protests now, saying we have been peaceful for nine times and these people are not answering us. When we want a meeting for the councilor, mayor, just to come and see us, and just to talk to us, to see how is the progress—there's nothing that they're doing to us like that. So these guys, the only language they understand is protest. Remember, getting the freedom, it was all about striking and everything. So you know what, we started to make protest and every-thing. Then after that, they came to us; they listened to us.[39]

This recollection underscored how popular mobilization under apartheid contin-ued to resonate decades later. Using the antiapartheid struggle to justify disrup-tive protest, Mandla illustrated how the legacy of racial inclusion came back to haunt the ruling party. He also made clear that the protest was as much about achieving recognition, through personal contact and attention from local politi-cal officials, as it was about specific economic resources. Crucially, the protest did bring the state closer, as officials came to meet with residents on the ground.

Thembelihle

In Thembelihle, blocking the nearby intersection at the edge of the informal set-tlement became a ritual. The word *robot*, referring to the traffic light at the in-tersection, became a rallying call that residents shouted when they were ready to protest. When I asked Thabo, a local activist, why there were so many protests in Thembelihle, he echoed the theme of misrecognition. He described how officials came to the area and made promises, only to leave them unfulfilled. He also insisted that, while residents attempted to "engage with the relevant stakeholders," positive responses were not forthcoming. This compelled residents to protest: "Government officials are not fulfilling their promises to the community. So that's why all the time we are going back to the streets. . . . We follow the [formal bureaucratic] procedures all the time, but they don't seem to be complying with their own procedures."[40]

This dynamic played out on a Sunday afternoon in February 2015. Residents decided to protest after a provincial-level official "failed to respond to residents' demands for housing." A public statement by local activists explained why they decided to barricade the road:

> Thembelihle, an informal settlement consisting of 20,000 people in Lenasia (South of Johannesburg) are fed up with waiting for what the government calls democracy and development. . . . As usual, the ANC makes promises, but fails to deliver. When they do not cooperate, residents are left with no other alternative but to engage in mass direct action. As one resident stated, "we cannot wait to apply for a march, after 20 years we still live in shacks, we need houses now." At a Thembelihle Crisis Committee (TCC) meeting held yesterday (Sunday), the masses decided to have a protest. They have been barricading the roads in Lenasia since 4 A.M. this morning.[41]

As in Motsoaledi, the statement illustrates how racial inclusion generated expectations that went unfulfilled. In a further parallel, disruptive tactics reflected both a demand for recognition and the legacy of resistance. Activists were well aware that the antiapartheid struggle was not as "peaceful" as sometimes portrayed. Thabo remarked: "If we can look back to apartheid, during the apartheid struggle—if these people were picketing every day, you know, peaceful, we were not going to achieve democracy."[42] If disruptive tactics were necessary to overcome apartheid, he suggested, they were also necessary to improve living conditions after racial inclusion.

Tsakane10

As a more recently established informal settlement, constructed by the state in 2007, Tsakane10 did not exist when the democratic transition took place. Yet the promises of democracy, and especially their failed realization, remained salient. Two prominent activists noted, "On TV government act[s] sugar sweet, they try and make us believe that they are very caring and democratic, but the reality is something different."[43] As in many local protests, residents of Tsakane10 directed much of their frustration toward local officials. One activist recalled: "The trigger for the protest was that the ward councilor didn't come to the community and account. Since we voted in the last municipal elections, she didn't come here. So we thought the best thing to do was to get on the street and force our issues."[44] Speaking on the sidelines of a protest action, another activist echoed the concern: "For now, they want the [councilor] to step down. . . . She is arrogant. Every time when she has to come to the residents and explain why there is a delay in answering their complaints, she is always busy. Because of that, we say she doesn't take us serious. She is not doing her work."[45] Tsakane10 residents burned tires and barricaded roads to garner attention from local politicians.

Kaya, a thirty-two-year-old activist, explained that legal marches and voting rarely produced the intended results. Disruptive protests and illegal tactics, she argued, were more effective: "Sometimes it is better if we scare them a little, because if we marched relaxed, they will think we are not serious. If we twist a little, they will see that we are serious."[46] Bobo expressed a similar sentiment. He argued that people were tired of waiting for representative democracy to deliver their basic needs. Instead, it was necessary for residents to use force to compel the local state to pay attention: "It shows . . . the office for the mayor that we are tired. . . . That is why we are burning the tires and put the stone in the middle of the road, just to show that the people are tired. So we need our needs in a force. Actually, we use the force."[47]

Bekkersdal

Residents in Bekkersdal also spoke about feeling alienated from the democratic state, noting at times that, like their counterparts in Motsoaledi, they did "not know" their local political officials.[48] As in the other three areas, Bekkersdal residents emphasized the need to protest to achieve recognition. One young protester, for example, expressed frustration with the unresponsiveness of government officials: "I feel like they are buying time because they always promise to answer; and when the time and date comes, they just do not answer. When it comes, they do not give us the feedback they promised that satisfies us. If they do not answer the way we expect them to, then forward we go with the protest. We won't stop."[49] In late 2013, a string of protests featured property destruction. Residents destroyed municipal structures, including a town hall that some asserted was only available to ANC members. During one protest, a large group began marching to the local municipal offices, only to confront a police blockade that prevented them from leaving the township. Frustrated protesters responded by vandalizing several public buildings. Dumisani, a twenty-one-year-old activist who was at the protest, explained the close link between the police blockade and burned buildings:

> MARCEL: So let's say the police had just decided to let you go [continue the march to the municipality]. Do you think those buildings still would have gotten burnt down?
>
> DUMISANI: I can say definitely, none of that thing could have happened. Because [before the police blockade] people went through those halls without breaking anything. It was just a march to go to town. But the police blocked us, to say, "No, you are not going there." People were not going to burn anything. But ever since the police started to fire the shots to them and to start firing the tear gas to people, that's what made people angry, to say, "We are going to burn these facilities because they belong to the municipality."[50]

Residents understood police repression as an act of misrecognition. It signaled the state's unwillingness to engage with them. As Moloetsi explained, about the very same event: "They don't want to listen to us. Yeah. We wanted them to come, or wait there, because we were going to them. So they don't take us seriously."[51] In this sense, disruptive tactics responded directly to the state's disregard for popular grievances, expressing the link between feelings of betrayal and demands for recognition.

If feelings of betrayal propelled demands for recognition, so did feelings of entitlement. Matsobane, a Bekkersdal activist, conveyed this in an especially direct and powerful way:

> We asked [the municipality] to explain reasons why the garbage is not collected at Bekkersdal, why there is no service rendered to the people. . . . We cannot beg as the community to have those services delivered. *That is what we are expecting, and it's not a favor but an obligation, which the municipality has to fulfill. We are governed by the government. Now this whole thing, the blame and everything, it goes back to the government. Then the government will be able to categorize in* terms of their failures for service delivery upon this community.[52]

This quote powerfully illustrates Chatterjee's notion of political society, which revolves around the state's obligation to take care of the poor within the ongoing passive revolution. For many residents, the postapartheid state was obligated to provide resources. Ordinary people put ANC elites in their government positions precisely for this purpose, first through the antiapartheid struggle and then through democratic elections. Material deprivation signaled a betrayal of that popular mandate. The idea of service delivery identified and condemned this betrayal.

Service Delivery

> I am also convinced that until we solve the economic problems in this country, we will not have peace.
>
> —Reverend Frank Chikane[53]

The notion of *service delivery* permeated everyday discourse in the impoverished townships and informal settlements. Whereas service denoted the object of desire, delivery referenced the state's obligation to provide it. Residents conceptualized services quite loosely. While demands for housing, water, and electricity were especially prevalent, protesters also sought tar roads, streetlights, toilets, refuse removal, jobs, and access to education, among others. The source—the state—represented the unifying thread. A common experience of material deprivation, due to unemployment, precarious work, and poverty, underpinned local protests. In the context of market-based insecurity, residents turned to the state to provide social protection. Some protesters expressed very specific demands, while others expressed a more general desire for service delivery or development. Demands for housing, electricity, and water were among the most common grievances among protesters nationally, and they loomed large in the four case study areas.[54] If residents shared common grievances, however, varying historical conditions gave notions of service delivery a distinctive local flair.

Motsoaledi

The Elias Motsoaledi informal settlement lay in the heart of Soweto, a massive conglomeration of townships built by the colonial and apartheid governments. It stood adjacent to a Coca-Cola plant, the enormous Chris Hani Baragwanath Hospital, and the Bara Taxi Rank, the largest and busiest transportation hub within Soweto. Residents established the settlement when they began squatting on an open piece of land in the early 1990s. When I first visited Motsoaledi in 2013, it was composed exclusively of tin shacks and wide dirt roads. The streets were dusty and prone to flooding during rainstorms. A small stream cut the settlement in half and was especially difficult to cross after rain. Surrounded by economic development, including the newly built Bara Mall and a KFC restaurant, each within a thirty-second walk, the poverty within Motsoaledi attested to the depth of South Africa's inequality.

Motsoaledi residents wanted formal housing. Constructed informally through a land invasion, the status of the settlement remained uncertain. Residents asserted that ANC officials consistently promised to provide them with housing. Some had vivid memories of visits from ANC leaders, which began before 1994. Thapelo recalled: "I remember the guy who was working for the municipality, who was the previous mayor, Parks Tau; he was one of the persons who normally come here with us. And Sicelo Shiceka, so many . . . leaders were coming. Sometimes they come frequently when it is toward the election time."[55] Despite consistent promises, however, as of early 2013 there was no physical evidence of a housing development other than a few underground pipes. One young resident described the confusion:

> Some of the councilors come up with, telling us that Motsoaledi is there on the map, and when we select another councilor, they tell us that no, it's not there on the map. So people were confused. . . . When you can go and check a map next to Bara [Taxi Rank], there is no place called Motsoaledi. But then physically it's there. So there was that—they need to approve it, that this place now exists. . . . So what can we do? Must we build our own houses, or must we wait for houses to come?[56]

It was in this context of uncertainty that protests exploded in April 2013. Residents wanted to make sure that they really were "on the map." They wanted to ensure that they did in fact exist in the eyes of the state and that government officials would follow through on their promise to build a formal housing settlement.

While in many instances protests only brought small concessions, in this instance the results were significant. Construction work began within six months. A combination of hope and uncertainty permeated the township, both before and during the construction. Rejoice, who moved to Motsoaledi in 1994, lived in a small tin shack with her daughter and grandchild. Recalling the experience of waiting for a state-provided RDP house, she explained: "Yes, [we have been waiting] for a long, long time! That is why we have been staying here, because no one has ever said we should move. Everyone comes here and makes promises that 'we will build houses for you,' but they have never delivered; until now we are seeing something happening, and yet we don't know if we [will] all get houses. . . . We have too many shacks."[57] Given the persistent promises, it is no wonder that residents focused their hopes and demands on the state.

The demand for housing encapsulated a variety of other demands, particularly around water and electricity. Motsoaledi residents had access to communal taps for water, and some residents extended them illegally into their own yards. But there was no electricity. The postapartheid state did provide streetlights at some point, only to later disable them because residents tapped into them for illegal connections. Residents understood that the state was unlikely to provide piped water and electricity inside of people's homes while they were still living in shacks. They first needed the state to move them into formal houses.

Residents discussed the challenges of living without electricity, such as the difficulty of studying for school, heating water for baths, or cooking and storing food. According to one pair of activists, the desire for electricity propelled protest action:

> ACTIVIST 1: [They said] they are going to build us proper adequate houses. You know they use those terms, building a "proper adequate housing," and we are going to make sure people have proper basic facilities like water, electricity. You see living without electricity man, *aiyiii* . . .
>
> ACTIVIST 2: Electricity is life.
>
> ACTIVIST 1: You can't do nothing [without electricity].
>
> ACTIVIST 2: You can't survive.
>
> ACTIVIST 1: It has become difficult for people to live without electricity . . . so I would say that as much as we seek houses, proper ones, as much as we do want proper sanitation, flushing toilets and water inside our houses, but if they can just put electricity.[58]

This description, of life without electricity, was a small window into the difficulties experienced by residents of informal settlements. In Motsoaledi, the demand for electricity came to the fore during protests. As a public statement associated with a 2010 protest explained, "There are plenty of things we want but for now we want temporary or permanent electricity."[59]

Thembelihle

Only a twenty-minute drive from Motsoaledi, the informal settlement of Thembelihle also fell within the Johannesburg metropolitan municipality. Residents established the settlement through informal squatting in the late 1980s. Composed of tin shacks and bumpy dirt roads, Thembelihle also attested to the depth of inequality and poverty. It was unique, however, due to its location within the predominantly Indian and more middle-class suburb of Lenasia. Inequality thus played into a localized racial and class tension between Black shack dwellers and Indian residents, who owned nearby businesses and brick homes that surrounded the shacks of Thembelihle. In contrast to promises of housing in Motsoaledi, residents in Thembelihle confronted the constant threat of eviction. The city of Johannesburg developed plans to relocate the population in the early 1990s. In 2002, the city declared the land unsuitable for human settlement due to the presence of dolomitic rock. Residents resisted. In June 2002, they disrupted a celebration of the historic Freedom Charter to protest their eviction, and shortly afterwards erected barricades to prevent forced relocation.[60] While some residents did relocate, most held their ground and remained in the area.

Despite introduction of a new national housing policy that prioritized in situ (in the original place) upgrading, the city remained firm that the decision to relocate residents was final and nonnegotiable.[61] By the early 2010s, Thembelihle residents had varied demands. Some preferred relocation to Lehae, a new housing settlement nearby for which construction began in 2005. This demand was consistent with the government's desire to eradicate the informal settlement, but the construction took time and the state also sought to accommodate residents from other areas. At a public meeting in 2013, upset residents began to rally the crowd around the idea of marching directly to the houses to occupy them, exclaiming that people must just "take their sponges and move!"[62] The frustration eventually spilled over into protest action.

Others were more concerned with local development than they were with relocation. Various service delivery grievances featured over time, from water to toilets to electricity. Thabo explained how the toilet issue sparked his initial involvement in local activism in the mid-2000s: "There were no toilets at the time. There were just these pits toilets that, when it's full, you have to close the hole and dig another one. The yard is getting full now with toilets, you know? So that's when I said, no, this thing must get to an end now. The government must provide services to the people."[63] The state eventually provided what they referred to as "VIP toilets." Rather than piped sewage, however, these toilets still emptied into pits below, and service providers had to come periodically to suck out the waste. Residents complained about the infrequency of the service and that the structures were falling apart.[64] Electricity, however, became increasingly central to local organizing and protest. In 2009, local activists began to connect to the grid illegally. The state responded by disconnecting them and moving the supply boxes, forcing residents to buy longer and more expensive cables. These reactions sparked resistance, but eventually the situation stabilized. Thabo bragged, "Even the police were told that now, if you are going to arrest these people who are connecting electricity, we are going to riot."[65] With the illegal connections in place, activists began to set their sights on the installation of formal electricity.

Thembelihle activists were especially proud of a series of major protests for "proper electricity" in late 2011 that lasted a full week. During the protest, residents burned supply boxes to shut down electricity in the surrounding Indian neighborhoods. Thabo explained that the purpose "was to keep the Indian communities in dark, as we are also living in the dark."[66] A similar cycle of disconnections, protests, and burning of electricity boxes occurred again in 2014. In a public statement, local activists pronounced, "We will not be treated as second-class citizens. Apartheid is over. If we can't have electricity, then no one will."[67] Electricity was the most prominent demand, but it was not the only one. Another statement from 2016 explained, "We have had many strikes [protests] in Thembelihle. Why? Because we want houses, roads, electricity, water, clinics, sports facilities, etc. right here in Thembelihle."[68]

The land issue remained unresolved. While government officials continued to insist that the land was unsuitable for human settlement, local activists countered that the existing geotechnical studies were insufficient. Consistent protests in the area nonetheless began to bear fruit. In April 2015, the Gauteng provincial government declared the formal registration of Thembelihle as a housing project. It noted that the government, including the city of Johannesburg, would begin providing public services to the area, pending a final geotechnical report about the land.[69] About one year later, however, with the public release of the report still pending, the government began installing formal electricity within the shacks. Declaring that "electricity is not a gift from the ANC—we fought for it," a public statement by local activists celebrated their long struggle: "We fought against the bulldozers. We stopped the forced removals with people's power. That is why Thembelihle is still here. The ANC did not want us to be here. . . . We know that this government will never give us anything unless we fight for it. It is our struggle that is bringing electricity to Thembelihle."[70] The reference to people's power underscored a connection between popular mobilization before and after racial inclusion. Conversely, the ANC also celebrated the electrification project as an indicator of state-driven development. In practice, the two celebrations went hand in hand.

Tsakane10

Located on the East Rand within the Ekurhuleni municipality, the informal settlement of Tsakane10 lay adjacent to a conglomeration of impoverished Black townships. The postapartheid state constructed the residential area in 2007 by relocating residents from other areas where officials determined that the land was unsuitable for human settlement. This was precisely the outcome that Thembelihle residents consistently opposed. Beginning in 2008 and continuing for years afterward, Tsakane10 residents protested with the hope of improving their situation. They targeted local municipal and provincial officials. Revolving around service delivery issues, the demands resembled those in Motsoaledi and Thembelihle.

Bobo was thirty-five years old, unemployed, and living in a shack when we met in 2014. He explained how issues of service delivery lay at the core of the protests: "Last week we marched to the mayor here in Tsakane, because we need the better services. It is not the first time to organize the march. I think it is the fifth time. So we are going there to submit the memorandum. . . . When we talk to them in Germiston [the municipal government], he said we have a budget [allocated funding]. . . . But since we are here, we haven't seen anything. . . . Actually the community is crying. That's why the [protest] happened."[71] The demands were plenty. Residents sought better access to water, the installation of electricity, tar roads, and the replacement of "bucket" toilets with something more dignified. As one protest leader put it: "It's like we are living in a bush [rural area]. We are just neglected."[72]

Residents' most central demand was for the government to separate families into their own stands. When the state relocated residents to the area, it combined families in groups of three on small plots of land, or stands. Residents wanted the state to dedensify the area. They complained that the stands were too small and that it was uncomfortable and unsanitary for three families to share a single toilet. Ayanda explained the demands of a recent protest: "Our first priority is to be separated. We want one stand for one family, one toilet for [one] family. We don't want to share as we believe it's unhealthy to share the toilet. We demand clean water, streets, and we also demand to have playgrounds for our kids, of which we believe that is what is going to limit crime in our area."[73] These engagements produced limited results. By the middle of 2017, the state had moved more than one hundred families into formal RDP houses in a newly constructed settlement nearby. Even with this action, however, most of the residents remained in the area, and their grievances persisted.

Bekkersdal

The township of Bekkersdal was located on the West Rand, forty-five kilometers from the Johannesburg city center. Unlike the large metropolitan municipalities of Johannesburg and Ekurhuleni, which boasted three to five million people each, Bekkersdal was part of the much smaller Westonaria municipality, which contained just over one hundred thousand people (in late 2016, Westonaria dissolved into the larger Rand West City municipality). Bekkersdal included a formal housing settlement, built in the 1940s, as well as various informal settlements that emerged in the late 1980s and early 1990s.[74] Protests incorporated both areas, though the formal housing settlement represented the epicenter of local activism. Residents began to protest around various issues in the late 2000s and early 2010s, but protests exploded forcefully in 2013.[75] A decision by the municipality to raise the fee for gravesites, making it more than seven times the previous amount, provided the initial trigger, but frustration spilled over into other issues.

Charles grew up in Bekkersdal and was recently involved in activism when we met in early 2014. He described how the scope of the protests quickly expanded:

> You see, in the process of the struggle, one issue will open up another issue. For example, when the protest started, there was an issue of the grave fees. The first day the grave fees were R270, and the next day when we woke up the grave fees were R1960. . . . We wrote a letter and submitted it to the minister and said we have a problem of service de-

livery, and guys who work in the municipality do not collect waste, and we also have a problem of sewer. You cannot tell the difference between sewer water and rainwater.[76]

If grave fees provided the impetus for gathering residents together to discuss their grievances, the issue of running sewage in the streets eventually took center stage. The media seized upon it.

Beneath these trigger issues lay a wide range of grievances. Once the lid on the boiling pot of poverty and frustration blew open, any number of issues could propel protests forward. New to activism, the twenty-three-year-old Tumelo thrust herself into the 2013 protests. Several months later, her excitement was still palpable. She underscored several reasons for joining the protests: "We demanded—my demands specifically were . . . You can see I have a baby. Our kids cannot play; they are not safe. We needed our municipality to come and unblock the drains. Secondly, unemployment rate, we needed them to do their job and employ youth. Thirdly, as they had promised to assist us with schools, we heard the money was out, but the municipality, we hear, misused that money. So we thought, if we speak our voice, we will be heard."[77] The encapsulating notion of service delivery was powerful because it summarized a whole range of frustrations, grievances, and demands—from fixing the sewage problem, to employing young people, to providing funding for education. Residents directed all of these demands toward the state, especially the local municipality.

Perceived failure of a major development effort, the Bekkersdal Renewal Project (BRP), propelled further frustration.[78] The project adopted wide-ranging goals, including new parks; a clinic and community center; formal housing; roads; improved access to water, toilets, and electricity; and the reduction of crime and unemployment.[79] Activists complained that state officials squandered the money for the project. They asserted that some funds had disappeared, while the rest went toward what activists commonly referred to as "white elephant" projects: infrastructure, such as a new community center, that did little to benefit the majority of residents. Sizwe, a prominent activist, explained:

> A pledge was signed that R1.2 billion should develop Bekkersdal. Ten years down the line, we still get nothing for the R1.2 billion that you can see or point that it has been done. . . . For about four years now, [the buildings they built] have not been utilized, and the intention was that they should uplift the lives of the community. Why are they not operational? Why are they not even monitored? That's how some of them were even vandalized. They are just white elephants; and we said, but look, we cannot continuously have problems caused by government and not speak out.[80]

The apparent failure of the BRP to bring meaningful development to the area only exacerbated frustration with various service delivery issues, such as running sewage and rubbish in the streets, overflowing toilets in the informal settlements that needed draining, and slow progress on a new housing development nearby. Sizwe continued: "The activities of service delivery came in now, to say that we cannot continue to have sewer network problems for so many years. . . . Over and above is the question of maladministration and mismanagement of funds and nepotism taking place upon our local government. And we say, look, we are not going to allow that situation to continue anymore."[81] Discourses of administrative failure were especially prevalent in Bekkersdal. Nonetheless, popular demands revolved around service delivery and the public provision of resources. That many Bekkersdal activists lived in formal houses rather than tin shacks did not change this basic defining feature. The emphasis on service delivery, in Bekkersdal and elsewhere, reflected popular disappointment with the postapartheid state amidst conditions of economic insecurity.

Economic insecurity sparked a vibrant reaction from society. Ravaged by poverty and unemployment, the residents of Black townships and informal settlements responded with widespread and often militant protests. Local protests called on the state to provide social protection in the form of resources, such as housing and electricity, or what residents and the media frequently called "service delivery." Beyond just livelihood, service delivery was also about fulfilling the promises of national liberation and racial inclusion. This became evident through the ways in which residents identified with and demanded recognition from the state. Reactivating the popular energy that lay beneath the antiapartheid struggles of the 1980s, protesters condemned government officials for failing to fulfill their historical mission of redemption for the Black majority. In short, local protests challenged South Africa's passive revolution. They called on government officials to stop the betrayal that passive revolution inevitably entailed and to meet the expectations it left unfulfilled.

Given their common vocabulary of service delivery, their common emphasis on recognition, and their common usage of disruptive tactics, the protests appeared to represent a unified movement. Even at a surface level, however, the emergence of fragmentation was evident. The different historical trajectories of local areas penetrated popular demands for service delivery, suggesting that widespread protests were not as unified as they might have appeared. In the following chapter, I show how popular struggles on the terrain of political society reinforced localization and division.

Part 2

FRAGMENTATION

COMMUNITY

One might have expected South Africa's local protests to cohere around a broader social movement. Not only did they share common repertoires of struggle and mobilize a significant section of society, but residents also had a recent example from which to draw. The antiapartheid struggle represented a vibrant national movement that unified otherwise disparate local mobilizations. Like postapartheid protests for service delivery, protests in the 1980s frequently emanated from impoverished Black urban areas, and they often revolved around demands for public resources. The broader political context, however, differed dramatically. Protesters in the postapartheid period confronted not official racial exclusion but an outwardly sympathetic government that claimed to be catering to their interests. In the wake of racial inclusion, how did protesting residents constitute a collective identity and give their struggles moral appeal? In this chapter, I show how residents turned to place-based notions of community to propel their struggles, with a mixture of positive and negative consequences for movement building.

Popular understandings of community were also central to antiapartheid resistance during the 1980s. Common opposition to apartheid racism helped to create bridges between disparate local areas. Many local organizations, for example, joined the United Democratic Front (UDF), which opposed apartheid racial exclusion. As a leading proponent for democratization and racial inclusion, the Congress of South African Trade Unions (COSATU) also facilitated connections between local struggles and the national antiapartheid movement. COSATU provided a unifying class lens that linked workplace and residential struggles. As Gay Seidman explains, unions brought "an understanding of class relations" into popular struggles, with labor activists "often redefining community issues in terms of working-class interests."[1] The passive revolution undermined these bridges through demobilization and absorption. The UDF disbanded in the early 1990s after the unbanning of the ANC, and COSATU entered a formal partnership with the ruling party. The latter pulled trade unions closer to the state and away from struggles within residential areas.[2] Passive revolution thus produced narrower visions of community, which became increasingly detached from unifying national categories of race and class.

The absorption of trade unions and community groups into the orbit of the ANC left activists on their own to build new vehicles of resistance. They did so by identifying and mobilizing place-based communities in the residential areas where they lived. This resonates strongly with Chatterjee's analysis of strategic politics within political society, which require segments of the population to constitute themselves as deserving of government welfare. Community is a versatile and malleable social construct that varied actors may deploy to advance a wide array of political projects. It invokes a sense of history, pride, and strong social ties, enabling activists to infuse their claims with emotions, values, and moral weight.[3] As Patricia Hill Collins remarks, "When individuals cease seeing themselves as part of a mass, a mob, a collectivity, a population, or a public, and instead claim a sense of belonging to a community, they are primed for political analysis and action."[4] This is precisely what political society demands. For Chatterjee, notions of community are crucial because they enable segments of the population to infuse "their collective identity with a moral content."[5] In South Africa, residents deployed place-based notions of community to secure recognition and varied forms of service delivery.

Postapartheid deployments of community had contradictory effects. They proved especially valuable for navigating the complex and often hostile terrain of politics after racial inclusion. The passive revolution empowered a single political party, the ANC, but failed to deliver on its promises. The ANC's perceived betrayal underpinned both a distrust of political parties and growing political division as opposition parties gained ground. An emphasis on place-based community enabled activists to negotiate this tricky landscape of deepening party competition. But community had its limits. On the one hand, notions of community isolated local activists and, to a certain extent, pit them against each other. On the other hand, because notions of community often glossed over important underlying differences with respect to employment, they also fed into internal antagonism toward workers. Organizing around community thus enabled a limited form of class formation defined by narrow and fragmented solidarities.

Participation and Community in Transition

In their groundbreaking work on poor people's movements, Frances Fox Piven and Richard A. Cloward note, "It is typically by rebelling against the rules and authorities associated with their everyday activities that people protest."[6] In postapartheid South Africa, local government and local political party dynamics represented key focal points. Local government inherited activist commitments to popular participation, as previously expressed through ideas about people's power.[7] The new democratic constitution, provisionally laid out in 1993 and formally adopted in 1996, identified the local state as one of three key spheres of government, alongside the provincial and the national. The constitution mandated that local government should be "democratic and accountable," "encourage the involvement of communities and community organizations," "ensure the provision of services to communities," and "promote social and economic development."[8] The local state thus inherited an enormous dual role: to enable popular participation and to provide services and development. Given widespread unemployment and poverty, handling these responsibilities was quite a heavy task. The *local* became a key site for managing popular expectations and economic insecurities.[9]

The Local Government Transition Act of 1993 called for consultation and engagement with civil society to establish Land Development Objectives and Integrated Development Plans (IDPs). Despite the promise of participation, however, technocratic decision making and emphasis on top-down service delivery predominated, relegating residents to the role of clients and consumers.[10] Patrick Heller concludes that the initiatives "served largely as instruments for exerting political and bureaucratic control and as vehicles for marketization, rather than as institutional spaces for democratic participation."[11] In many instances, rather than incorporating input, government used planning processes to legitimate decisions taken elsewhere.[12] A long-standing popular emphasis on *delivery* gave legitimacy to the top-down approach. Some activists imagined their primary role as ensuring that local government delivers. The popular demand for timely delivery—already evident in the last years of apartheid—undermined emergent efforts to incorporate Black participation into urban development planning.[13]

The politics of national liberation reinforced these patterns. For some within the ANC and allied organizations, people's power was always more about insurrection and challenging apartheid than it was about popular decision making. This stemmed from the ANC's view of itself as the true bearer of national liberation and the only organization with revolutionary potential and correct politics.[14] In the wake of racial inclusion, this same view undermined efforts at participatory democracy because the ANC understood its own program as synonymous with the interests of the public.[15] Internal dynamics within the ruling party took precedence over participatory mechanisms. Within the ANC, the center dominated over local branches, giving ordinary members little say over party policy or local branch leadership.[16] Ward councilors had little power to shape political agendas, and they were more accountable to party structures than they were to voters. Despite prominent rhetoric about the value of popular participation in decision making, officials often viewed it more as a nuisance than as a key priority.[17] At the same time, local government became an important source of upward mobility and enrichment for politically connected individuals. This only furthered popular frustration.

Notions of community often further enabled technocratic, party-driven, and top-down decision making. The liberation movement fostered deep skepticism of representative democracy, and some within the movement emphasized the continued importance of civil society participation even after the democratic transition.[18] Local government represented the site for this participation, and *community* became its civil society counterpart. Crucially, though, activists often used notions of community to justify the domination of singular groups, which claimed to represent the interests of residents within specific geographic areas.[19] Such views followed from the ANC's claims to represent the people. Organizations aligned with the ANC presented nonaligned organizations as opposed to the general will of residents in the area.[20] State officials reinforced these claims by recognizing certain groups as representatives of the entire community.[21] Under apartheid and after racial inclusion, notions of community thus enabled the ANC to limit popular participation and extend its domination over civil society.[22]

The hollowing out of participatory mechanisms, the ANC's domination of civil society, and the prominent emphasis on technocratic decision making were all elements of South Africa's passive revolution. They enabled elite empowerment and the demobilization of society, and they focused activists on the temporal and contextual aspects of government administration that Chatterjee associates with political society. This history of participation in transition had crucial implications for local organizing. First, it made available the idea of place-based community: an apparently homogenous group of residents who live within a specific geographic area. Community became a popular and important source of local solidarity, especially for those seeking to challenge aspects of the state. If the ANC used notions of community to challenge apartheid, after racial inclusion activists used them to challenge the ANC.[23] Second, however, community represented an important site of ANC dominance. This created a hostile terrain for activists with critical or oppositional positions, who had to contend with supporters of the ruling party. Protesters responded by muting their political challenges. Third, community became a technocratic category associated with local government and the delivery of public goods. State officials could use self-declared representatives of the community, and the geographic boundaries that they promoted, as tools for implementing development projects. Rather than building bridges across areas, activists thus became entangled in bureaucratic, top-down mechanisms.

Hostile Terrain

The proliferation of local protests took place against a backdrop of simultaneous ANC dominance and decline. Writing in 2015, at the beginning of South Africa's third decade of democracy, the prominent ANC analyst Susan Booysen remarked that the ruling party "is strong but flawed, and increasingly frayed. . . . It is on the borderline where famed-liberation-movement-turned-political-party could become an ordinary contestant in a multiparty democracy or—worse—predatory strongman." The ANC, she continued, still "leads with substantial margins over its political rivals" and controls powerful state apparatuses. Nonetheless, patronage and corruption threatened the functioning of public institutions, growing doubts loomed about the party's moral leadership, and opposition parties were gaining strength. It was "still the time of ANC dominance and hegemony," but the "liberation dividend" was "wearing thin," and the ruling party was beginning to lose its grip.[24]

ANC dominance reached its apex in the mid-2000s, just as local protests began to emerge (figure 4). During national government elections, for example, support for the ruling party increased from 63 percent in 1994 to 70 percent one decade later. This pattern held locally in the case study areas. As of 2004, ANC support in the municipalities of Johannesburg (69 percent), Ekurhuleni (70 percent), and Rand West City (73 percent) matched ANC support at the national level. Support for the ANC in local government elections, which peaked at 64 percent nationally in 2006, revealed a similar pattern. The tides began to turn for the ruling party in the second decade of democracy. Between 2004 and 2019, support for the ANC in national government elections dropped steadily from 70 percent to 57.5 percent nationally, with similar declines evident in Johannesburg, Ekurhuleni, and Rand West City. The ANC fared even worse in local government elections, where support reached new lows in 2016: 54 percent nationally, 53 percent in Rand West City, 49 percent in Ekurhuleni, and 45 percent in Johannesburg. The 2016 local government elections sent a wakeup call to the ruling party, which lost control of three metropolitan municipalities, including Johannesburg and Tshwane in Gauteng Province and Nelson Mandela Bay in Eastern Cape Province. In these three municipalities the Democratic Alliance (DA) assumed power with support from the Economic Freedom Fighters (EFF).

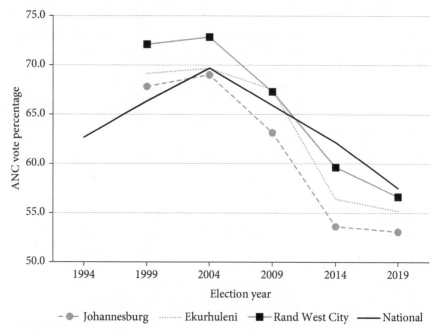

FIGURE 4. ANC support in national government elections, by municipality, 1994–2019.

Source and notes: Electoral Commission of South Africa, http://www.elections.org.za/content/default.aspx. Rand West City formed in 2016 through a merger of the Westonaria and Randfontein municipalities. Figures for previous years combine the election results for these two municipalities.

Despite this decline, the ANC continued to dominate the state apparatus, including at the local level. As of 2015, for example, more than 65 percent of local ward councilors in Johannesburg and Ekurhuleni were ANC members, while in Westonaria (merged into the Rand West City municipality in 2016), ANC members accounted for 94 percent of local ward councilors. Even in the Johannesburg municipality, where a DA-EFF coalition briefly overtook the ruling party in 2016, the ANC still had more city councilors than any other party and managed to regain control of the municipality in 2019.[25] ANC members held all of the ward councilor positions in the four case study areas. Because protesters typically directed their frustrations and demands toward the state, ANC dominance of local government meant that protests often appeared to oppose the ANC. Charles, a twenty-eight-year-old activist from Bekkersdal, explained that the local struggle was not "anti-ANC" but rather "about poor service delivery and poor performance of government. . . . This month, we will be celebrating twenty years of democracy, but we don't have democracy in Bekkersdal." He did, though, acknowledge the blurry distinction between party and state: "We are not fighting [with any particular party]. But we are trying to raise our concerns towards government, and government is led by the ANC. But the struggle is not [op]posed to any political party; it is [op]posed to our local government. But now our local government is led by the ANC. Now the ANC thinks that the struggle is directed to them."[26] Even if activists did not intend to oppose the ANC, protest actions often assumed such a character. To the extent that protests appeared threatening to the ruling party, declining ANC support only exacerbated the tension.

Confronting what they viewed as threats to ANC dominance, or even their own personal benefits associated with relations of patronage, party loyalists inside and outside of the state moved to suppress collective resistance.[27] In describing the difficulties of organizing within this hostile terrain, activists highlighted a combination of intimidation and attempts at incorporation. State employees and loyalist members pressured them to join the ANC, offered them bribes to keep quiet, and subjected them to physical violence and arrest. Tido, for example, an activist in Tsakane10, described how ANC loyalists kidnapped, beat, and threatened him with death, only to later offer him a bribe to keep quiet.[28] In Thembelihle, Thabo explained how ANC members, including government employees, offered him political positions, land, and housing to cease organizing efforts. Police also arrested him multiple times, leading to ongoing court appearances. Connecting his arrests to political motives, Thabo described how one officer explicitly defended the ruling party: "[The officer] says, 'I will deal with anyone who is disrupting the ANC. I will not tolerate you people to discredit the ANC.'"[29]

The story of Mpho, a young activist from Motsoaledi, illustrated how politically motivated intimidation discouraged involvement in resistance activities. Mpho became involved in local activism and social movements when he was in high school.[30] Local ANC members repeatedly, but unsuccessfully, tried to recruit him into the ruling party: "They came back again, more than five times actually, and it's different people. . . . At first it was just talking, and they started telling me that if you sign here, our party is gonna do this; we gonna do that for you; just sign here, forcing me to sign something I didn't want to sign."[31] With his persistent rejections, Mpho's activism became a threat to the ANC. In return, he began to receive direct, physical threats: "My mother was worried because she found out that I got a lot of threats from other politicians. . . . Some even threatened to end my life if I didn't quit politics. . . . They were coming from different political parties, especially our own political party, the one that is carrying South Africa at large [i.e., the ANC]."[32] Mpho's unwillingness to explicitly name the ANC reflected a tinge of ongoing fear. Out of concern for his personal safety, Mpho removed himself from local activism.

These accounts echoed Fanon's concerns about the nationalist party devolving into dictatorship and using force to silence dissent. They underscored the difficulty of organizing for social change in the postapartheid context. Remaining an activist over an extended period required deep commitment and thick skin. The challenges were not only personal. Beyond managing hostile responses from ANC loyalists, local activists also had to negotiate a political terrain characterized by growing political divisions. Party competition presented an even bigger obstacle than direct intimidation and repression.

Fluid Party Loyalties

If repression represented one side of the ongoing passive revolution, political fragmentation was the other. As the betrayal of ANC leaders came into focus for many residents, the opposition gained strength. The main opposition party nationally, the DA, slowly began to shed its long-standing appearance as a party primarily for white voters. The party elected as its leader a Black man from Soweto, Mmusi Maimane, and sought to make inroads into predominantly Black residential areas. The DA also campaigned on its record as the ruling party in Western Cape Province from 2009. Even more important, however, was the formation in 2013 of the EFF, led by the former ANC Youth League president Julius Malema. The EFF's introduction into the electoral sphere, with a prominent focus on Black economic empowerment, provided voters with a way to punish or abandon the ANC without leaving the fold of the national liberation movement. EFF support grew modestly at the national level, from 6 percent in 2014 to 11 percent in 2019. In many impoverished Black townships and informal settlements, however, it quickly became the main opposition party.

Survey evidence shows that many residents maintained an emotional attachment to the ruling party, due to its significant role in achieving racial inclusion, while others had faith in the ANC's ability to govern. Not surprisingly, residents who received welfare benefits, such as free housing or a cash transfer, were more likely to vote for the ANC.[33] Age was crucially important. Whereas the ANC drew its strongest support from older voters, who were more likely to have participated in antiapartheid struggles, the EFF performed best among younger voters. This hinted at a possible changing of the guard, with younger Black residents taking control of South African politics. The situation, however, was remarkably more complex. Perhaps most importantly, declining loyalty to the ANC did not translate into close attachments to opposition parties. By 2018, more than half (53 percent) of residents nationally did not feel close to any political party.[34] Party dealignment meant that many eligible voters chose not to vote at all, with abstention rising from 16 percent in 1994, to 42 percent in 2004, to 49 percent in 2019.[35]

This instability underpinned the fluid party loyalties of residents in protest areas. Feelings of betrayal often centered on disappointment with ANC officials in government, though some activists remained loyal to the ruling party. They wanted to see the ANC improve so that it could fulfill its historical mission. Mandla from Motsoaledi, for example, hinted at the possibility of mobilizing support for the EFF. But his loyalties were clear: "We told them, if you do not pull up your socks, Malema is coming. We can call him now. . . . But we do not want to do that. We grew up with ANC."[36] While Mandla sought to engage and reconfigure the ruling party, others had little interest in doing so. In Bekkersdal, for example, the Black Consciousness tradition and the socialist-oriented Azanian People's Organization (AZAPO), an ANC rival, had an important legacy that helped to inspire support for the EFF. Matsobane, a Bekkersdal resident who "grew up under the ranks of AZAPO," explained that Bekkersdal "has always been a home of socialists. . . . That is why the 'son of the soil' Julius Malema came to the township. . . . He has been saluted by the AZAPO members because the EFF policies and manifesto are similar to that of AZAPO, and that is why the ANC hates us so much. This is the home of the socialists."[37]

The political consequences of betrayal thus ran in a multitude of directions. If some residents continued to thrust high expectations onto the ANC, others were willing to give opposition parties a chance to fulfill the promises of national liberation and racial inclusion. The tension between these different positions permeated residential areas, households, and even individuals who shifted their views over time. Kaya, a Tsakane10 activist, illustrated the complexity as she sought to manage a tricky balance of multiple political allegiances. Kaya was disappointed with the ANC's performance and was active in protests directed at the local ANC-led government. It was therefore not surprising that she supported the two main opposition parties: "I want EFF and DA to win local government. DA councilors worked in the Western Cape, so I think they can put pressure on [the ANC] and represent the community." While supporting opposition parties locally, however, Kaya did not support change at the national level: "ANC has come a long way. The person that fought for the freedom [Nelson Mandela], even though he is gone, I feel that the party should always be there so that he may also rest in peace. But I wish for the name not to die."[38] At the same time, she wanted to replace current ANC national leaders because "they only feed their pockets."[39] Kaya's nuanced position demonstrated the instability and fluidity of popular politics.

Activists were well aware of the challenges associated with deepening political party competition. While frustration with the ANC mounted, organizing around opposition to the ruling party was a losing battle because opposition parties still claimed limited support. Many residents remained loyal to the party of Mandela and national liberation. Andrew, a prominent Tsakane10 activist, explained: "Even now, if someone can come from that corner, inviting the community to a meeting wearing political colors, only those who believe in that political party will go. If you come not wearing any political colors, then people will come and join you."[40] During one protest in Tsakane10, for example, ANC members did not support a protest because they worried that it was "politically motivated" and intended to "disrupt their organization not to win the elections again."[41] While the precise political character and trajectory of local organizing varied, tensions around party competition permeated all protest areas. Emphasis on the state represented a common thread across the various political viewpoints. Regardless of where their allegiances lay, many residents agreed that the state should, could, and would cater to their basic needs. In the fluid political climate of crumbling ANC leadership, faith in the state proved to be much more stable than allegiance to specific political parties.

One did not have to vote or belong to a political party to protest and place demands on the state. Tebogo, an unemployed, twenty-six-year-old Bekkersdal resident, demonstrated this reality when a newspaper journalist asked him to explain his participation in recent protests. He described an array of challenges, such as dirty sewage in the streets, lacking recreational facilities and job opportunities, and corruption within the local municipality. His sense of betrayal and despair translated into deep frustration with the ruling party: "We are tired of poor service delivery in this area. . . . We are sick and tired of empty promises from the ANC." Tebogo wore a red beret, the signature symbol of the EFF. But he was not a loyal EFF member: "We want change now. . . . I am not an EFF [member]; neither am I an ANC member. I am just a fed-up resident of Bekkersdal who wants to see change taking place in my community, as in yesterday. We have lived in this dump for too long while holding on to the empty promises of the ANC. It's time we forced them to bring change to the people of Bekkersdal."[42] Like many residents, Tebogo clung dearly to hope for a better life. The EFF may have represented his best outlet for anger and frustration, but the opposition party was not his object of desire. Nor was it the ANC. His object of desire was the postapartheid state, which he hoped would one day deliver on the promise of national liberation and racial inclusion.

From the other side of the political spectrum, Thapelo from Motsoaledi expressed a similar longing for state social protection. A longtime ANC member, he was active in struggles against apartheid and later within his local ANC branch. He was loyal to the ruling party, but this did not distract him from the main prize of service delivery. After the DA took control of the city of Johannesburg following the 2016 local government elections, I asked him whether he had any hope for change under the new local regime. He replied:

[The Johannesburg municipality] can be under DA. As long as things are happening on the ground, we do not mind. Because look, as long as service is coming to the people, even if it was an independent [i.e., nonparty] somebody to be a councilor, I do not mind, as long as he delivers what people they want on the ground. We cannot always be politicizing service delivery. . . . If we do that, we are making people to suffer more. . . . As long as service is being provided to the people, people they won't complain.[43]

By focusing on the state, and especially public service delivery, residents began to move beyond their different political party affiliations. Local activists seized on this approach. To reduce political division and link their struggles to the postapartheid state, they emphasized a category that was especially legible to state officials: community.

Community, Not Politics

Activists deployed discourses of community to imbue their struggles with moral legitimacy and rally popular support. This emphasis stemmed from South Africa's passive revolution, which empowered nationalist elites associated with the ANC—at the expense of redistribution and a more participatory democracy— and engendered a hostile climate of repression and political division. Within this context, political parties represented a tainted and divisive terrain. The fluidity and competitiveness of party politics, rooted in ANC decline and the weakness of opposition parties, meant that invoking political parties necessarily invited division. Further, the process of passive revolution and racial inclusion exposed the flaws of individual activists-turned-politicians, who abandoned the ideals of the liberation movement in favor of their own personal advancement. The betrayal of ANC leaders thus left a negative stain on political parties, which came to represent upward mobility for individuals rather than improvements for the masses.

Community represented the opposite. Activists used the term to refer to all residents within a given geographic area, regardless of their political affiliation. Crucially, community symbolized detachment from party politics. To a certain extent, if not always completely, such detachment enabled activists to sidestep party competition and intimidation from ANC loyalists. Whereas political parties, whether the ANC or an opponent, necessarily claimed only partial support within each area, the community could potentially encapsulate every single resident. Equally important, if not more so, activists used detachment from party politics to signal that they were not attempting to secure political power in the form of government positions. By eschewing party politics, through appeals to community, local activists could avoid accusations or suspicions that they were using local mobilization to pursue narrow ends.[44]

In all four areas, activists explicitly claimed to represent community interests rather than political party interests. They understood the latter to be narrower and less legitimate. This pattern held across areas with different political compositions. In Motsoaledi, for example, where the ANC was especially dominant and many activists identified as ANC supporters, the main local organization, Motsoaledi Concerned Residents, defined itself as "an organization formed by the community of Motsoaledi irrespective of their political affiliation."[45] On the other end, while some prominent activists in Tsakane10 supported the DA, as one activist affirmed: "We all come from different political parties, but when we march, we march with one voice—community. . . . I am a member of the DA. But when we are working, we are not working as DA. We are working as community."[46] Leading activists in a 2014 protest explicitly banned political party symbols. Ayanda explained, "We are not fighting against anyone, and we are not trying to organize. So no one wore a T-shirt for any political party. It was just a peaceful march for Extension 10."[47] The legitimacy of the protest, therefore, rested on a close connection to the community, distance from party politics, and dissociation from explicit attempts to secure political power or government jobs.

Notions of community were especially prevalent in Bekkersdal, where hostility toward the ANC loomed large. While some prominent activists adopted an anti-ANC stance, when acting as a collective, they emphasized the needs of the community. Sello, who grew up in Bekkersdal and participated in recent protests, explained: "If I am fighting for service delivery, I am not fighting for me. I am fighting for the *whole* community. *Everyone living in the community is community.* So if one is going there, another there, then it is not working."[48] This emphasis informed the dominant activist structure in the area, the Greater Westonaria Concerned Residents Association (GWCRA), which included individuals from various political parties: "Within the leadership of this Concerned Residents' [Association], we are apolitical as a structure. But we have representatives from different political parties. . . . They are accommodated here, as a mandate that comes from a public meeting to say that: if we want to push the struggle, this struggle cannot be pushed by a certain group or political party or a group of people, but we need to amalgamate as a community in concern."[49] Maintaining an "apolitical" stance proved challenging, as activists in Bekkersdal consistently targeted ANC-affiliated officials within the local municipal government. To preserve this position they continued to emphasize the centrality of community, which required the independence of local resistance from either broader political challenges or the narrow interests of individuals.

The local struggle in Thembelihle was an exception that proved the rule. Beginning in 2006, the leading protest-oriented organization in the area, the Thembelihle Crisis Committee (TCC), joined the Operation Khanyisa Movement (OKM) electoral front, which contested local government elections in Johannesburg. Despite this opposition, as a small group with no ties to national opposition parties, it did not present a major challenge to the ANC. Significantly, OKM drew primarily on local networks and claims about community. Simphiwe Zwane, a longtime Thembelihle resident and OKM representative, explained: "I think the special thing about us is that we are a community-based movement. So we are able to deal with the community's challenges directly, and as such have grown a lot of trust between ourselves and the community of Thembelihle."[50] TCC and OKM thus relied heavily on their ability to address the place-based demands of Thembelihle residents. While activists did sometimes appeal to broader challenges and party politics, especially around election time, their legitimacy rested primarily on notions of community. This permeated the consciousness of the organization. As one activist put it clearly at a TCC meeting, community well-being was significantly more important than the competition between political parties: "I don't care about DA; I don't care about EFF; I don't care about ANC. But I care about the community that we live in."[51]

Discourses of place-based community enabled solidarity and participation in a context of heightened political division. They also facilitated localization by discouraging joint struggles across local areas. Among the four case study areas, activists in Tsakane10 and Thembelihle made the greatest efforts to coordinate struggles with other areas. In each case, they ran into difficulties. In Tsakane10, an internal tension emerged as some activists sought to contain the struggle to a small area while others sought to include a broader range of areas. Ayanda defended the hyperlocal focus of one march, explaining, "We decided to do it on our own—go out by ourselves, in numbers—so that the mayor can see that we are serious, and no one is pushing us. No motives. We just demand to be separated and service delivery."[52] For him, the legitimacy of the protest depended on its dissociation from any outside influences or political ambitions, thus limiting the struggle both politically and geographically.

For Tsakane10 activists who turned outward, political intimidation reared its head. This did not reflect a greater emphasis on political parties. Consistent with the widespread prevalence of "apolitical" approaches, Jakobo noted that they were "not necessarily anti-ANC" and did "not attack political parties as much as we attack the government . . . and the system the government is operating under."[53] Even with this stance, however, they confronted hostility from ANC members in other areas, who sought to act as gatekeepers. As George, another Tsakane10 activist, put it, "They ask, from whom did we get the permission? They say we must address them first. And you find that the community is interested but the parties are the stumbling block."[54] This intimidation represented the ANC's persistent claim, before and after racial inclusion, to be the sole legitimate representative of Black communities.

Localization was also evident in Thembelihle, despite explicit attempts to connect the local struggle to other areas through OKM. Shifting patterns of OKM support provide a useful window. The local struggle in Thembelihle advanced more rapidly than it did in other initial OKM strongholds. Over time, as OKM support declined overall, it also became increasingly concentrated in Thembelihle. Between the local government elections in 2006 and 2016, the number of OKM votes in Johannesburg municipality dropped from 3,312 to 996. Meanwhile, the proportion of OKM votes coming from Ward 8—where Thembelihle was located—increased from 3 percent to 46 percent.[55] Rather than a broadening alliance of community struggles, OKM thus relied increasingly on the singular community struggle within Thembelihle.

The experiences of Tsakane10 and Thembelihle suggested that discourses of community did not necessarily preclude links to either other residential areas or broader-reaching social movements. In both instances, activists sought to establish wider connections and combine an emphasis on community with critiques of the state and capitalism. Yet there were other forces at play. Most vital was a prominent emphasis on administrative fixes, which exacerbated localization and isolation.

Administrative Fixes

Rather than outward-looking solidarity and class formation, notions of community were more likely to feed into technical and bureaucratic processes of government delivery. As James Scott has shown, a key part of modern state power is the administrative ordering of society to make it legible, arranging the population to simplify state functions. Such order becomes especially dangerous, he suggests, when combined with authoritarian rule, a weak civil society, and a "high-modernist" ideology of self-confidence in rational, technical, and scientific progress.[56] Within South Africa, these processes gained prominence as the ongoing passive revolution elevated state power and technocratic decision making over popular participation.[57] Community, in turn, enabled residents to insert themselves into administrative processes.[58] As Chatterjee's analysis of political society suggests, giving "the empirical form of a population group the moral attributes of a community" allows residents to make themselves legible to the state and thus eligible for government welfare.[59] In this sense, notions of community helped to reduce struggles around service delivery to narrower questions of bureaucratic administration rather than broader questions about redistribution. Struggles from below thus reflected and reinforced maneuvers from above.

Demands for service delivery expressed deep-seated hopes and expectations, as residents believed that the state should and could provide for their basic needs. Protests put these beliefs, which sometimes bordered on faith, into action. Residents wanted to make the system work better and in their own favor. They wanted to call attention to current failures so that government officials could correct them, and the concept of community helped activists to identify place-based groups within the population who had experienced particular neglect. To be sure, some activists had grander visions of socialist transformation. Even in residential areas where such views were prominent, however, protests typically revolved around demands for administrative fixes: narrow bureaucratic adjustments that would deliver resources to a specific residential area. This emphasis reinforced localization and fragmentation by confining resistance within circumscribed geographic areas. It also fed into subtle competition between residents in different areas, which only further reinforced fragmentation.

Popular hope for administrative fixes often focused attention on problematic individuals, rather than broader systemic problems. Sometimes the individuals were specific people, such as local ward councilors, and other times they were problematic individuals in general. Rejoice, a longtime Motsoaledi resident who had her hopes set on a new RDP house, remarked: "They keep on promising. Yes, they will promise you, this and this, jobs and whatever, but there isn't anything that's happening. They are greedy; they are keeping it to themselves. Chances are there, but they are keeping it to themselves and not spreading it. Even when one gets a tender, he just misuse[s] the money. . . . Maybe that's why we don't see that the government is working for us?"[60] Like Rejoice, many residents believed that the state was "not working" due to the poor performance of public servants, who put their own individual interests ahead of community interests. Complaints about corruption and maladministration frequently accompanied protests for improved service delivery.

Residents reserved special disdain for local ward councilors, who they frequently perceived as distant and neglectful. Part of the frustration, however, stemmed from the fact that some residents, including prominent activists, understood local ward councilors as key agents of democratic inclusion and service delivery. In explaining why Thembelihle residents marched to the local municipal offices to protest about electricity, Thabo noted that it was because the local ward councilor was an important "messenger of the community" and thus responsible for taking their grievances to the electricity utility City Power. A Tsakane10 activist similarly suggested that ward councilors resembled union shop stewards, but working in the realm of government rather than the workplace. Just as a shop steward communicates the views of rank-and-file workers to union leaders and managers, he explained, the councilor "comes through to the community to take the problems. . . . [Then] he goes to the housing [department] or to the mayor to put that problems [on behalf of] the community. It's the same tools, actually."[61] Desire to repair these democratic mechanisms frequently underpinned collective resistance.

In all four case study areas, fixing local government became a top priority. Activists in Tsakane10 sought to remove the twice-elected local ward councilor. As one activist explained during a 2014 protest, "We took a decision that the person who is oppressing us is the councilor—no delivery. That is why today the community is this much. . . . The councilor must step down because she has failed this eight years."[62] Likewise, in Bekkersdal, the popular demand to remove and replace the municipal mayor was a common rallying point. The GWCRA wanted higher levels of government to take over the municipality. Sello explained, "Here we have got [a] crisis . . . lack of service delivery; money is being chopped [corruption]. . . . We said we want to remove the councilor and the mayor. . . . Let the administration [higher levels of government] control the municipality. . . . Everyone must be removed because it is corrupt."[63] Elections represented another possible way to change municipal leaders. Activists in Motsoaledi, Thembelihle, and Tsakane10, for example, sought to improve local government by getting their own sympathetic candidates onto their respective town councils, though their efforts met with little success.[64] Prioritizing efforts to change who held local government posts, these approaches frequently isolated activists from each other and displaced broader political challenges.

While protests often appeared to challenge the state, they were also vulnerable to co-optation. Attempts to secure administrative fixes frequently led to engagements with local government officials. Tebogo Mokgope, a prominent Tsakane10 activist, explained that residents were quite willing to engage: "Most communities, we're always willing to work with government to make sure that they address certain things. . . . Most community forums that I know, when the government calls the meeting, [residents] come to the meeting."[65] Protests enabled residents to secure meetings and government attention to local grievances. Contrasting with the sense of urgency that typically accompanied protest action, activists frequently assured me that they were willing to wait for the government to deliver. As Mokgope put it, "We don't have the resources to build houses. The government must build houses. [If they do,] the protests will stop. Simple. Quick solution."[66]

Protest action and subsequent negotiations with government officials often bore fruit. In Motsoaledi, within six months of a major 2013 protest, the state began to construct formal houses within the settlement. In Tsakane10, following a surge of protests in 2014 and 2015, the state relocated more than one hundred households to a new formal housing settlement. In Thembelihle, the provincial government officially registered the area as a formal housing project in April 2015 and the following year began to install formal electricity. In Bekkersdal, protests led to a major new project to rebuild the sewage infrastructure. To a certain extent, then, protests worked. At the same time, concessions dampened resistance. Activists often remarked that it was difficult to sustain struggles over time, precisely because residents disengaged after even small concessions. As Jakobo from Tsakane10 put it, for unemployed activists it is "too hard to keep on holding the flag forever." Once "the government delivers what it has promised," he noted, "you find that the opportunity to mobilize people around any other issue just becomes an issue."[67] Mobilization for administrative fixes often led to quick demobilization.[68]

The incorporation of activists into patronage networks also facilitated demobilization. In all four case study areas, prominent activists developed important relationships with state officials. These relationships provided local leaders with privileged access to information and sometimes even job opportunities. Local activists sat on steering committees for development projects, giving them knowledge about timelines and plans. Some had privileged access to housing allocation lists and potentially even the opportunity to influence such lists. Others secured government contracts or coveted positions as community liaison officers (CLOs). Not only did these connections divert attention from mobilizing and organizing residents, but they also generated frustration, resentment, and division, exacerbating demobilization.

Possibly even more important, demands for administrative fixes prompted a subtle sense of competition over access to scarce state resources.[69] If existing development projects renewed hope or faith, they also generated jealousy. Residents were aware that development was happening around them and expressed frustration that the state was not incorporating them. This dynamic was evident in all four cases. In Motsoaledi, residents often complained that the state neglected them while prioritizing the nearby area of Freedom Park for development. In one public statement, activists bemoaned, "We have been denied the right to benefit from the economic growth in our country."[70] Another statement put it plainly: "Elias Motsoaledi people must be prioritized."[71] In Tsakane10, some residents expressed concern that the state was relocating people from other areas into new housing before them. Kaya lamented, "We were told that we just arrived; those other people have been here for long in the shacks, so they must be sorted first."[72] Similarly, in Thembelihle, some residents worried that the state was prioritizing other areas for relocation to a new housing settlement at Lehae. In Bekkersdal, some activists complained that the government had developed the nearby township of Mohlakeng, while letting their own township devolve into decay.

Mpho, the young activist introduced above, was unemployed and living in a shack with his mother and several extended family members. Using a vivid familial metaphor, Mpho related the underdevelopment of Motsoaledi to parental neglect of an older brother:

> Let me go back to this example. . . . At home they know you love this watch, and they buy it for your brother, and your brother is younger than you. How would that make you feel? . . . Freedom Park was our little brother. [It] came way after Motsoaledi. But look at it, everybody has houses. . . . Now they have proper sanitation; they have electricity; *they have everything that we do not have.* And actually it makes some of the people very angry, some to the extent that they do not even want to see the councilor or hear from the councilor. They don't even want to talk to the councilor; that is how sad and angry people get. . . . This is the first place that came before Freedom Park, before a couple of other places, but only to find those places have already been built. They have been developed, but Motsoaledi is still . . . [73]

Feelings of betrayal, therefore, had an important spatial and relational dimension. They were not only about market exclusion and economic insecurity but also inferior treatment compared to peers in other residential areas. As Mpho's analysis underscored, residents frequently directed their frustration toward a local government official, the ward councilor.

Matsobane, a Bekkersdal activist, offered a remarkably similar analysis: "Three kilometers from us is the Mohlakeng township. It has developed far better than Bekkersdal, and yet it was developed after Bekkersdal. But today it has eleven extensions. It has recreational structures. Infrastructure is one hundred percent satisfactory. They may have certain issues of service delivery here and there, but it is not like us. We have been neglected in Bekkersdal."[74] Matsobane attributed government neglect of Bekkersdal to poor local leadership. In Mohlakeng, he argued, local officials were "bona fides" who lived in the area and therefore knew "the dos and don'ts." Bekkersdal was a different story because the local officials were not originally from the area: "You find people whom we don't know. . . . It becomes a problem when you deploy someone who does not come from that area because that person does not have the interest of that community at heart."[75] Just as Mpho placed blame on the local councilor, Matsobane attributed the lack of development in Bekkersdal to poor local governance, due especially to the deployment of ANC officials from other areas.

When focused primarily on administrative fixes, the politics of community thus had important limits. It encouraged localized activism, incorporation into official bureaucratic mechanisms, and competition between residential areas. In turn, the localization of resistance generated tension by creating pressure to produce unity and participation within residential areas. Notions of community ultimately proved thin, as expressions of local solidarity often gave way to internal antagonism. One of the most important antagonisms emerged in the division between the employed and the unemployed.

Attacking Workers

In the struggle, they usually say there is no struggle without casualties.
—Themba, Bekkersdal[76]

Moments of protest were crucial for constructing community and giving it physical expression. The stay-away tactic, which gained prominence during anticolonial and antiapartheid struggles, was central.[77] Resembling a general strike that extends across workplaces, the stay-away entailed a boycott of outside activities for the day, including primarily work and school.[78] Indeed, residents often referred to local protest as "strikes."[79] Yet, whereas during the 1980s trade unions often helped to organize stay-aways, in the postapartheid period, unions grew distant from resistance within residential areas. Further, unemployed activists were prevalent, and workers within specific urban areas held jobs at a wide variety of workplaces.[80] Without the support of collective workplace organizing, workers had to decide whether to join stay-aways on an individual basis. When working residents chose work rather than protest, they often confronted retaliation.

The declining significance of workplace organizing underpinned an important shift in the goal of stay-aways. Whereas unions can influence the economy by organizing the collective withdrawal of labor power, this strategy was less central to proliferating local protests in the postapartheid period. Rather than drawing a picket line around workplaces, with the goal of keeping workers out, activists drew picket lines around residential areas, with the goal of keeping residents in. The primary goal was to increase the pool of potential protesters and thus the impact of the protest. Kaya explained a stay-away in Tsakane10 by noting, "We wanted a strong march and [to] send a message so that they fulfill our needs." If some residents went to work, she added, they would not have a "good outcome."[81] Mpho, from Motsoaledi, echoed Kaya's account: "If everybody went to work and every student and learner went to school, how many people will be involved in the strike, so it will have impact? . . . So that's why a lot of people are told not to go to work. Just participate."[82]

A successful stay-away required disrupting transportation. Activists frequently attempted to secure support from drivers of local minibus taxis, known as *kombis*, sixteen-passenger vans that represented the primary mode of transport in most low-income areas. These attempts typically met with limited success. Unable to convince taxi drivers (or their bosses) to give up business for the day, activists often turned to more coercive methods. The latter included barricading roads to block transportation and establishing checkpoints to make sure that no workers left the area for work. Kaya remarked, "We would just stop them and make them join."[83] In some instances, activists punished escaping workers with physical attacks. While not all protests took the form of stay-aways, physical confrontations with workers took place in all four of the case study areas.[84]

Resentment underpinned antagonism toward workers. Residents expressed frustration that workers, who were also members of the community, skipped protests even though they stood to benefit. In Motsoaledi, Mpho argued that workers were obligated to sacrifice like everybody else: "*Workers are people who live in this community as well*, and they are rushing to their jobs. . . . That's not fair—let's be honest—while others are sacrificing. Why they cannot sacrifice? Because we [are] fighting for the same thing at the end of the day. So some other workers were kept; others were even slapped a little so that they get it inside their skull that this is a strike."[85] Similarly, in Thembelihle, Thabo explained that activists expected workers to struggle for the good of the community, which meant prioritizing their interests as residents over their interests as workers:

> What makes people angry is that at the end of the day, when we achieve this thing, everyone is going to achieve, not only those who are participating in the protest. So you will find those people wanting to go to work, [but] some of the people they sacrifice their job and be part and parcel of the protest. So that's why we end up fighting amongst ourselves, you see? Those who want to protest will fight with those who don't want to participate. [Protesters] will start beating them up because they are sell outs, you know?[86]

In Bekkersdal, Tumelo echoed these sentiments: "People who are unemployed felt that people who are employed were ignorant, because they work. So they wanted their support to say, 'Our brothers are sitting here in the township, doing nothing, doing drugs.' So it turned out that those that are unemployed were fighting the employed ones. They did not want them to go to work. At some point, they say it was a stay-away, and if they find you in the taxi or on your way to work, they beat you up."[87] In all of these instances, activists expected workers to make individual sacrifices for the greater good of the community. Physical altercations during protests, between unemployed residents and working residents, demonstrated that communities were fragile. While activists frequently claimed to speak on behalf the community, inevitably protests only partially represented the diverse intentions of residents in the given area. This held true despite the fact that public meetings, where residents frequently took decisions to protest, were impressively democratic and often boasted participation from hundreds of residents and households. Workers exposed this weakness when they chose to skip protests and go to work.

With the political incorporation of antiapartheid resistance organizations into the state, local activists had to build new vehicles of mobilization from scratch. In meeting this challenge, notions of community provided a solution to a practical problem: the difficulty of organizing and uniting population groups that were rife with divisions based on political affiliation and employment. Community proved to be a powerful rhetorical tool, enabling localized solidarity between individuals that might have otherwise aligned themselves with different struggles. Yet this solidarity had crucial limits. When combined with popular faith in the state and expectations of service delivery, notions of community and emphasis on administrative fixes encouraged the narrowing of struggles to local areas. This isolated activists from each other and created a subtle sense of competition over access to scarce resources. Pronouncements of community also met practical limits, particularly during stay-away actions, when activists confronted neighbors who did not want to abandon their jobs for the collective good. In these instances, physical confrontation and community solidarity were opposite sides of the same coin.

In contrast to the 1980s, powerful movements against state-driven racial oppression or employer-driven class exploitation no longer permeated notions of community. This did not mean that activism was entirely devoid of transformative agendas. Especially in Tsakane10 and Thembelihle, for example, prominent activists participated in broader social movements, which in turn reinforced their commitments to class-based and socialist-oriented transformative politics. Even in these cases, however, a narrow politics focused on administrative fixes—with the end goal of improving service delivery in a specific residential area—prevailed much of the time. Compared to transformative solutions, such as broad-reaching changes to the state and its economic policies, administrative solutions promised more immediate and straightforward benefits. The context of widespread unemployment and deep poverty made such solutions especially attractive.

Isolation reinforced inward turns against local targets. This was not a new phenomenon. The long and varied history of working-class resistance across the globe is full of examples where groups with similar long-term interests developed antagonistic relationships. For every picket line, there is a scab. In this case, popular frustration with poverty and unemployment, the isolation of local activism, and the absence of workplace organization all brought antagonism between the employed and unemployed to the fore. Physical attacks against employed residents were only one form of inward-looking antagonism. As I show in the next chapter, attacks against foreign-born residents were another.

NATIONALISM

In May 2008, a wave of antimigrant attacks spread through the townships and informal settlements of South Africa. Over the course of a few weeks, Black South Africans physically attacked foreign-born Black Africans, chased them from their homes, looted their property, and demanded that they return to their countries of birth. This was not the first instance of xenophobia after racial inclusion. Smaller-scale and more geographically limited attacks began as early as 1994 and persisted through the first decade of democracy. Yet the 2008 attacks were more widespread, demonstrating a remarkable surge of xenophobic antagonism. They left sixty-two people dead, many more injured, and up to one hundred thousand displaced from their homes.[1] Most of the victims were foreign-born, though roughly one-third of those who died were native-born, including those who were married to foreign-born residents, who refused to support the violence, or who the attackers nonetheless deemed as outsiders to local areas.

Shattering the myth that South Africa had somehow moved beyond the racial antagonisms of the apartheid past, the 2008 attacks shocked the nation and made international headlines. One group of commentators remarked, "The surprise and anxiety triggered by the violence of May derive from the implosion of fantasy—the fantasy of an inclusive 'rainbow' nation whose citizens regard difference not merely with tolerance, but with respect."[2] Also shocking was that the attacks targeted Black migrants from other African countries. This "intraracial" antagonism reversed the legacy of Black solidarity against white colonial rule, which spread across southern Africa. Indeed, the apartheid state defined all Black

African residents as foreigners and noncitizens within white South Africa, whether they were born abroad or within the boundaries of South Africa. In response, popular struggles against apartheid did not emphasize native/foreigner distinctions, and oppositional forces in exile drew heavily on support from recently decolonized countries in the southern African region.[3]

Antagonism toward foreign-born residents continued after the 2008 eruption. Ongoing attacks featured two different forms of nationalist exclusion: a more generalized *anti-African nationalism*, which entailed the horizontal exclusion of international migrants from the African continent; and a more specific *antitrader nationalism*, which entailed the vertical exclusion of small-scale shop owners and managers from East Africa and South Asia.[4] In both instances, residents targeted groups that they deemed as national outsiders, but anti-African nationalism drew a larger boundary of exclusion that encompassed a wider range of groups. Antitrader nationalism sought to exclude a more specific group of outsiders, whom residents distinguished through a combination of ethnoracial and economic markers. Notably, in neither instance did residents target migrants that they identified as white or European. While present in the country, these latter groups were noticeably absent from the impoverished Black townships and informal shack settlements. Like local protests, xenophobic attacks stayed close to home, focusing on nearby targets rather than distant ones.

These exclusionary nationalisms were often closely tangled and difficult to separate. While the 2008 attacks featured a generalized hostility toward migrants from the African continent, characteristic of anti-African nationalism, they also included collective attacks against foreign-run businesses. Antitrader nationalism nonetheless grew increasingly prominent after 2008. Typical incidents included residents looting shops owned or managed by East African and South Asian migrants, as well as physical attacks against the migrants themselves. Drawing on news reports, Jonathan Crush and Sujata Ramachandran identified 241 episodes of collective violence against migrant traders between 2005 and 2014, excluding the outbreak in May 2008. The attacks increased dramatically over time, from an average of 12 attacks per year between 2005 and 2009 to 35 attacks per year between 2010 and 2014.[5] While anti-African and antitrader nationalisms coexisted and sometimes intermingled, the latter became increasingly prominent. When subsequent waves of xenophobic antagonism emerged in Soweto in 2015 and 2018, for example, they revolved around attacks against foreign-born traders.

Among scholars in South Africa, there is debate over the precise relationship between local protests and xenophobic attacks. Some scholars emphasize their differences and their separation, while others emphasize their commonalities and entanglements.[6] I aim to steer a course in between these two perspectives. I argue that xenophobic antagonism drove a further wedge within already fractured communities. Especially important, it distracted attention from other targets, such as large-scale capital or state policy. Protagonists of protests and protagonists of xenophobic attacks were often, though not always, different people. They also expressed very different, though not necessarily mutually exclusive, politics. It is therefore important to distinguish between protests aimed at local municipalities and xenophobic attacks directed at foreign-born neighbors. At the same time, it is also crucial to acknowledge that xenophobic antagonism did, in some instances, overlap and intermingle with protest action. Some residents viewed the two forms of mobilization as compatible and reinforcing.

It is impossible to make sense of these dynamics separately from the elite-driven politics of South Africa's passive revolution. Crucial elements of this process included demobilization of popular resistance, heavy emphasis on state-led social transformation, and narrow elite struggles over access to state resources. As Neocosmos argues, South Africa followed much of the African continent in equating the nation with the state. This meant abandoning people-driven forms of citizenship from below—as expressed during the antiapartheid struggle through notions of people's power and worker control—in favor of state-driven citizenship from above. Within this process, "citizenship is reduced to passive citizenship and nationhood is reduced to indigeneity."[7] Such processes do not mean, however, that ordinary residents will remain passive. As Fanon warns, the narrow struggles of elites from above may encourage popular xenophobia from below. In South Africa, official postapartheid nationalisms frequently cast migrants as a threat to the nation, linking the ongoing project of national liberation and racial inclusion to a politics of migrant exclusion. Some residents reinforced this exclusionary politics while others challenged it, turning the issue of xenophobia itself into a terrain of struggle.

Popular xenophobia reflected the competitive and strategic terrain of political society. Whereas the previous chapter revealed how this terrain generated narrow struggles for administrative fixes, this chapter shows how claims rooted in indigeneity further fragmented popular resistance. All four of the case study areas experienced xenophobic attacks, which frequently occurred alongside and during protests for service delivery. I illuminate antimigrant antagonism by pointing to three interweaving dynamics: the resentment of foreign-born residents, driven by conditions of economic insecurity; the reconstruction of apartheid-era racial categories to include foreign-born residents, particularly migrant traders; and resistance, including both the coincidence of protest and xenophobic antagonism and the ways in which activists sought to counter xenophobia through discourses of solidarity. Before turning to these dynamics,

I establish the broader political context of official nationalisms that defined South Africa's ongoing passive revolution.

Official Nationalisms

It is impossible to understand popular xenophobic antagonism independently of postapartheid nationalism and elite discourses. As scholars of nationalism have long understood, state formation processes frequently distinguish between national insiders and outsiders. While state elites seek to constitute the populations within their territories as homogeneous polities, the inevitable reality of incomplete integration feeds into patterns of exclusion and ethnic boundary making.[8] International migrants are prototypical outsiders. Their exclusion represents the familiar dark side of nationalism. Following World War II, the rise of national liberation movements, decolonization in Africa and Asia, and the solidification of the nation-state system reinforced these processes. They exacerbated both nationalist ideologies and divisions between natives and migrants.[9] In these senses, South African hostility toward foreign-born residents was not exceptional. The nationalist struggle against apartheid and the persistent reality of widespread economic insecurity helped to amplify the distinction between national insiders and outsiders.[10]

Postapartheid nationalism and the project of racial inclusion featured attempts to redress the historical disadvantages of Black residents and to repair the tenuous relations between various racial groups. While cloaked in a language of inclusion, however, this nation-building project had limits. Based on a shared national history of division and oppression, it often excluded residents who migrated from beyond South African borders. The ANC's negative portrayal of migrant labor, which underpinned the apartheid regime of police surveillance and workplace exploitation, reinforced the political exclusion of nonnationals. Within this view, racial inclusion entailed abolishing migrant labor.[11] Further, state-driven and popular discourses alike distinguished South Africa as exceptional, due to its democracy and development, contrasting with backwardness, poverty, instability, disease, and authoritarianism in the rest of Africa. Nationalist discourses also established a close link between citizenship, birthplace, and race, suggesting that a shared indigeneity entitled Black South Africans to certain privileges.[12] Consistent with this idea, the new South African constitution preserved some rights for citizens only and did not protect against discrimination by nationality.[13]

From the very beginning of the democratic era, official discourses treated foreign-born migrants as a threat to national well-being. A news report on early parliamentary discussions about immigration noted that "politicians from all parties lashed out at illegal immigrants . . . calling them a threat to the Recon-struction and Development Program, a drain on South Africa's resources, and branding them potential criminals, drug smugglers and murderers."[14] The new minister of home affairs, Mangosuthu Buthelezi, put it bluntly in his first speech to parliament in 1994: "If we as South Africans are going to compete for scarce resources with millions of aliens who are pouring into South Africa, then we can bid goodbye to our Reconstruction and Development Program."[15] State dis-courses on migration softened in subsequent years, but traces of hostility re-mained. More than two decades into democracy, Home Affairs Minister Hlengiwe Mkhize explained how the 2017 *White Paper on International Migra-tion*, which prioritized admissions for migrants with skills and capital, sought to address the problems of weak borders and undocumented migration. Noting that such problems exacerbated unemployment, poverty, and inequality, she re-marked, "We cannot be too liberal as though we are not dealing with a real sit-uation that affects people on a daily basis. . . . If we do not manage the process of free movement within the continent, we could end up with a crisis."[16] Nor was the ANC the only culprit, as the leaders of opposition parties also called for bor-der enforcement and migrant exclusion.[17]

Officials frequently downplayed the significance of xenophobia or racism, portraying attacks against foreign-born residents as merely the work of crimi-nal elements.[18] In early 2015, for example, President Jacob Zuma both condemned a recent outbreak of attacks and acknowledged the grievances that under-pinned them. The latter, he suggested, included the following: "That the num-ber of illegal and undocumented migrants is increasing, that they take their jobs as some employers prefer workers who are prepared to accept lower wages. There are also complaints that foreign nationals benefit from free government services, and that they run businesses illegally. There is also an accusation that undocu-mented foreign nationals commit crimes in the country. We reiterate that none of these complaints can justify attacks on foreign nationals and the looting of their shops."[19] While taking care not to explicitly support the attacks, Zuma also appeared to condone them by affirming their popular justifications. While argu-ing that the attacks stemmed from scarce resources and "the legacy of poverty, unemployment and inequality," but he also placed blame on other African coun-tries: "As much as we have a problem that is alleged to be xenophobic, our sister countries contribute to this. Why are their citizens not in their countries and are in South Africa?"[20] Taking a similar position, Deputy Minister of Police Bon-gani Mkongi worried that Johannesburg's heavy concentration of immigrants might signal a broader problem: "If we don't debate that, that necessarily means the whole of South Africa could be 80 percent dominated by foreign nationals and the future president of South Africa could be a foreign national."[21]

Fears of migration and the policing of mobility marked continuity with the apartheid era. As Loren Landau has shown, postapartheid patterns of migration control mirrored the strict regulation of Black movement and residence enacted by the apartheid state: "Whereas the Apartheid state sustained an onslaught on South African citizens' residential rights, the post-Apartheid state has employed similar techniques to alienate and isolate non-nationals."[22] Evidence suggests that law enforcement officials were especially brutal to foreign-born residents, subjecting them to harassment, extortion, and abuse alongside legal bureaucratic practices of arrest, detention, and deportation.[23] According to a 2004 survey of Johannesburg police officers, for example, 87 percent agreed that "most undocumented immigrants are involved in crime," justifying harsh treatment.[24] Building on the legacy of policing movement under apartheid, the practices of the South African Police Service helped South Africa to become one of the most prominent deportation regimes in the world.[25]

Responding to the outbreak of xenophobic attacks in early 2015, the South African National Defense Force launched Operation Fiela—meaning to "clean up" or "sweep away the dirt"—in hotspots of violence. What at first appeared to be an antiracist maneuver quickly turned into an exercise in rounding up migrants, both documented and undocumented, for detention and deportation.[26] On a weekend in early May, the operation turned its attention to the Central Methodist Church in downtown Johannesburg, which had long been a sanctuary for African migrants, who slept in the stairways and pews.[27] During the 2008 attacks, the church took in thousands of migrants who fled for their safety. Seven years later, Operation Fiela cleared out the church during an early morning raid, including five hundred arrests.[28] The bureaucratic response to the 2015 attacks thus followed the imperative of the attacks themselves: expulsion of foreign-born residents. Including official deportations and the displacements that the attacks encouraged, between April and July 2015 more than fifteen thousand undocumented migrants left the country.[29]

Mirroring and encouraging the shifting character of popular xenophobia, official nationalisms increasingly marginalized foreign-born traders. They portrayed a situation in which international migrants from East Africa and South Asia were dominating the sector of *spaza shops*—very small grocery stores found within townships and informal shack settlements—and thus taking away opportunities from native-born residents. There is some limited evidence that migrants from Somalia, Ethiopia, Pakistan, and Bangladesh were especially prominent among small-scale traders in Gauteng Province.[30] It is important to note, though, that native-born residents still dominated the sector. According to a representative 2015 survey of Gauteng businesses, 82 percent of informal sector business owners were born in South Africa.[31]

Set against a backdrop of widespread poverty and unemployment, even the limited penetration of foreign-born migrants into the trading sector could appear threatening to native-born residents. Public statements helped to constitute the threat. Major Kobese, a senior official in the Department of Home Affairs, the government agency tasked with regulating migration, explained: "If you go to Alexandra, you go to Sunnyside [Black townships], you go everywhere, spaza shops, hair salons, everything has been taken over by foreign nationals . . . they displace South Africans by making them not competitive."[32] The national police commissioner, Bheki Cele, similarly noted: "We can't have a country that's run by people who jump the borders. . . . Our people have been economically displaced; all these spaza shops are not run by locals. . . . One day, our people will revolt, and we've appealed to DTI (Department of Trade and Industry) to do something about it."[33]

Just weeks before widespread looting of foreign-run shops in Soweto in January 2015, Minister of Water and Sanitation Nomvula Mokonyane—previously premier of Gauteng and a close ally of President Jacob Zuma—echoed these sentiments in a Facebook post: "Almost every second outlet or even former general dealer shops are run by people of Somali or Pakistan origin. . . . I am not xenophobic fellow comrades and friends but this is a recipe for disaster which I will raise with the authorities relevant. . . . This phenomenon needs a coherent formal attention. Our townships cannot be a site of subtle takeover and build up for other situations we have seen in other countries."[34] These public proclamations reproduced popular beliefs that migrants were dominating township economies. They reinforced a politics that privileged native-born South Africans over their foreign-born counterparts, and they called for action to prevent the situation from worsening.

Some government officials with mandates to manage the economy also promoted these ideas. At a 2013 summit on small, medium, and micro enterprises (SMMEs), the deputy minister of trade and industry complained about the "scourge" of native-born South Africans "selling and renting their businesses to foreigners," which undermined economic growth in the informal sector. She echoed Mokonyane's frustration with Somalian and Pakistani migrants, noting that despite the "African names" of many spaza shops, "when you go in to buy you find your Mohammeds and most of them are not even registered."[35] Responding to the breakout of attacks in Soweto in 2015, Small Business Development Minister Lindiwe Zulu affirmed the need for stricter regulation of foreign-owned businesses in the townships: "Foreigners need to understand that they are here as a courtesy and our priority is to the people of this country first and foremost. A platform is needed for business owners to communicate and share ideas. They [migrant entrepreneurs] cannot barricade themselves in and not share their practices with local business owners."[36] Such statements clarified the second-class status of international migrants, who were only welcome if they shared their business knowledge with native-born residents.

These state practices and official discourses legitimated popular hostility and antagonism toward foreign-born residents, especially traders. Nationalism created a bridge, linking discourses and practices from above and below.

Resentment

Popular attitudes toward migrants and migration control mirrored hostility from the state. A nationally representative 2010 survey, conducted by the Southern African Migration Project, found that 53 percent of South African residents supported the deportation of migrants who were not contributing to the economy, and 62 percent supported the use of electrified fences at the national border.[37] About one-quarter of respondents indicated that they would act to prevent foreign-born migrants from either moving into their neighborhood (23 percent) or operating a business in their area (25 percent).[38] Popular reflections on the 2008 attacks were especially revealing. Only 11 percent of respondents opposed the 2008 attacks, while 54 percent supported them and 35 percent were indifferent.[39] This was a remarkable level of support for physical violence against foreign-born residents. Further evidence from national surveys shows that support for immigration among Black residents declined steadily following the 2008 attacks. Whereas shortly after the 2008 attacks more than 45 percent of Black residents indicated that they "generally welcome" all immigrants, by 2016 the figure was below 25 percent.[40]

Ethnographic research from the violent hotspots of the 2008 attacks revealed strong concerns that foreign-born residents were depleting scarce resources that should have gone to native-born residents.[41] In my interviews, as well as popular media and secondary accounts, residents complained about foreign-born migrants taking resources—most notably jobs and housing—by working for low wages (jobs) and using bribery and corruption (housing). As one resident put it: "We don't have houses, we don't have jobs, we don't have anything. . . . So, we are fighting over the little we have."[42] Many native-born residents believed that they should have priority over foreign-born residents. Nyeleti, who lived in a small but immaculately maintained shack in Motsoaledi, demonstrated this view. Having lost her job as a domestic worker, she was eking out a living by selling kitchen items on commission. Explaining to me her frustration with poverty and government neglect brought her to tears. She explained: "They [government] have to start with us, to take care of us. After, then they have to help the people from outside. . . . Because we [are] born here, and they [politicians] want us to help them, and they want our vote; they can't go to Zimbabwe and say we want your vote. That's why they have to help us first."[43] Establishing a clear hierarchy with native-born residents at the top, Nyeleti articulated a common sentiment: the state was obligated to provide for voting citizens before nonvoting migrants.

Expectations generated by racial inclusion, such as the ANC's promise to deliver a "better life for all," underpinned xenophobic attacks. Witnessing accounts of humanitarian aid to victims of the 2008 attacks, some native-born residents expressed jealous frustration about their access to state resources. One woman remarked, "We are amazed to see government providing free food for foreigners when we are also hungry but are not catered for. . . . Our children go to bed on empty stomachs on some days."[44] Residents also held the government accountable for xenophobic violence. While some blamed the government for failing to secure the national border, others highlighted government failure to provide resources. In the wake of the 2008 attacks, for example, some residents threatened further attacks if the government continued to neglect them and failed to address their grievances.[45] As Lucky Ngobeni, a prominent leader in Motsoaledi, remarked: "We don't want this [xenophobic violence] to happen again in our country but the solution is with political parties and government to bring basic needs to the people."[46] These sentiments reflected a state-centered politics that linked citizenship to indigeneity and associated national liberation with migrant exclusion. Filling in for the weakness of the state, popular xenophobia from below reinforced the ongoing liberation struggle by restricting foreign-born residents from accessing scarce resources.[47]

Resentment about the privileging of foreign-born residents also fed into antitrader nationalism. The latter resembled the social dynamics that Edna Bonacich identified in the early 1970s as revolving around "middleman minorities": ethnic groups, typically migrants, that occupy an "intermediate" economic position and concentrate in occupations related to trade and commerce.[48] Bonacich argues that these intermediate groups generate hostility from indigenous groups, who resent their competition and their perceived drain on domestic resources. The economic success of middleman minorities, she suggests, "appears devastating to host members, who believe their country is being 'taken over' by an alien group."[49] Such resentment leads to "ever more extreme reactions" and "harsh measures" in order to restrict or expel the threat.

My interviews with young Bekkersdal residents revealed how closely Bonacich's analysis resonated with antitrader nationalism in South Africa. Thirty years old, Moeletsi was surviving through occasional work on temporary jobs and support from his family, including his grandmother's government cash transfer. In explaining recent attacks against foreign-run businesses, he noted: "It is because the shop owners are Somalis. These guys are closing Black guys' [native-born] businesses here. They are taking over." Moeletsi understood migrant traders as a threat: "How [do] they make us feel when they do business here? For me personally, it is not good. When you see people from outside come and do business here, when we have our own people who can do business . . . I think if he comes and opens a business, and he is cheaper, so he is killing that guy [who might be] a breadwinner for his family."[50] Moeletsi was not a trader himself, but he sympathized with native-born shop owners who were supporting families. Tumelo, a twenty-three-year-old Bekkersdal activist, admitted to participating in recent attacks against migrant traders. She echoed Moeletsi's concerns:

> The youth felt that these Somalis are taking their jobs. They come from where they come from, and they get jobs here in SA, and they come and open shops. . . . The shops that were broken down were Somalis, and the Black shops [native-born South Africans] were not broken down or stolen from them. . . . Some of them were even beaten up. That is why I say there is no excuse for what they did. . . . But I will not point fingers. I was also in the strike, and what we did was stupid.[51]

This was a rare admission. While antimigrant attitudes were certainly not rare, residents were often quite wary of openly expressing them. Tumelo's regret was palpable. Dumisani, a twenty-one-year-old Bekkersdal activist, was less bashful. Lamenting the lack of opportunities for youth in the area, his own uncertain future made him visibly upset. He identified with the attacks:

> People said, "Somalis are running our community; they are busy coming in and out. So we need to start to tell them to go back home so that we as the community can open our own businesses." So they said the only way to stop this is to loot the shops, and they did. It is to show them that they need to go back home and we can open our own business and not depend on them. . . . I can say it was a xenophobic attack. Because some of the people started to say the Somalis are raping our sisters, taking our businesses, [using] our IDs to make fraud. . . . I do not support the idea of attacking foreigners, but however, people see that attacking is the only way to alert people. Because if you tell them to leave, they will not listen. So you need to do so by taking charge, looting, and that is what they did.[52]

Dumisani sympathized with the attackers and appeared to share what he understood as their primary goal: the expulsion of migrant traders.

These accounts were remarkably parallel to the hostility that Bonacich describes. They illustrated how some residents viewed migrant traders as an economic threat and as "taking over" the country. Those views articulated with processes of ethnic group formation. Bonacich notes, "Middleman groups are charged with being clannish, alien, and unassimilable. They are seen as holding themselves aloof, believing they are superior to those around them (a 'chosen people'), and insisting on remaining different."[53] In parallel ways, residents in South Africa constituted migrants not just as economic threats but also as racial and national Others.

Racial Reconstruction

Antitrader nationalism frequently targeted migrants from East Africa and South Asia, particularly Somalia, Ethiopia, Pakistan, and Bangladesh.[54] Residents distinguished these groups from both native-born South Africans and migrants from other southern African countries, such as Zimbabwe and Mozambique. Drawing on phenotypical markers, social patterns, and economic activity, residents linked these distinctions to apartheid-era racial categories. The apartheid state classified residents into four primary racial groups: white, Black/African, Indian/Asian, and Coloured. These categories remained salient in the post-apartheid period.[55] Official surveys and censuses continued to use the categories, race remained correlated with resource distribution, and residents continued to embrace racial identities. Racial categories were also, to a certain extent, fluid and malleable. Residents continually reworked them. In this instance, residents often referred to migrant traders from Somalia, Ethiopia, Pakistan, and Bangladesh as Indian, including them within the apartheid-era racial category.

Some residents distinguished East African and South Asian migrants on traditional racial grounds, referring to phenotypical differences. Thabo, from Thembelihle, explained their difference from Zimbabwean migrants in clear terms:

> These Zimbabweans, they are more like the [Black] South Africans, you see; and these Somalians are more likely to the Asian. . . . You will hear people calling these Somalians Pakistanis, because of their skins and the appearance of their face looks like the Asian people [Indian]. . . . They are far different from the Zimbabwean, from Malawian. They are far different. Even if you can look at their skin and then look at their hair and [then] look at the Zimbabwean, the Zimbabwean are like me. Everything of Zimbabwean is the same like mine.[56]

Thabo's account grouped Zimbabwean migrants with native-born Black residents, and Somalian and Pakistani migrants with native-born Indians. When I asked whether there were any differences between Indians and Somalians, he remarked, "Well, the difference is that they can identify themselves. The Indian can identify that, no, this guy is a Somalian, you know? There is not much difference [between] them. But they are the ones [who can tell]."[57] While acknowledging the presence of two distinct groups who could differentiate themselves from each other, from his perspective, native-born Indians and foreign-born Somalian migrants belonged to the same racial group. Thabo went further to describe how the difference went beyond phenotype to include patterns of socialization: "These Somalians, they [are] always in the shop. They don't go around; they don't socialize; they don't make friendship with the peoples. So they always in business. So these Zimbabweans, they walk around you know. They go to *shebeens* [taverns] as South Africans are doing. . . . And in most cases these Zimbabweans, some of them may be married to a Xhosa girl, all these tribes that we have in South Africa."[58] Thabo later speculated that this social distance reinforced antagonism toward Somalians, who were unable to locate suspects after an attack. In contrast, Zimbabweans could easily identify perpetrators, refer them to the police or community members, and ensure their punishment.

Lindiwe, a young Bekkersdal activist, echoed these themes, but with reference instead to Mozambicans (also referred to here as *shangaan*) and Pakistanis: "They [Mozambicans] stay on our yard, and they are living in the same. They help, the people of Mozambique, not Pakistani. . . . They keep themselves separate, and they even fight with us when we are on strike. That is why people take their things. . . . The *shangaan* are the same as us. It is the Pakistani that we do not want."[59] Like Thabo, Lindiwe underscored the social distance between Black South Africans on the one hand and migrants from East Africa and South Asia on the other.

It was impossible to separate these phenotypical and social distinctions from economic distinctions and, in turn, the legacies of apartheid. The apartheid state officially discriminated against all three nonwhite groups—Black, Indian, and Coloured—but it also treated them very differently. State oppression targeted Black residents for the harshest treatment, including tight restrictions on business development. Within the urban areas, the apartheid state effectively abolished legal Black businesses.[60] In contrast, facing fewer restrictions, Indian residents managed to work around apartheid racial oppression to develop a significant number of successful businesses.[61] The Indian racial group developed a reputation for small business, especially in the trading sector. It is thus not surprising that Black-Indian tensions figured prominently in Bonacich's account of "middleman minorities" in colonial and apartheid South Africa.[62]

Several decades later, the popular 2002 song "AmaNdiya" by Mbongeni Ngema demonstrated the persistence of these tensions. Ngema described how Indians were "suppressing" and "dispossessing" Black residents and lamented the failure of Black leaders to deal with the situation. Ngema concluded, "It was better with whites, we knew then it was racial conflict."[63] My interviews echoed these themes. Nandi, a Motsoaledi resident who was attempting to sell bread informally within the local area, complained about her inability to compete with foreign-run shops, especially Pakistani-run shops: "Now Indians in our locations, they are opening the shops. What about those people who got spaza [small shops]? Now those people [local residents] are running to the Indians; they do not go there now [to the South African shops]. Pakistanis are all over here. Me, I'm selling with R9.50, and they come they sell it R6. . . . They want to drag us down."[64] In lumping together "Indians" and "Pakistanis," Nandi extended the apartheid-era racial category to include traders from Pakistan. Robert, a Tsakane10 activist, elaborated on the idea:

> Here in the location, we call them Indians. So we do not know [if] this guy is from India or [not]. We call them *amakula*; that is the word we use. But we do not know where they are coming from, Somalia or Pakistan; we do not know where they come from. . . . You know all those who are selling, we call them amakula. It is either tuck shops or they are selling in the streets, blankets. We call them amakula, *amaNdiya* (Indians). . . . People from Zimbabwe are selling brooms, something like mops. They are not selling at tuck shops. They do not have [wealth] like amaNdiya.[65]

Robert thus assimilated, or reconstructed, the apartheid state division between Black and Indian into a popular division between Zimbabwean migrants and Pakistani or Somali migrants. The economic success of the latter group affirmed their equivalence to native-born Indians.

Residents constituted foreign-born traders as outsiders, distinguished by their physical appearance, their social patterns, and their economic activity. Many adopted hostile views. National survey evidence, for example, shows that Black residents frequently mentioned Somalians among those who they least wanted to come and live in South Africa.[66] Not all residents, however, had exclusionary intentions. Some of the very same people that emphasized racial differences between foreign-born traders and native-born Blacks also took strong and public stances against xenophobic antagonism. In such public pronouncements, they sought to undermine any differences, portraying foreign-born traders as "one of us" and part of the community. While such appeals often appeared quite effective, popular resentment worked as a countervailing force. The boundary between us and them was constantly under negotiation. Collective resistance around service delivery brought this negotiation to the fore.

Resistance

If the twin processes of resentment and racialization created an undercurrent of antitrader nationalism, collective resistance put it into motion.[67] The connection between collective resistance and antitrader nationalism was twofold and contradictory: xenophobic attacks often took place during local protests around service delivery issues, but leading activists consistently promoted opposition to xenophobic antagonism. Far from straightforward, the relationship between resistance and exclusive nationalism was variable.

Xenophobic attacks often escalated during moments of protest. Migrant traders described their heightened vulnerability during these times. They described how residents arrived at their shops, in unfriendly groups, while singing protest songs. It was typical for protests to generate a volatile mixture of frustration and energy. As one Thembelihle activist explained, "A person who is in a protest is uncontrollable. [They] can do anything, can throw the stone to the car; he can steal, just to satisfy himself that no, he is angry."[68] Protests created a ripe environment for economic opportunism, with some residents taking advantage of chaotic situations to steal groceries and money from migrant-run shops. Government officials seized on such opportunism to deny the extent of antimigrant sentiment, portraying attacks as products of "criminal elements" rather than xenophobia.[69] This denialism failed to appreciate that such criminality targeted national outsiders exclusively.

Migrants were aware of the unevenness of antitrader activity. Daniel, an Ethiopian shop owner in Thembelihle, remarked clearly: "It is obvious we are foreigner. The shops that are owned by local people, they are not going there [to loot or attack]. There is another shop owned by South African in another street, but they attack me. . . . It is only the foreigner shops that are attacked. Because you are foreigners, that is why they are attacking you."[70] The attacks were not only about theft. They also targeted migrant themselves. Daniel noted, "They come to you as a group singing the protest songs . . . if they find you in the shop they will kill you. So no one is staying around, we go and hide."[71] Other migrant traders noted that, during protest actions, residents approached them by calling them "foreigners" and derogatory names. While the anti-trader attacks certainly had an economic dimension, they tended to downplay class antagonism. Rather than redistribution from the petty bourgeoisie to the working class and the poor, they sought redistribution from foreign-born residents to native-born residents.

It was impossible to disconnect antitrader nationalism from collective demands for service delivery. One important dynamic revolved around a perceived lack of solidarity. In explaining the 2008 attacks, some native-born residents accused foreign-born residents of not participating in local meetings or service delivery protests.[72] Similar explanations of antitrader attacks emerged in my interviews. In all four areas, activists suggested that migrant traders were not active participants in local struggles. Some residents justified looting as retribution for nonparticipation. Norma, who participated in protests but attempted to keep a healthy distance from the police, recalled the looting of Somalian shops in Motsoaledi: "The shops for the foreigners [were targeted] because they didn't participate in the march. . . . They have to be included in the march. That is why they have looted their shops. . . . Some of them [e.g., Zimbabweans and Mozambicans], they used to participate when there are riots. But this one, the new group [e.g., Somalians], is not participating; and [residents] have told them that if you are not participating, we will loot your shops. And they have done that."[73]

Lindiwe, from Bekkersdal, made the connection between nationality and protest participation more explicit: "The Pakistani, when we strike, they do not go to the strike. They just sit and watch us. We do not fight for ourselves but them too. They must help us when we fight for our community. . . . The people of Mozambique help us when we have a strike. . . . We were told that it's a stay-away and there is no one who is going to sell. But they open [their shops]; that is why [they were attacked]."[74] Like attacks against workers (chapter 3), some residents attacked migrant traders because they failed to participate in protests and stay-aways. Themba, another Bekkersdal activist, argued that such attacks were effective means for building solidarity. He suggested that prior to the attacks, migrant traders "didn't even bother supporting us." In contrast, however, "after people started burning their shops . . . they started to participate."[75] From this perspective, antitrader nationalism was necessary for building resistance.

Another important dynamic revolved around a collective relationship to the state. Alongside other disruptive tactics, such as barricading roads and destroying property, some residents viewed attacks on foreign-born traders as a key tool for achieving recognition and service delivery. Such dynamics were evident in Motsoaledi, where a string of protests included attacks against Somalian and Ethiopian shops. When I asked a group of young activists to explain the attacks, they offered the following interpretation: "They looted the shops that belong to Ethiopians . . . so then the government can see that their lives is in danger. [It was] not [that] they looted the shops because they did not want them to sell, because even now they will let them open their shops. They have done what they wanted. . . . They do want them to sell, but then they wanted to attract the attention of the government."[76] Rather than seeking to expel migrant traders from the area, Motsoaledi activists suggested that the attackers were using them to demonstrate anger and attract attention. Indeed, some residents believed and appreciated that migrant shops offered lower prices.

The desire for state attention was a popular justification. Even Nandi, introduced above, who expressed concern about migrant traders stealing business opportunities from native-born residents, drew a link between xenophobic attacks and state-citizen relations. I interviewed Nandi along with Kabelo, an older male resident. They both spoke with scorn about their situations, the neglect of local political officials, the poor state of public services and, especially, the negative impact of migrants. Kabelo, who celebrated xenophobic attacks in the area as "very good," understood the connection between protests and xenophobia to be straightforward: "Because we say to the government: if we march because we want a house, and [migrants] put their own thing, we fight them, and we [will] take everything from them." Nandi agreed: "That was good, marvelous. . . . That is how we pass the message to the government. How can we allow the stranger to come here?"[77]

More than simply coinciding and intermingling, protest and xenophobia had deep political and ideological entanglements. Yet the relationship was far from straightforward. While activists did sometimes reveal underlying negative attitudes toward migrants, as illustrated above, more commonly they were at pains to illustrate distance and opposition from such views. Most activists viewed xenophobia as a distraction. They drew a sharp distinction between attacks against migrant traders and local struggles for service delivery. Their own organizations, they argued, focused on service delivery and had nothing to do with xenophobic attacks, which they attributed to separate groups and individuals. Some organizations even went further by actively opposing xenophobia within their areas. In short, xenophobia became an important terrain of struggle.

I found evidence of antixenophobia organizing in all four areas. Such organizing appeared to be weakest in Motsoaledi. Even in that case, however, prominent activists denounced attacks against foreign-born residents in informal conversations and acknowledged the participation of foreign-born residents in protests during public meetings. Residents reported that a local branch of the South African National Civic Organization, which eventually joined forces with the activist group Motsoaledi Concerned Residents, held a public meeting in 2015 to oppose xenophobia. The meeting effectively limited the spread of xenophobic activity in the area. A similar dynamic unfolded in Bekkersdal, where the Greater Westonaria Concerned Residents Association (GWCRA) held a public meeting to promote an antixenophobia message. Tumelo recalled the messages that local leaders emphasized during the meeting: "They emphasized on *ubuntu* and humanity and that we are one, so we can never kill one another over the struggle of jobs. People from outside who are the so-called foreigners are not the ones who are taking our jobs, and they are not the culprits or the victims here. So we need to understand that they are also in the struggle. So we need not to kill them or do anything bad to them, but actually hold each other's hands and fight this thing."[78] Tumelo's recollection underscored the contingency of collective action, which could swing toward targeting either the state or foreign-born neighbors. GWCRA leaders called for the former by appealing to the notion of ubuntu, a popular South African idea that refers to a common humanity and kindness toward others.

Opposition to xenophobia was even stronger in Tsakane10 and Thembelihle. In Tsakane10, local activists held public meetings to promote an antixenophobia message. George, an activist associated with the Kwatsaduza Community and Worker Forum (KCWF), explained, "We emphasized unity, that we are all people, and we are the same; we have to treat each other equally." KCWF activists also went door-to-door to hand out antixenophobia pamphlets and promote an antixenophobia march. Like activists in Bekkersdal, they sought to redirect attention from foreign-born residents to the government, portraying the latter as the primary target. Through these actions, activists gained the support of their migrant neighbors: "The foreigners looked up to us as they heard that they are being attacked in areas like Soweto and Alexandra. They wanted to know, what are we saying about that? We told our people that, let us deal with our government so that it gives what we want. Like, if it can give our youth the jobs, what we call xenophobia can drop because it is caused by the lack of something to eat."[79] Billed as the Far East Rand March against Xenophobia, the flyer for the April 2015 antixenophobia march raised a call to arms: "Fight poverty not immigrants. Workers of the world unite. Immigrants are welcome here."[80] Gathering about two hundred people, activists affirmed that the march was significantly smaller than a typical protest around service delivery issues, which might include thousands. They were still happy with the turnout and their impact. George celebrated the fact that they "played a big role . . . in changing the mind-set of people."[81]

The Thembelihle Crisis Committee (TCC) had a longer history of opposing xenophobia. When the outbreak of attacks began in 2008, residents attacked and robbed a migrant trader in the area. Rumors began to spread about further collective action against migrants. TCC activists responded by calling a public meeting, which after heated debate decided to not allow further xenophobic attacks. Affirming the antixenophobia position, TCC established patrols of the neighborhood to prevent further attacks and organized a soccer game with foreign-born and native-born residents to promote solidarity. Evidence suggests that these actions were crucial in ensuring that the attacks did not spread to Thembelihle.[82] TCC also helped to spearhead the formation of the Coalition against Xenophobia (CAX), which coordinated a six-thousand-person march in Johannesburg at the height of the 2008 attacks and held an overnight vigil to call for the closure of the Lindela migrant detention center.

Antixenophobia activities remained subordinate to struggles around service delivery in Thembelihle. One activist regretted that, "unfortunately, we did not put in place a program to tackle the xenophobia question on a long-term basis."[83] Nonetheless, TCC activists continued to take an antixenophobia stance, which became crucial during moments of antitrader nationalism. In 2015, for example, some residents began to attack migrant traders during a protest around service delivery issues. Local activists decided to temporarily suspend the protest and address the antagonism by calling a public meeting. Not only did they spread a message of solidarity, but they also put the message into practice by inviting migrant traders to the meeting. TCC activists also went door-to-door to recover stolen goods and managed to return sixteen stolen refrigerators to their migrant owners.[84] Due to these various efforts, TCC won the Most Integrated Community award at the 2016 Mkhaya Migrants Awards, sponsored by the Department of Home Affairs.

Struggles around xenophobia highlighted the inherently political character of collective anger and resistance, which were highly contingent and could run in varied directions. Anti-immigrant nationalism, including antitrader nationalism, represented an exclusionary form of resistance that sought to limit resources to native-born residents. Such exclusion reproduced official nationalisms and broader nation-building projects, which drew a sharp line at the national border and a sharp distinction between national insiders and national outsiders. They also reflected an inward turn, with residents turning against their neighbors. The inward turn of nationalist exclusion represented a narrowing or contraction of popular struggles, distracting residents from external targets and potentially even broader networks of solidarity.

Local politics had high stakes. To the extent that residents took a strong stand against xenophobia, they could refocus attention on service delivery issues and protect their migrant neighbors. In Motsoaledi, Bekkersdal, Tsakane10, and Thembelihle, leading activists in service delivery struggles were often the most outspoken opponents of xenophobia, though their responses were far from uniform. The antixenophobia stance was weakest in Motsoaledi and strongest in

Tsakane10 and Thembelihle. These varied responses reflected larger differences. While activists in all four areas confronted the challenges of isolation and inward-looking antagonism, they did so with different ideologies and organizational structures. Due partially to their isolation from each other, activists in different areas pursued very different political projects. I turn to this divergence in the next chapter.

CLASS POLITICS

To the extent that local activists were interested in developing social movements with a transformative agenda, they confronted several challenges. Living in areas defined by high levels of unemployment and poverty, they lacked material resources. Political dynamics created additional obstacles. Many residents remained committed to the postapartheid state or the ruling party, and the potential constituents of social movements were often more concerned with achieving narrow administrative fixes than they were with pushing for deep social change. Activists also faced state repression and hostility from ANC loyalists, both inside and outside of the state. Further, they had to negotiate antimigrant xenophobia, which emanated from both above and below and distracted attention from broader aims and targets. These varied challenges reflected the dynamics of South Africa's ongoing passive revolution. Given such challenges, it is perhaps unsurprising that forces of the Left often found themselves stuck, despite the vibrant legacy of left-leaning activism within the country.

Local struggles remained in what Gramsci calls the economic-corporate phase: they focused primarily, if not exclusively, on the immediate needs of small groups rather than the longer-term interests of a broader class. Drawing on Gramsci's metaphor of class struggle as "trench warfare," Ira Katznelson highlights the peculiar feature of American "city trenches" that distinguished and separated workplace and community politics.[1] While a similar division between labor and community increasingly took hold in South Africa, in this chapter I show how trench warfare under South Africa's passive revolution gave rise to a further division between community activism in different residential areas. In pursuing economic-corporate struggles, activists in different areas developed different ideologies and practices, as expressed through local organizations and networks. Some of the ideologies and practices remained narrow. Others began to hint, or at least pose the question, of broader class struggles, even if activists confronted difficulty in implementing such visions. The divergence reinforced fragmentation. Even so, the divergence suggests that economically insecure groups were not a malleable mass that external forces could easily manipulate. They were, instead, active agents expressing their own politics.

Gramsci describes the shift from narrow economic-corporate struggles to broader economic-class struggles as involving two dimensions: one focused on group solidarity, the other on the state.[2] The group solidarity dimension revolves around whether activists demonstrate a growing consciousness of "the solidarity of interests among all the members of a social class."[3] Along this dimension, I distinguish between expressions of local solidarity, which pertain to groups within specific residential areas, and expressions of class solidarity, which extend to similar economic groups in other residential areas. With respect to the state dimension, Gramsci suggests that economic-class struggles seek "politico-juridical equality with the ruling groups," and the right "to participate in legislation and administration."[4] I distinguish here between struggles that primarily aim to pressure the state by publicizing and registering popular interests and those that also seek to supplement the state through some form of popular governance.

Fanon and Chatterjee underscore how passive revolution shapes the terrain upon which these struggles unfold. Fanon focuses on the group solidarity dimension. He emphasizes how the anticolonial passive revolution, marked by elite pursuit of narrow interests, undermines national unity. Nonetheless, in stressing both the transformative potential of economically marginalized groups and the necessity of unifying the nation through social and political consciousness, he hints at the possibility of moving beyond localized identities to form broader solidarities. Chatterjee focuses on the state dimension. He argues that passive revolution relegates the rural and urban poor to political society, where the primary task is to pressure government agencies to provide for their basic livelihood needs. In Chatterjee's analysis, however, the activities of political society grope toward a reinvigoration of democracy, deepening popular participation without quite reaching the hypothetical ideals of civil society. These accounts of postcolonial passive revolution accentuate the diversity of possible responses from below.

In this chapter, I examine the divergent forms of group solidarity and state engagement that predominated across the four case study areas (table 3). Activists in Motsoaledi and Bekkersdal focused primarily on local solidarity. Whereas Motsoaledi activists deployed a *concerned residents'* politics by pressuring the state to meet their basic livelihood needs, Bekkersdal activists began to develop

TABLE 3. Politics of local community organizing

STATE DIMENSION	GROUP SOLIDARITY DIMENSION	
	Local solidarity	Class solidarity
Popular pressure	Concerned residents (Motsoaledi)	Union alliance (Tsakane10)
Popular governance	People's parliament (Bekkersdal)	Socialist party (Thembelihle)

autonomous local decision making through a *people's parliament* politics. Activists in Tsakane10 and Thembelihle also emphasized local solidarity, but they began to situate local efforts within a broader class struggle. Demonstrating a *union alliance* politics, Tsakane10 activists sought to bolster their immediate livelihood struggles by joining hands with organized workers. Conversely, activists in Thembelihle adopted a *socialist party* politics, which bolstered livelihood demands by linking them to grassroots mobilization, socialist ideas, election campaigns, and involvement in local government. These varied politics reflected the "community trenches" of South Africa's fractured militancy.

My analysis here challenges portrayals of local protests as primarily about internal factionalism within the ruling party, or a "parallel political world in which voters directly engage with *their* ANC."[5] Local organizing frequently took place beyond the ruling party and often adopted oppositional positions. This reflected activism on the terrain of political society, which denotes precisely that part of society that political leadership, via the passive revolution, is unable to fully incorporate. As Chatterjee notes, political society revolves around "temporary, contextual and unstable arrangements arrived at through direct political negotiations."[6] This is about pressuring the state in the right places to secure welfare and security. It is important not to overexaggerate the strength and autonomy of local resistance. Organizations remained weak, and potential co-optation by the ANC was a consistent possibility. Even so, this did not mean that protests emerged from within the ruling party. Further, co-optation was never complete. Oppositional energies persisted. While residents failed to register significant challenges to ANC dominance or capitalist inequality, they did begin to imagine alternative possibilities.

The Electoral Terrain

Before turning to the four case studies, it is useful to situate the political and organizational dynamics surrounding local protests in relation to electoral and party politics. The importance of this arena stemmed from the features of passive revolution: the ANC's hostility to an independent civil society, the closing down of participatory space, the centralization and insulation of local government, and the prioritization of technocratic and market-driven processes of public provision.[7] Protests both reflected and responded to these conditions. They sought to pry open a bit of participatory space, but they also demanded the effective functioning of the state administration, or what I have referred to as administrative fixes (chapter 3). Despite a common rejection of political parties, albeit to varying degrees, activists in all four areas did pursue elections in some way. In the absence of participatory mechanisms, local government elections represented a possible alternative pathway to the state. Standing up to the mighty ANC, though, proved extremely difficult. These efforts met with very little success.

To capture local political party dynamics, I briefly examine the election results for key voting stations that were close to the center of organizing and protest in each area. As shown in figure 5, the national pattern of simultaneous ANC dominance and decline held in each of the case study areas. Between 2004 and 2019, support for the ANC dropped by 16 percentage points in Thembelihle, 20 points in Motsoaledi, and 24 points in Bekkersdal. In Tsakane10, which formed in 2007, ANC support dropped by 23 percentage points between 2009 and 2019. Despite this decline, however, the ruling party continued to dominate. The organizations and networks that propelled local organizing and protest could not compete. This included efforts by activists in Motsoaledi to put forward an independent candidate in the 2011 local government elections, as well as the growing involvement of Thembelihle activists in the Operation Khanyisa Movement (OKM), a left-leaning electoral front that sought to use elections to gain access to the Johannesburg city council. The ANC crushed the former, while the latter bore only limited fruit: OKM managed to secure a single proportional representation seat on the city council between 2006 and 2016 but eventually lost the seat amid diminishing support. OKM candidates never won a ward councilor position.[8]

The ANC's two main competitors nationally, the Democratic Alliance (DA) and the Economic Freedom Fighters (EFF), occupied most of the void left by ANC decline.[9] The DA is a descendant of the liberal Progressive Party, founded in 1959, which participated in the all-white parliament under apartheid but opposed apartheid policies. The DA sought to challenge prominent views that it was primarily a "white party." In the context of racial inclusion, however, where notions of national liberation remained prevalent, the opposition party had difficulty penetrating impoverished Black urban areas. Among the case study areas, the DA never surpassed 6 percent in the focal voting stations within

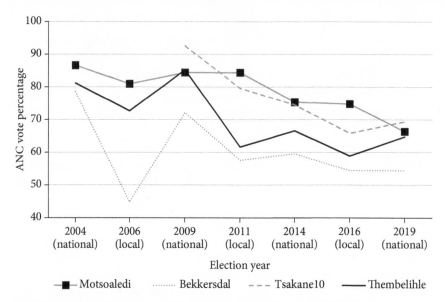

FIGURE 5. ANC electoral performance in the four case study areas, 2004–2019.

Source and notes: Electoral Commission of South Africa (http://www.elections.org.za/). The results pertain to the following voting stations: 32862719 (Motsoaledi), 33270083 (Bekkersdal), 33030515 (Tsakane10), 32862641 (Thembelihle).

Motsoaledi and Bekkersdal. The country's main opposition party fared only marginally better in Tsakane10, where some local activists aligned with the DA, and in Thembelihle, where support for the DA was prevalent in the predominantly Indian and more middle-class surrounding areas. In both places, the DA had a brief surge during the 2011 local government elections, securing 15–16 percent of the vote, but declined steadily afterward.

If the DA was the main opposition nationally, within the four case study areas the main opposition locally was the EFF, founded in 2013 by former leaders of the ANC Youth League. Emerging from within the national liberation movement, the breakaway party quickly reshaped politics within the impoverished Black urban areas. The EFF gained particular traction among younger voters and provided a solid option for residents who wanted to challenge the ANC but remain within the ambit of national liberation politics. As shown in figure 6, the breakaway party secured 15–25 percent support in the case study areas during its first three elections, with the exception of slightly lower support in Motsoaledi in 2014–2016. While this positive performance suggests that the EFF may have greater staying power than did previous ANC breakaways, it still paled in

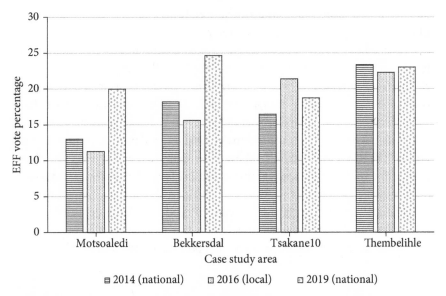

FIGURE 6.   EFF electoral performance in the four case study areas, 2014–2019.

Source and notes: Electoral Commission of South Africa (http://www.elections.org.za/). The results pertain to the following voting stations: 32862719 (Motsoaledi), 33270083 (Bekkersdal), 33030515 (Tsakane10), 32862641 (Thembelihle).

comparison to the ruling party.[10] Between 2014 and 2019, the EFF never came within 30 percentage points of the ANC in any of the four areas.

As challenges to local political leaders, protest movements may have contributed indirectly to EFF support. For the most part, though, the party's rise occurred separately from local resistance in each of the four areas. Bekkersdal and Thembelihle represented the greatest potential for overlap. In Bekkersdal, the EFF resonated with the popular Black Consciousness tradition, and some prominent activists identified with the emergent party. Nonetheless, the main activist organization in the area eschewed party identification (chapter 4), keeping the EFF at bay. Elections did little to connect the struggles in Bekkersdal to those in other areas.[11] In Thembelihle, some activists attempted to facilitate a local coalition between the OKM and the EFF. The former lacked a major national brand, while the latter lacked a local organizational presence. A meeting between representatives of the two organizations failed to produce tangible results, and they campaigned separately. According to some OKM activists, the partnership failed to materialize because EFF leaders were unwilling to forfeit a substantial proportion of their councilor salary, as per the OKM's common practice. Rather than bolster local struggles and build bridges between them, the EFF appeared to siphon or repurpose their energy.

The shifting terrain of electoral politics, marked especially by the declining dominance of the ANC and the rise of the EFF, shaped the context in which class politics unfolded in the four areas. While activists rejected political parties as the primary vehicle of organization and mobilization, they nonetheless entertained elections as a possible route to the state. In doing so, they pursued very different pathways. Challenges to the ANC differed in both magnitude and type. With respect to magnitude, for example, opposition to the ruling party was stronger in Thembelihle, and to some extent Bekkersdal, than it was in Motsoaledi. Activists also developed their own distinctive political orientations and visions of the future. In each case, activists contended with the terrain of political parties, but the latter did not fully encapsulate popular politics. The bulk of local organizing took place separately from political parties and elections.

Motsoaledi: Concerned Resident Politics

From the inception of Motsoaledi in the early 1990s, the ANC dominated. The informal settlement emerged in the context of bloody conflict between competing political groups, which spread across the country during the final years of apartheid. Many of the early residents were ANC supporters fleeing violent battles with isiZulu-speaking supporters of the Inkatha Freedom Party (IFP). Pro-ANC "self-defense units" were active in the area. Thapelo remarked that, during the early years, "that group of Zulu nation, they were not welcomed here."[12] Even before the first democratic elections in 1994, the ANC helped residents to negotiate with the local apartheid state to prevent eviction. In the early 2000s, the ANC-led municipality began to assert control of the area by numbering the stands (plots of land) and preventing the building of further shacks. Many residents understood this process as affirming the legitimacy of their residence, which in turn raised expectations for local development. ANC-affiliated officials frequently visited the area with promises of formal housing and development.

A small anarchist group sparked initial efforts of collective resistance in the early 2000s.[13] Through the Phambili Motsoaledi Community Project (PMCP), which drew support from outside activists associated with the Zabalaza Anarchist Community Foundation, they launched various projects including a library, food garden, tool-lending operation, and newspaper. Xolani, a leading PMCP activist, explained: "People had an idea about the constitution, that staying in the shack without electricity, without anything, it is unacceptable. . . . I would always engage people about the state of delivery and how the ANC gov-

ernment has failed them and how it is important to come up with something
that is not politically aligned, which includes everyone."[14] For Xolani, the PMCP
sought to "consolidate that thinking that people can do things themselves."[15]
Though short-lived, these anarchist-inspired projects raised political awareness
and prompted further resistance.

In 2005, PMCP activists and other residents launched Motsoaledi Concerned
Residents (MCR), which became the main vehicle for organizing local resistance. Reflecting the prominence of young residents, MCR held its first major
protest on June 16, or Youth Day, a national holiday commemorating the uprising by Soweto students in 1976. Hand-made signs called attention to poor
service delivery and government failure:

"It's too long. 12 years in shacks. We need water, electricity, housing, toilets."
"Stop empty promises please."
"We demand, proper, adequate, housing."

Popular frustration with the ANC was evident. One of the biggest signs featured
a marked-up poster with a large image of ANC president Thabo Mbeki, painted
over with a big white question mark. Xolani celebrated that, saying, "We were
the first people to make people in Motsoaledi stand up by themselves. . . . People
were very scared, and we were the first to organize the demonstration that
challenge[d] the ANC government officials."[16]

At this moment, it seemed possible that activism within Motsoaledi might
extend outward, joining other local movements to register a broader challenge
to the ANC. MCR affiliated with the Anti-Privatization Forum (APF), a prov-
incewide umbrella of oppositional social movements. Some activists in the area
supported the OKM electoral front, which grew out of the APF.[17] Over time,
however, local activism moved closer to the ANC.[18] Repression played a role.
Some activists recalled how ANC loyalists came with weapons to break up MCR
meetings or visited them individually with threatening messages. Infiltration,
however, was likely more important. Between 2000 and 2011, the ANC confronted a local organizational crisis as the state redistricted Motsoaledi from
Ward 24 to Ward 26, and then back to Ward 24. Not only did the relevant local
ANC branch switch along with these changes, but also meetings consistently
took place outside of the informal settlement. As ANC presence in the area
declined, some members—especially younger residents from the ANC Youth
League—began to participate in and shape MCR activities. A stance rooted in
tense negotiations with the ANC gradually crowded out both the original anarchist current and the possibility of a broader alliance through the OKM.[19]

Xolani recalled a 2009 incident that illustrated how the organization's politics began to shift. In preparation for a major protest, he went to draw a big white

question mark on a poster over the image of the new president, Jacob Zuma, like he had done to the Mbeki poster four years previously. Whereas the marked Mbeki poster figured prominently in the 2005 protest, this time another activist confronted him: "He said, 'You dare not do that.' . . . That is when I realized that there is underground work here happening from the ANC Youth League."[20] Residents were not necessarily happy with the ANC. Frustration with the ruling party was palpable during the 2009 protest, and television interviews show residents threatening not to vote for the ANC if it did not deliver development. In the wake of another major protest in January 2010, in which residents demanded electricity and the immediate resignation of the local ward councilor, the government officially adopted a housing plan for the area. The city of Johannesburg promised publicly that they would begin construction in April and that they would begin moving people into houses by the end of the year. These events reinforced hope, though development remained elusive.

With no signs of progress, MCR activists took a middle road between opposing and embracing the ANC. In the 2011 local government elections, they put forward an independent (i.e., non-party-affiliated) candidate, Lucky Ngobeni, for the position of local ward councilor. The Ngobeni campaign did little to build solidarity with activism beyond Motsoaledi. It did not contribute, for example, to the citywide OKM campaign for a proportional representation seat on the Johannesburg city council. Residents could still vote for the ANC on the proportional representation ballot, which determines overall representation within the city council, while voting for Ngobeni on the ward councilor ballot. Within Motsoaledi, Ngobeni secured 25 percent of the vote on the ward councilor ballot. This was an impressive showing, even if the ANC candidate dominated with 64 percent. Less than 1 percent of Motsoaledi residents voted for the OKM on the proportional representation ballot.

In explaining the move to contest local elections with an independent candidate, one of Motsoaledi's leading activists argued that independent candidates provided a direct link from civil society to the state: "You will be having someone . . . who will not be controlled by a certain political party. . . . You have to respond back to the community, not to a political party; he will be mandated, actually, by the community. Someone when we march, he will be part of the march and not get constraints from leaders up there to say, 'Why are you doing that?' . . . They will put more pressure on the state because they are unpolitical." This position prioritized accurate representation within the state over movement building and working-class solidarity. It emphasized that officials should share residents' lived experience: "When I light with the candle, he is lighting with the candle. . . . [If] I am lighting with the candle and he is lighting with the electricity, obviously . . . I am the one being used." Crucially, the activist understood independent candidates as compatible with loyalty to the ruling party: "I support them [ANC] ideologically, because of my forefathers and everybody in my family. Remember the history and the freedom that we got from Mandela, Oliver Tambo, and the others. That history obviously won't be deleted . . . If we have the party [ANC] there on the national . . . but on the local ones have people who will stand for the community—that is when we will see more service; there will be service delivery."[21] This inward-looking approach lent itself to a highly localized solidarity and a muted oppositional stance.

The 2011 election marked a brief foray into electoral politics that did not last or return. Local activists placed greater emphasis on pressuring the ANC to deliver. Such efforts reached new heights in April 2013 when, with little evidence of the promised housing project other than some underground pipes, residents took to the streets again in militant fashion. Protesters burned down the local KFC restaurant and toppled a traffic light. By this time, MCR's profile was waning. Some protesters did not even know what it was. One young protester remarked, "There is no organization that is helping us. We are helping ourselves. . . . We are striking as a youth."[22] Yet MCR activists remained visible as local leaders and played significant roles in negotiating between protesters, police, and the media. One journalist captured Ngobeni's frustration: "We're going to continue until they respond positively. . . . For about 20 years we've been fighting for simple things, basic services. We will wait for electricity, water, sanitation and housing. . . . We are tired. We are saying enough is enough. They must respond."[23] While seeking to pressure the ruling party, his admission that "we will wait" hinted at a desire to avoid a broader challenge.

After the protest, forces of co-optation moved in from multiple angles. One force was the ANC itself, which formed a steering committee to manage the local housing project. A local ANC leader explained, "When we look at it, the steering committee won't be nominated in a public meeting because ANC is no longer popular there. The people who are popular are the MCR people; they will take over all positions."[24] The ANC organized the steering committee behind closed doors to ensure adequate ANC representation. They allocated only two of the ten positions to MCR members, including Ngobeni, and they offered Ngobeni a paid position as a community liaison officer for the housing project. In July 2013, just three months after the protests, MCR activists joined the ward councilor in presiding over a mass public meeting to distribute temporary jobs in the housing project, which they did by lottery. When I asked about their surprisingly positive relationship to the ward councilor, one activist remarked: "We are not fighting with the person; we are only fighting with the things they are not delivering."[25] They were now working closely with the ANC to promote the housing project.

The other co-opting force was a group of ANC members who launched a local branch of the ANC-affiliated South African National Civic Organization (SANCO) within Motsoaledi. MCR and SANCO activists clashed around the time of the 2013 protests. The former called for action while the latter called for patience. Unfolding developments around the housing project, however, helped to bring them together. After the ANC incorporated MCR activists into the housing project, rumors began to spread about activist involvement in corrupt activities, such as illegally selling access to houses or allocating them to family and friends. This provided an opening for SANCO activists, who both worked to expose the corruption and reached out to those involved. As one SANCO leader explained: "I sit with them, and they told me they have done some mistakes, but they are willing to work for the community. . . . That is why I said, 'Let us join hands and fight.'"[26] For a while, the two groups represented the merger with a new name: Motsoaledi Activists. Over time, however, MCR dissipated further, and SANCO increasingly led local efforts to promote civil society. While SANCO did continue to put pressure on the ANC to develop the area, there was little evidence of a broader challenge to the ruling party or connections to local organizing in other residential areas.

In May 2016, after the state had already built hundreds of houses and relocated many residents, I met a group of activists who were prominent in MCR and the 2013 protests. This was a difficult time for the ruling party. Just two months earlier, the Constitutional Court ruled that President Zuma had violated the constitution by failing to pay back public money spent on his personal homestead. Despite this, the activists expressed strong commitments to the ruling party. They also defended Zuma, arguing that he had "done a great job as a Black person" to amass the Nkandla estate and adding that, "because of apartheid, there are white people who are richer than Zuma. Zuma has got nothing in Nkandla."[27] It was a remarkable defense of the ANC leader, at a time when oppositional forces were beginning to align and mobilize against him. Though only representing the views of a few activists, the episode hinted at the way in which the ANC had managed to mute and incorporate the opposition.

Bekkersdal: People's Parliament Politics

Oppositional currents were more prevalent in Bekkersdal and had deep historical roots. Like many low-income Black areas, in the late 1980s and early 1990s the township became an important site of both antiapartheid resistance and bloody political violence between competing forces. As in Motsoaledi, the violence often found the ANC pitted against the Zulu nationalist Inkatha Freedom

Party (IFP). In Bekkersdal, however, the Azanian People's Organization (AZAPO) figured prominently as well. By one report, as of 1990, AZAPO "was unquestionably the dominant organization in the township."[28] This laid a foundation for opposition to the ruling party. AZAPO emerged from the Black Consciousness movement (BCM), and the BCM legacy persisted after racial inclusion. In June 2015, for example, a flier posted on the wall of the Greater Westonaria Concerned Residents Association's (GWCRA) one-room office announced the launch of the Bekkersdal Black Consciousness Philosophy Academy. Prominent local leaders included activists associated with AZAPO, the Socialist Party of Azania (SOPA), a breakaway party from AZAPO, and the Pan Africanist Congress (PAC), which broke away from the ANC in 1959 to promote a more "Africanist" position. Most significant, however, was the emergent popularity of the newly formed EFF, which emphasized Black economic empowerment. Some residents expressed the overlap by mixing their T-shirts and hats, with an AZAPO logo on one and EFF on the other.

Anti-ANC sentiment burst into the open in October 2013, when the provincial premier Nomvula Mokonyane—a leading figure within the ANC and close ally of President Jacob Zuma—visited the township in the midst of ongoing protests. In a heated exchange with frustrated residents during her public speech, Mokonyane snapped at residents: "People can threaten us and say they won't vote but the ANC doesn't need their dirty votes." Thabang Wesi, spokesperson for the GWCRA, retorted that "it is fine," because residents would take their dirty votes "to other political parties that will wash them and once they are clean utilize them effectively, taking care of the voters, unlike the ANC."[29] The infamous "dirty votes" comment amplified the already sizzling tension within Bekkersdal. In March 2014, residents protested when the ANC attempted to campaign in the area for the upcoming national elections, and on the eve of the election, residents chased away ANC Youth League members attempting to rally in a public park. In explaining the incident, Themba—a longtime Bekkersdal resident and AZAPO member who helped to launch the GWCRA—made clear his special disdain for the ruling party: "We started to say we don't need ANC around here because of our dirty votes. . . . EFF was here. AGANG was here. COPE was here. AZAPO was here. All of these political organizations. But I said there is no way that we gonna allow ANC to come and canvas around."[30]

This oppositional thrust, however, did not feed into broader solidarities or connections to activism in other areas. Prioritizing place-based community and administrative fixes, activists instead promoted a self-governance project. Residents referred to the GWCRA, including the one-room building that served as the group's headquarters, as "the Parliament." The label reflected activists' belief that they knew best how to govern the area. In explaining the origins of the name, Vuyo recalled social gatherings with "guys that are thought to be the brains of Bekkersdal." Echoing the stories of other prominent local activists, he explained their realization: "We are a government ourselves. That's how the concept of Parliament came about."[31] Notions of local community control and self-governance underpinned hostility toward broader movements, which some activists understood as opportunistic attempts to use the community for narrow ends. As one activist explained: "You cannot come and want to orchestrate a struggle of the community that you don't stay in and want to lead it. Give the communities the power. The power is within us; we are the government."[32]

The Parliament's self-governance project peaked on Freedom Day in 2014—a national holiday celebrating the democratic transition of 1994—when activists sought to launch a new hub for creating local development solutions. The GWCRA spokesperson Thabang Wesi explained, "This will take our grievances and issues to a higher level. We cannot depend on government to deliver in terms of the effective services they should render to us." Launching a broader attack, the GWCRA chairperson Wonder Modise remarked, "This is the first thing in 20 years where the community of Greater Westonaria can claim to say they have freedom. There was nothing to celebrate before today."[33] After listening to speeches extolling the virtues of self-governance and outlining potential development projects, the crowd of a few hundred broke into working groups to discuss service delivery, local economic development, education, and the environment. Time was short, limiting opportunities for discussion. The working group I visited revolved more around the ideas of prominent leaders than it did around genuine dialogue and widespread participation. Yet the significance was clear. Local activists were *asserting* their ability to resolve local development problems, despite their very limited organizational capacity.

The project stalled. The GWCRA was a small organization with few resources, no clear membership base, and limited ability to implement development projects. Further, the prospect of participating in official governance proved enticing. Sizwe, for example, argued that state officials "should not underestimate" the capacity of residents to do more than just protest. He emphasized the need for deeper state-community collaboration: "We need to have a continuous engagement with government, so as to have clear solutions and guidelines within the policy frameworks of the country. . . . We must better the communications of communities and government for us to have a proper democratic country."[34] State engagement reached new heights in June 2014, when GWCRA activists met with provincial-level government officials. The engagement built on previous meetings with high-profile leaders in late 2013, when key representatives of the ruling Alliance—ANC, SACP, and COSATU—moved in to quell the ongoing protests.

The goal of the June 2014 meeting was to discuss plans for local development, and the activists looked forward to sharing the results of their Freedom Day event. After a closed-door meeting, GWCRA activists and government officials jointly presided over a press conference in the Westonaria municipality board-room. The officials ran the press conference and assured the media that the government would address all of Bekkersdal's issues in due time. Activists ex-pressed confidence in the government's ability to deliver and affirmed their own cooperation. The GWCRA spokesperson, Wesi, exclaimed that the meet-ing was "very much fruitful." When a reporter asked the activists if, given the official cooperation, they were going to denounce violent protests, Wesi re-sponded: "We are leadership; we are not hooligans. That is why we are always engaging with relevant stakeholders." Echoing the sentiment, the GWCRA gen-eral secretary Wonder Modise noted, "As a community we will not necessarily have reason to protest anymore." He also affirmed Wesi's optimism, expressing hope that "the lack of services that has been raised is going to be addressed in a new manner moving forward."[35]

In the wake of the meeting, the Parliament began to lose steam as popular en-ergy dissipated. Some residents complained that GWCRA leaders no longer held regular meetings or provided feedback about government projects. Rumors began to circulate about them abandoning the struggle and accepting bribes. While the evidence was thin, some GWCRA activists did manage to secure access to jobs and subcontracts through a new sewer project, which was the most visible conse-quence of the 2013 protests. When combined with the official meetings between the GWCRA and the government, such evidence of patronage demonstrated the power of the ruling party to co-opt and incorporate local movements. Years later, one young EFF activist remarked with no hesitation that the Parliament was *ifile* (dead). She complained that local leaders had "sold out" the struggle for their own personal benefit.[36] Seeking to find a bright spot, I asked about the former mayor, who the ANC transferred to a new post after the 2016 election. Removing the mayor was a primary demand during the protests, but this did not appease Non-konzo: "We don't think so, because still the ANC won." Thuli affirmed: "And she [the old mayor] is still serving on some ANC committees."[37] Disappointment loomed large.

The 2016 local government elections further fragmented local organizing. For a brief moment, following participation in an activist workshop in Cape Town, a few Bekkersdal activists joined discussions with other participants about a new electoral campaign platform—the People's Movement, or PEMO—that would promote locally selected independent candidates. PEMO rejected exter-nal organizations, especially political parties: "This will be a Councilor of the people, for the people, by the people. His/Her mandate will come from the people,

AND NOT FROM A POLITICAL PARTY!!!"[38] Similar to the MCR's brief flirtation with electoral politics in Motsoaledi, the PEMO idea reflected a localized attempt to insert an authentic community representative into local government. PEMO rejected outside influences and asserted the capacity of activists to solve local development problems. These positions were consistent with the Parliament's self-governance project. By the 2016 elections, however, the project had fizzled. Instead, activists went their separate ways by supporting different parties, including the ANC, EFF, AZAPO, PAC, and others. The GWCRA did not produce their own candidate.

A few days after the elections, Sizwe was visibly disappointed. He noted the fragmentation of activists who were working separately on different tasks and the influence of bribery and patronage from local officials and the ANC. He lamented that the Parliament was no longer the formidable entity that it once was. Sizwe expressed hope about forming a "shadow community council" to monitor the official town council, though it was unclear from where he would draw the popular energy to make it work. People's parliament politics in Bekkersdal fed into an emphasis on bureaucratic fixes that was compatible with ANC rule, and it rendered activists vulnerable to incorporation into official governance procedures. It also reinforced localization. With residents isolated from broader movements and racked by internal division, mobilization had dissipated.

Tsakane10: Union Alliance Politics

In contrast to Motsoaledi and Bekkersdal, activists in Tsakane10 developed a more explicit class politics. They sought to move beyond local solidarity by joining forces with organized workers, specifically the National Union of Metalworkers of South Africa (NUMSA). At a Special National Congress in December 2013, NUMSA charted a new political pathway for organized labor. Delegates resolved to withdraw support for the ANC and the SACP, explore the possibility of forming a new socialist-oriented political party, and establish the United Front of progressive forces opposed to neoliberalism. Given NUMSA's historical legacy and strength, these decisions offered significant potential for reshaping popular politics in the country. In the 1980s, NUMSA was a bedrock of antiapartheid resistance and a consistent prosocialist voice. By the 2010s, the union boasted more than three hundred thousand members. The NUMSA break reinvigorated left-wing activists. As one local activist later recalled, "It was like a new dawn, a hope of a South African."[39]

Local activists in Tsakane10 and nearby areas sought to seize the moment by building the United Front from below. Rather than waiting for NUMSA to act, they took the initiative to bring the United Front to them. Such efforts were controversial. Residents began protesting several years before NUMSA's decision to build the United Front, and popular resistance featured fluid politics. Some activists recalled fondly the support they received from the APF, which brought shirts to some of their early protests. Over time, local organizing fed into support for the main opposition party, the Democratic Alliance (DA). A prominent local activist built ties with the DA and briefly convinced some residents to put their support behind the opposition party. Local support for the DA never reached above 15 percent and declined sharply after 2011, but the opposition party did maintain a limited presence in the area. In April 2014, for example, some activists claimed that DA members organized an "after party" for a local protest.

The April 2014 protest marked a point of tension. One group wanted to incorporate NUMSA and the United Front. The month prior, some residents from Tsakane10 participated in the United Front's first major public action—a march in Johannesburg against unemployment—so momentum was building.[40] Another group, however, sought to preserve the local character of resistance. Ayanda, one of the localist-oriented activists, remarked: "[NUMSA] is against the ruling party. . . . I do not think we need to entertain that. It is their problem; they need to sort it out. Even if they took the resolution to support community marches, they have to meet the leadership and explain on which grounds and why now. [Because] they were not supporting our marches all along . . . we don't want to be used. We don't want people to benefit indirectly, using the community. That is my fear."[41] Labor's growing distance from service delivery struggles reinforced wider concerns about outside influences.

From the other side, Andile, a NUMSA organizer who lived in a neighboring area, recalled the "sensitivity" that he confronted: "Looking at the gap from 1994 till now, *people feel that they have been used.* . . . in Extension 10, I think I was lucky that those people accepted me, because those people were very sensitive [about] who [is] coming [from] far away, because different people came with the aim of helping them, only to find out that these people had their own issues to thrive."[42] Fortunately for NUMSA, local activists from nearby areas within Tsakane helped to integrate the union. Some of them had ties to the Democratic Left Front, a social movement that championed the NUMSA break and threw its limited weight behind the United Front initiative. The pro-NUMSA position gradually gained steam. In July 2014, just a few months after the April protest, residents took to the streets again. This time, with support from the United Front, they marched alongside protesters from nearby areas who had their own grievances. They also enjoyed support from NUMSA workers in the engineering sector, who were on strike. In a political environment defined by fragmentation, it was a remarkable showing of solidarity.

Local activists worked to build a political discussion forum (PDF)—a NUMSA idea—by incorporating workers into their weekly meetings. NUMSA envisioned PDFs as a key vehicle for implementing the United Front locally. The Tsakane Community Forum, an APF affiliate that originally began organizing in Tsakane Extension 1 and later began to support protests in Tsakane10, provided a base for the effort. As Andrew, a longtime Tsakane activist, explained, the organizers changed the name of the group to incorporate their union counterparts: "We added 'Workers' after the resolution of NUMSA to actually form a United Front and do all these things of PDFs and so forth. Because that resolution of NUMSA led them to say, 'No, before you become a worker, you are a community member.' So we must organize together with workers. . . . Then we were forced by the participation of workers at that time to change the name to the Community and Workers Forum."[43] Turning their own organizing space into a local forum for the United Front, they renamed the group to be the Kwatsaduza Community and Workers Forum (KCWF). This was an impressive development, hinting at solidarity between organized workers and their more precariously situated counterparts. It also reflected an aspiration to link the local struggle to nearby areas in the three adjacent townships of Kwa-Thema, Tsakane, and Duduza.

These efforts began to bear fruit. Whereas the April march garnered little response from the state, the United Front–backed July protest led to a formal meeting between provincial-level officials and local activists from various areas, including Tsakane10. The United Front appeared to be on the rise. At the local level, within Tsakane10, it was helping to build new solidarities—between unionized workers and the unemployed and between different local areas—and to advance struggles for service delivery, even if progress remained slow. Beyond the local, the United Front was also building regional and national structures. In December 2014, the United Front held a National Preparatory Assembly and appointed a National Working Committee to guide the organization. These gains, however, proved short-lived.

Marrying the fluid and more spontaneous character of local protests to the bureaucratic and more deliberate approach of the union was one of the most significant difficulties. Local activists often expressed frustration with NUMSA's slow pace, which reflected the hierarchical and bureaucratic structure of decision making. Jakobo, a longtime activist who worked hard to integrate NUMSA and the United Front into Tsakane10, noted, "I find that if there is no NUMSA top official, whatever we are going to discuss may not hold, so we have to wait for the influence of their rubber stamp."[44] In contrast, local struggles moved quickly. Residents could take to the streets immediately, at any time. They were also more likely to deploy disruptive or illegal tactics. Andrew lamented the distance:

Whenever there is a march, you will have them [NUMSA representatives] coming as speakers, and that's not our tradition. . . . On a day of a march we must wake up as early as we can, four o'clock. We go [to] all routes [to] make sure that no one goes to work. . . . But [NUMSA representatives] don't come. You will see them when the gathering is at ten A.M. They will come at nine fifty-five A.M., take [the] podium, and leave. So you see, we [are] introducing them to community politics and ideas of which in a long run they disapprove.[45]

NUMSA's substantial organizational and financial resources, contrasting with the fluidity and financial weakness of local organizations, amplified these difficulties. Due to the imbalance, local activists sometimes found themselves waiting for support from their union counterparts.

NUMSA also sought to harness and, to a certain extent, discipline local activism. NUMSA leadership often portrayed unemployed residents and local protests as disorganized and politically backward.[46] The union's official declaration following its landmark Special National Congress in 2013 portrayed local protests as "largely leaderless."[47] NUMSA's deputy general secretary Karl Cloete argued that local protests represented "a leaderless resistance. It has no direction. Sometimes the protests get violent and the anger and frustration is not properly directed."[48] These sentiments surfaced at the local level. Andile, for example, clarified Numsa's role in Tsakane10:

We need to play a big role in terms of educating our community. Because people are doing those things—burning libraries, schools, halls, and all those—simply because they see those buildings as the symbol of the person they are talking to, which is government, who do not want to respond to them. . . . That is why NUMSA said the community does not have a leader. If there was a leader advising, as we are doing as NUMSA, obviously people were not going to burn what they have.[49]

While many local activists appreciated NUMSA's support and their critical stance toward the ANC, some resented their heavy hand. One activist complained, "They like to take decisions alone, and when they come to us on the ground, you find that they have already taken the decisions, and which end up with a bad outcome."[50] Another noted, similarly, that they could "discuss and take a decision, but your decision [would] be overturned. . . . NUMSA wanted to control the show by all means."[51] Andrew argued that NUMSA was afraid to "let go" of the process: "They want to remain the drivers. . . . I think [they are] imposing. . . . They have got that worry that we are losing this organization to other people."[52] Jakobo summarized: "Most comrades feel that NUMSA is still playing a big brother role where some of the things can only be done if they get approved, and that has its negative effects. It means that the level of activism is not as quick as you want it to be."[53]

The limited involvement of ordinary workers presented another challenge. Beyond the impressive July 2014 protest, a handful of union officials accounted for most instances of NUMSA involvement in Tsakane10 activism. This reflected broader patterns. To the extent that NUMSA members lived in protest-affected areas—and many did not—they represented a small proportion of residents. The fact that NUMSA failed to attract other COSATU unions to the United Front project reinforced this weakness. After supporting the ruling party for more than two decades, NUMSA leaders also had difficulty winning over rank-and-file members to the new oppositional stance.[54] Rather than building solidarity with rank-and-file workers on the ground, local activists in Tsakane10 worked primarily with NUMSA officials.

As time progressed, labor and community activists drifted apart. Within one year, they split into two meetings: one for KCWF and another for the local United Front. While the split stemmed partially from different views about what areas to include within their organizing scope, it also had deeper roots in varied political orientations. Tsakane10 activists sought to address immediate grievances within local areas, and KCWF meetings focused on hearing such grievances. United Front meetings were more concerned with building United Front structures, including planning for higher-level meetings and official launches of new structures. They also discussed theory about economic crisis and social change, which Jakobo referred to as "advanced politics." Andrew put the difference this way: "Kwatsaduza [KCWF] takes issues on the ground and creates programs whereby you can go and demand whatever services you can that are lacking. But United Front currently is more shaping the way forward, is not into action that much. . . . The only program was recruiting people to the United Front, inviting more people to the United Front, [and] also planning the submissions of the national launch."[55] Whereas service delivery struggles were immediate and urgent, United Front activists sought to build a durable organizational structure that could lead in the longer term.[56]

The split coincided with the general decline of the United Front. Locally, the United Front structure eventually ceased to have regular meetings. Nationally, the United Front began to fade into obscurity. In a reflexive self-evaluation in December 2015, the Political Coordination Committee of the United Front argued that, despite favorable conditions for organizing the Left within the country, "the UF is in crisis. It is going nowhere politically." Noting the organization's distance from "fighting movements, organized communities, [and] new and old layers of militants," the assessment warned that "it is not an exaggeration to posit that the UF initiative is not far from withering away into oblivion."[57] Subsequent developments did little to reverse this warning.

The 2016 local elections illustrated and reinforced the decline. From its inception, the question of electoral politics represented one of the stickiest issues within the United Front. NUMSA leaders worked hard to separate the United Front from its simultaneous Movement for Socialism, which referred to plans for a socialist and worker-oriented political party. Despite these efforts, the media and activists alike consistently conflated and confused the two. In Tsakane10, for example, some activists understood the split between the KCWF and the United Front as one between apolitical "community" struggles and party-linked "politics."[58] Thato, a Tsakane10 activist, expressed concern that turning the United Front into a political party would reduce support by half: "Maybe we can be seventeen in United Front, but going to the Movement for Socialism [political party], some ten may drop and go to seven."[59]

In Tsakane10, the KCWF chose a local resident to stand in the election as an independent candidate. Stressing the importance of raising residents' confidence, Jakobo explained that the effort was important to "instill hope in our working class that we can still do things ourselves." He remarked, "We do not need things to be done by political parties. I think it is that hope which is missing where people feel they need to always rely on political parties, someone who is big, the messiah."[60] Some also expressed hope that having a Tsakane10 representative on the local town council would give them an inside voice and push the state in their favor. Election officials dashed these hopes when they rejected the application for an independent candidate, due to the supporting names not having proper identification numbers. The technical blunder reflected weak organizational capacity, stemming partly from the weak support of a declining United Front.[61]

These obstacles, however, did not mean complete failure. In response to the various protests and meetings, some of which included support and participation from NUMSA officials and workers, the state agreed to relocate more than three hundred families to a nearby housing settlement. Officials also promised further development within the informal settlement. Whether and when these promises become reality is quite another question. The brief attempt to build the United Front also influenced popular consciousness. After learning of the split between the KCWF and the United Front, I asked Andrew if they planned to remove "Workers" from the name. His response was clear: "No we keep the name. . . . We can't just take out 'Workers' because [now] we understand the importance of combining the two struggles." After the NUMSA intervention, activists began to appreciate the tactical importance of workplace organizing:

> When you do these stay-aways, you will have people crying, saying, "But I will get fired." . . . Because when you plan things during the day, they will be at work. . . . [The next morning,] they wake up to a burning tire; they have a problem. . . . So we are excited to bring them [workers] closer to us. And that will mean understanding all workers, not only NUMSA members.[62]

This was a major leap. While the United Front eventually collapsed in Tsakane10, such awareness underscored the project's great potential.

Nor did the local struggle disappear. The KCWF continued to meet in Tsakane10 and hold public meetings. They continued to focus on service delivery issues, most importantly housing. While activists appreciated the importance of having an independent candidate in the elections, this was never a central goal. They were more concerned with putting pressure on the state to deliver. The distinctive aspect of the struggle in Tsakane10 was their approach to group solidarity, which centered on uniting workers and the unemployed. Activists confronted significant obstacles. Most notable were the different organizing approaches of union activists and local activists and the lack of participation by ordinary workers. To the extent that class solidarity did materialize, residents were not able to sustain it for very long. Nonetheless, the struggle in Tsakane10 demonstrated a politics that began to look outward, beyond the highly localized solidarities that predominated across the country.

Thembelihle: Socialist Party Politics

> Vote OKM. Vote against: forced removals; evictions; electricity cut offs; pit toilets; corrupt housing officials; unemployment. Vote for: free basic services for all; socialism.
> —poster at the Operation Khanyisa Movement annual general meeting, Thembelihle, May 2013

Thembelihle represented one of the most sustained attempts in the country to connect local struggles to left-leaning class politics. The Thembelihle Crisis Committee (TCC) lay at the center of that politics. Like the activists in Tsakane10, TCC activists sought to move beyond local solidarity by building a broader class solidarity, and like the activists in Bekkersdal, TCC activists also sought to participate in popular governance through the local state. While TCC was more successful on both fronts, they still confronted significant challenges. In this sense, the Thembelihle case illustrated the limits of militant local resistance after racial inclusion.

The TCC formed initially through efforts to improve access to water. In 2001, residents coordinated the installation of water pipes to connect communal taps to individual yards. They organized into street committees and collected money to purchase pipes. The urgent threat of eviction the following year became the TCC's formative moment. In 2002, the city of Johannesburg declared Thembelihle unsuitable for human settlement, due to the presence of dolomitic rock, and notified residents of plans to relocate them to the nearby area of Vlakfontein. The TCC responded by securing a lawyer, educating themselves about the dolomite issue, opposing their eviction in court, and organizing protests. The latter included defending residents against forced eviction. Having commissioned their own study of the geotechnical reports, with help from their lawyer, TCC activists consistently opposed the city's claim that the area was not suitable for human habitation.[63] Over the next decade, the dolomite issue lay at the center of the broader struggle for service delivery.

The TCC's powerful resistance to forced removal attracted attention from activists associated with the Soweto Electricity Crisis Committee (SECC), who visited Thembelihle and invited activists to join their meetings. The TCC and SECC became the two core affiliates of the OKM, which adopted a socialist orientation and the central demand of free basic services for all, including housing, water, and electricity. As local resistance accelerated in Thembelihle, including major protests in 2007 and 2011 around housing and electricity, the TCC continued to raise its profile. This reinforced support for the OKM. Between the local government elections in 2006 and 2011, the OKM support in Ward 8, which included Thembelihle, increased from 86 votes to 443 votes. In 2011, the ANC still dominated locally and secured the ward councilor position. Nonetheless, combining support from Thembelihle and Soweto, the original OKM stronghold, the electoral front mustered enough votes on the proportional representation ballot to retain a single seat on the Johannesburg city council. Whereas the previous OKM councilor position went to an SECC activist, after the 2011 election the organization appointed a TCC activist, Simphiwe Zwane. This decision reflected the growing importance of Thembelihle and the TCC to the OKM.

The OKM enabled Thembelihle activists to make their voices heard within the formal spaces of government. Thabo explained that the OKM "was not formed as part of the political party, but [an] electoral front so that we can have representatives inside, who will [advance] the interests of the working class and the poor, who will represent the interests of the unemployed inside the city council."[64] Consistent with this view, TCC activists were adamant that the OKM was a "movement" rather than a "political party." In between elections, the TCC did appear to operate that way. The organization spent more time holding meetings and organizing protests to address issues of service delivery than it did trying to sign up potential voters and convince them of the OKM's superiority. Indeed, when it was not election time, the topic of the OKM rarely emerged during public mass meetings, which the TCC organized as nonparty community gatherings.

OKM activists sought to demonstrate that public officials could operate differently, and in line with socialist and democratic principles. Representatives had to sign a pledge in which they agreed to follow mandates from the organization, consistently engage working-class and poor residents, and support collective struggles. Further, they had to contribute their monthly government salary to the OKM and in return receive a smaller salary from the organization. Zwane explained that the OKM was different from regular political parties because it sought to advance the demands of a movement rather than work to enrich individuals. She concluded, "Actually, if you were an opportunist, you would not agree even to be a candidate of OKM."[65] In the lead-up to the 2016 local government elections, the OKM sought to underscore the distinction between itself and political parties by developing a "voters' pledge" for rank-and-file supporters. The preamble explained that capitalist elections were a "time for lies and false promises." It also emphasized the OKM's commitment to "be there in struggle with you and your community in struggle as you organize and mobilize to solve your problems." The pledge itself asked voters to commit to "join and support the struggle of the working class," such as by actively participating in community organizing.[66]

This emphasis on working-class movement played out within the Johannesburg council, as Simphiwe Zwane from the OKM clashed with representatives from mainstream political parties. Two episodes stood out. One involved a situation in which Zwane played a leading role in a protest march directed at the local ward councilor. While the OKM pledge mandated her to do so, it was a breach of the code of conduct for councilors. Her colleagues in the council chamber ridiculed her, and the ethics committee referred her to the integrity commissioner. When the integrity commissioner questioned her actions in a private meeting, she responded by clarifying where her loyalties lay: "[The integrity commissioner said], 'You were not supposed to do that as a councilor, because you are an employee of the city of Joburg.' And I said, 'No, no, no. Not me, I am not employed by the city of Joburg. I did not come here with my CV, but I came here with votes. . . . I was not appointed to be here. But I was voted.'"[67] Shortly after the meeting, the police arrested her for intimidation of the local ward councilor. She spent three days in jail before the judge dropped the charges. The second episode involved a debate within the council over whether to raise the salaries of council members. The OKM did not agree with the salary increase, and Zwane had to represent this position within the council. Responding to her colleagues, Zwane argued that their pay was already high enough and that they should instead use the money to pay for child-care centers, old age homes, and houses for homeless people. She remarked to me that the OKM was different because, rather than simply enriching individual politicians, it took the needs of people seriously.[68]

In early 2015, the situation in Thembelihle began to shift. Frustrated with disregard from local municipal officials, activists attempted to meet with Jacob Mamabolo, the provincial-level executive in charge of housing. Mamabolo initially failed to respond, but a mass march of two thousand residents encouraged him to visit a public meeting in the area. Three months later, after Mamabolo failed to return with a progress report that residents claimed he had promised, militant protests erupted over three weeks. As in previous instances, the protests invited police intimidation, arrests, and detention. Yet one month later, in April 2015, the Gauteng provincial government and the city of Johannesburg declared Thembelihle a formal housing project. The government noted that they would only deliver services upon a positive "final geotechnical report" about the land. Crucially, though, they announced immediate plans to install formal electricity. The decision to electrify marked a significant material concession.

Both the ANC and TCC/OKM claimed responsibility for electrification. Just over one month ahead of the 2016 local government elections, in a highly publicized media stunt, President Jacob Zuma visited Thembelihle to symbolically "switch on the lights" in three shacks. The event illustrated how the ruling party could swoop in to claim material concessions as an indication of its own effectiveness. Moving quickly to reject the ANC narrative, the OKM released a statement declaring, "Electricity is not a gift from the ANC—We fought for it." The statement recounted how the TCC and OKM "stood with the people of Thembelihle through thick and thin in the struggle for development" and concluded, "It is not Zuma and the ANC who are bringing electricity here, it is our struggle."[69] Affirming their commitment to struggle, the OKM and TCC led a protest march, from Thembelihle to the local municipal offices, to complain about the slow pace of the electricity project.

Through the OKM, the TCC sought to harness solidarities both within and beyond Thembelihle. On the one hand, the TCC and OKM relied heavily on local ties and claims about place-based community to sustain legitimacy. As Zwane explained, "I think the special thing about us is that we are a community-based movement, so we are able to deal with the community's challenges directly and as such have grown a lot of trust between ourselves and *the community of Thembelihle*."[70] On the other hand, activists attempted to bolster their local struggle by building ties with kindred struggles in other areas. The OKM facilitated this by uniting the TCC and SECC. In the days before the 2016 election, for example, activists from the two groups joined to campaign, together, in the various wards where they each had presence.

It proved difficult, however, to use an opposition party to forge working-class solidarity across geographic areas. Support for the OKM grew in Thembelihle but declined in the electoral front's original strongholds in Soweto. Thembelihle and the TCC increasingly carried the OKM flag on their own. Due to its poor performance in 2016, the OKM lost the single seat on the Johannesburg city council that it had held for the previous decade. As one news article remarked, it was a "David vs. Goliath" struggle.[71] The major parties, especially the ANC, overmatched the OKM. They boasted national profiles and organization and significantly more resources. Loss of the councilor seat also eliminated the OKM's income stream. Some activists lamented that they would no longer hold their weekly meetings to discuss local government issues. Within Thembelihle, the TCC began to experience internal conflict in the wake of the electoral loss.[72]

Despite these challenges, the TCC had a strong foundation. This included a committed base of activists, a practice of holding weekly membership meetings and semiregular mass meetings, and a commitment to socialist and participatory democratic politics. These features were crucial as the organization regrouped. An exchange during a regular TCC membership meeting in May 2017 illustrated the dynamic. As per usual, they devoted a segment of the meeting to "political discussion," which centered on a recent outbreak of protests around Johannesburg. One woman noted that the TCC needed to clarify their own demands before supporting others. Another activist affirmed, "We *toyi toyi* [protest] as Thembelihle, but nobody supported us. . . . We have been pushing our agenda alone."[73] Narrow interests were coming to the fore, but seasoned activists quickly challenged them. One remarked that struggles elsewhere were one and the same with their own, while another affirmed that the TCC constitution was clear: they were a socialist organization, meaning that solidarity was automatic rather than conditional. He went on to recount the many times that the TCC received support from other areas in previous years. A spirit of solidarity triumphed. With a healthy culture of spirited debate and militant struggle, the TCC seemed poised to keep alive a radical movement from below, despite weakness and isolation.

The divergent political orientations of prominent activists in the four areas reinforced division and isolation. This was especially evident with respect to Motsoaledi and Thembelihle, which were under the same local municipality

(Johannesburg) and located only fifteen kilometers apart. In the middle 2000s, it seemed possible that activists in the two areas might build a common struggle. Yet Motsoaledi activists increasingly aligned with the ruling party, while Thembelihle activists rallied around the oppositional OKM. Bekkersdal activists were more detached from, and at times openly hostile to, broader social movements. Activists in Tsakane10 and Thembelihle thus offered the best hope for solidarity across the four areas. Growing out of a shared commitment to social movements and socialist politics, a few activists from Tsakane10 did assist Thembelihle during the 2016 OKM election campaign. Yet physical distance made a more substantial solidarity expensive and challenging. The local solidarity within the OKM, between the TCC and SECC, seemed more promising. Even in this instance, though, OKM support beyond Thembelihle dwindled, increasingly leaving the TCC to carry the OKM on its own.

Division and isolation left local protest movements weak and vulnerable to co-optation. This was especially true in such places as Motsoaledi and Bekkersdal, where activists placed even greater emphasis on local solidarities. In Tsakane10 and Thembelihle, activists envisioned a broader struggle, whether aligned with unionized workers or other communities, though they confronted difficulty putting these visions into motion. Even in these two cases, election results show that popular support for the ANC predominated. The ruling party did cede ground to the EFF, the breakaway from its own youth wing, which gained prominence in all four areas. The EFF, however, did little to build bridges between activists. This trend is likely to persist as the breakaway party becomes further entrenched in parliament, moving closer to the state and away from society.

Despite these difficulties, local organizing persisted. As of late 2017, for example, activists in Motsoaledi, Tsakane10, and Thembelihle were still holding public meetings and putting pressure on local government officials to deliver services. The case of Bekkersdal represented an outlier in this respect, as much of the collective energy had dissipated, though some activists did suggest that they were still able to call meetings when urgent matters arose. Two years later, in June 2019, I met a group of young activists who had come together from various political parties (including the ANC and EFF) to renew local organizing in Bekkersdal. They had recently staged a highly publicized protest for electricity. They were adamant about their separation from both party politics and the GWCRA/Parliament, whom they viewed as co-opted by local ANC officials. Ongoing local organizing in the four areas attested to the vibrancy of popular resistance. Though dominant, the ANC was unable to fully absorb the popular energy stemming from protests. Persistent protests and organizing appeared to keep hope alive for a renewed politics of the Left, independent of the ruling Alliance, even if the organizational basis for such a politics remained very weak.

CONCLUSION

In the early 1990s, after decades of upheaval bordering at times on civil war, South Africa achieved a remarkable democratic transition. With the iconic Nelson Mandela at the helm, the African National Congress (ANC) assumed power, bringing new hope to Black South Africans and advocates for social justice worldwide. Against high expectations, however, democratization and formal racial inclusion did not fundamentally transform the economy or significantly reduce inequality, which remained racially skewed. Many Black residents continued to live under harsh conditions on the urban periphery. During the second decade of democracy, local protests erupted. Reactivating the popular resistance of the apartheid era, residents took to the streets to express feelings of betrayal. Protesters called on government officials to fulfill the promises of national liberation. They demanded that the state recognize their existence and value and provide essential resources, such as housing, electricity, and water. Residents were often quite militant, as they barricaded roads and sometimes even vandalized property to convey their anger and frustration. Despite the magnitude and militancy of the protests, they failed to generate a coherent and sustained movement for redistribution. Instead, popular resistance fragmented. Residents focused on securing gains for their own local areas, they turned against and attacked their neighbors, and they pursued varied political projects. It was a fractured militancy.

In the preceding chapters, I traced South Africa's fractured militancy to passive revolution, which defined the process of racial inclusion and the transition from apartheid to democracy. In this concluding chapter, I draw out the lessons

138

of the study for scholarship on social movements and racial inclusion and consider the implications for left politics and capitalism in South Africa. I suggest that, at least in the short term, local protests reinforced capitalist hegemony.

From Social Movements to Capitalist Politics

In recent decades, the triumvirate of resource mobilization, political opportunities, and framing has dominated the field of social movement studies.[1] These approaches offer useful clues about South African resistance, but they also have important limits. Following recent calls for greater attention to capitalism, class, and political economy within scholarship on social movements, I emphasize the political dimensions of capitalism and class struggle.[2] This alternative approach calls for three shifts: from resource mobilization to class position, from political opportunities to elite maneuvers, and from framing to the politics of solidarity and fragmentation.

In their classic account of the resource mobilization approach, John McCarthy and Mayer Zald assume that there is "always enough discontent in any society" to supply social movements. The key question thus becomes whether movement actors can muster enough resources—including the formation of social movement organizations—to support their cause.[3] From this perspective, it is difficult to understand mobilization by the poor, who have limited resources. In South Africa, though, the urban poor were the primary agents behind widespread local protests. Building on Fanon, who underscores the revolutionary potential of economically excluded groups, I showed how the urban poor in South Africa managed to overcome their economic vulnerability by condemning the betrayal of nationalist elites, building solidarity within place-based communities, and making demands for public service delivery. The South African case demonstrates that life toward the bottom of the class structure, where such economic threats as extreme inequality, financial crisis, and austerity policy are most devastating, can produce grievances that lead to mobilization.[4] One might say that South Africa's protests exemplified *mobilization without resources*.

Despite this important limitation, the resource mobilization perspective is likely correct in that the lack of resources did create obstacles to building solidarities across residential areas. This became apparent with the collapse of such organizations as the Anti-Privatization Forum, which previously provided resources to help connect activists from different areas. Equally important, however, is the way in which class positioning shapes the "arenas" and "targets" of mobilization.[5] For Gramsci, the economy and class structure set limits on the possibilities of class formation. In South Africa, many among the urban poor lacked not only material resources, but also access to workplace organizing. This amplified the significance of residential areas and demands for collective consumption. Resembling what many describe as struggles for a "right to the city," residents demanded service delivery—improved access to public goods, such as housing and electricity—rather than improved wages and working conditions. Such political orientations made the state, political parties, and community groups, rather than unions and labor organizations, the central players and institutions.

Taking political factors seriously, the political opportunities approach suggests that external factors, such as popular access to the political system, elite divisions and allies, and a lack of repression, enable social movements to thrive.[6] These factors undoubtedly contributed to the explosion of protest in South Africa. Democratization and the collapse of apartheid expanded popular access to politics, such as the legal right to vote, participate in government, and assemble in public. While state repression certainly did not disappear, as demonstrated by the dramatic example of the Marikana massacre, it was arguably less than under apartheid.[7] Further, not only did racial inclusion bring Black elites of the national liberation movement into power, but also elite power struggles within the ANC drew on and amplified popular antagonisms.[8] What still demands explanation in the South African case, however, is why these facilitating opportunities led to both mobilization *and* division rather than a coherent and sustained movement.

In her study of Black movements in Colombia and Brazil, Tianna Paschel calls for a "long march" view of social movements. This requires following the trajectory of social movements as they become institutionalized, including attention to "what happens after, in between, and sometimes along cycles of protest."[9] In South Africa, this means paying attention to the connections between popular resistance before and after apartheid, and especially to the ways in which racial inclusion reconfigured the political landscape. I turned to Gramsci's concept of passive revolution, which underscores the importance of elite compromises and maneuvers from above to dismantle oppositional forces and restore the existing order. I also drew on the classic accounts of Fanon and Chatterjee, which extend Gramsci by showing how anticolonial nationalism enables elites to demobilize society and promote their own narrow agendas. The democratic transition in South Africa resembled this process. White and Black elites negotiated a new political order that featured formal racial inclusion in the polity, alongside new conditions for globalized and financialized capital accumulation.

South Africa's passive revolution amplified economic inequality and preserved its associations with race and space. The continuation of concentrated urban poverty underpinned the resurgence of popular resistance, but under new political conditions. The process of demobilization, marked especially by the absorption of popular organizations into the ANC and the state, meant that activists had to build new organizations and communities of resistance from scratch. Connected to the process of demobilization, ANC leaders presented the state as the key vehicle of transformation. They prioritized technocratic solutions to service delivery over mechanisms of popular participation. These maneuvers redirected popular energies toward the state and engendered competition over access to scarce public resources. Rather than broader solidarities, class or otherwise, passive revolution encouraged narrow struggles for recognition and administrative fixes for particular residential areas.

This brings us to framing, the third major pillar of social movement studies. There were remarkable parallels between instances of popular resistance in different residential areas. Confronting parallel material conditions of economic insecurity and hardship, residents expressed similar feelings of betrayal and mobilized around similar notions of service delivery and community. Given this array of powerful frames, which clearly resonated with many among South Africa's urban poor, one might have expected to find a burgeoning movement that unified residents in a common cause. Instead, as I have shown, resistance fractured both within and between residential areas. Making sense of this fractured militancy called for emphasis on the politics of solidarity and fragmentation. The analytic of class formation, which underscores both the importance of material conditions and the contingency of collective action, is a useful tool. In the context of South Africa's passive revolution, class formation remained limited. Activism frequently contained solidarity within local areas and coupled it with antagonism toward workers and national outsiders. This fragmentation suggests that effective mobilizing frames are insufficient. Movement building also requires political orientations that enable solidarities across varied forms of division.

Racial Inclusion and Resistance, South and North

The South African case also helps to illuminate processes of racial change and their relationship to popular resistance. For Howard Winant, the process of racial inclusion initiates a shift toward what he calls "racial hegemony."[10] The term builds on Gramsci's well-known theory of hegemony but replaces Gramsci's emphasis on class with an alternative emphasis on race. At the core, Winant's racial hegemony involves concessions to nonwhite groups that do not fundamentally alter the racial order. This involves a reconfiguration of how subordinate racial groups relate to the state and economy. On the one hand, under racial hegemony the state distances itself from white supremacy. This means rejecting discrimination, colonialism, and formal segregation. On the other hand, racial inequality persists, with white residents continuing to possess disproportionate economic and political power. The former enables the latter by "dispersing" the sources of racial inequality, making them more difficult to recognize and resist.[11] Winant suggests that these conditions characterize the global racial order following World War II, with the United States and South Africa as iconic examples.[12]

My account here underscores the articulation of class and race. In contrast to Winant, rather than shifting the focus from class to race, I pay close attention to class struggles *within* the process of racial inclusion.[13] In South Africa, formal racial inclusion rested on a negotiated compromise that primarily enriched two sets of elites: a predominantly white layer of elites with close ties to the global economy and a predominantly Black layer of elites with close ties to the ANC party-state. Gramsci's concept of passive revolution calls attention to this process of elite class formation. It points us toward the ways in which elite maneuvers limit the transformations associated with racial inclusion. For Gramsci, the passive revolutionary route represents the weakness of elites and thus their inability to secure hegemony and popular consent across the entire social formation. My focus on the articulation of class and race thus leads to a different characterization: whereas for Winant the process of racial inclusion marks the achievement of (racial) hegemony, in my analysis racial inclusion represents one form of passive revolution, or the absence of hegemony.[14] The latter implies a more unstable social order. My characterization also underlines the centrality of class struggles to the future of racial hierarchy, racial inequality, and racial politics.

One of the strengths of Winant's analysis is that it encourages cross-national comparison. If South Africa's democratization was part of a global shift toward racial inclusion, what does this study of fractured militancy mean for Black movements elsewhere? As noted in the preface, widespread local protests in South Africa took place simultaneously with the emergence of the Black Lives Matter movement in the United States. Though more sporadic than the South African protests, which remained steady and consistent for over a decade, the US movement also spoke to the plight of low-income Black communities. The two sets of mobilizations nonetheless differed sharply with respect to both their demands and social composition. In South Africa, protests took the form of localized uprisings by impoverished Black residents for recognition and public service delivery. In contrast, in the United States, the Black Lives Matter movement called for ending police violence against Black residents, with some parts of the movement advocating for abolishing or defunding the police. Importantly, movement participation expanded to include the middle classes as well as diverse racial groups. This increasingly wide scope of participation was notably absent in South Africa. Following the logic of the preceding chapters, I argue that we can trace this divergence to the different forms of passive revolution that marked racial inclusion in the two places.

For Gramsci, passive revolution includes the absorption of oppositional forces into a conservative political project. Like in South Africa, Black elites in the United States entered the political establishment and capitulated to logics of capital accumulation while abandoning projects of radical redistribution.[15] The process of political incorporation, however, was much more limited. While Black leaders began to occupy prominent positions within local and national government, it was far from a wholesale transformation. The United States did not elect a Black president until more than four decades after passage of the Civil Rights Act. Further, the socialist and nationalist wings of the Black Power movement experienced repression and marginalization, while the demand for "equal opportunity" became the crowning achievement of the civil rights movement.[16] Conversely, racial inclusion in South Africa led to an arguably broader process of transformation, with the transfer of power to the ANC reshaping the state at all levels. The left wings of the national liberation movement remained central, as illustrated by the ANC's formal partnerships with two prosocialist organizations, the South African Communist Party (SACP) and the Congress of South African Trade Unions (COSATU). At least partly due to these alliances, the ANC's promise to undermine the legacy of apartheid and deliver a "better life for all" spoke to aspirations for redistribution that extended well beyond equal opportunity.

The greater extent of absorption in South Africa, including its consequences for the character of the state and popular expectations, help us to make sense of divergent protests. Three differences stand out. First, contemporary protests represented a continuation of the political projects that ushered in racial inclusion: equal opportunity for Black residents in the United States; redistribution of resources to Black residents in South Africa. Second, the ANC's rise to power in South Africa meant that feelings and expressions of betrayal were more central and prominent. Whereas South African protesters frequently criticized the shortcomings of Black political leaders, this was not a central theme within the Black Lives Matter movement. American protesters were more likely to attribute police violence to the legacy of slavery, ongoing white supremacy, and anti-Black state violence. Such opposition to overt racism suggests a closer parallel to the antiapartheid movement in South Africa than it does to contemporary struggles for public service delivery. This stemmed from the more limited change associated with racial inclusion in the United States. Put in Gramscian terms, in the combination of "restoration" and "revolution" that characterizes passive revolution, restoration weighed heavier in the United States than it did in South Africa. Racial inclusion was weaker, producing resurgent protests against racial domination.

Third, these divergent orientations likely influenced the social composition of the mobilizations. In contrast to demands for redistribution, which call for some restriction of capitalist markets and the inequalities they produce, demands for civil rights are entirely compatible with—and may even facilitate—capitalist markets and inequality. To the extent that middle classes fare well within market society, they may be more likely to defend the protection of civil rights than redistribution to the poor. Put more directly, I am proposing that the Black Lives Matter movement garnered greater middle-class participation precisely because it revolved around well-established twentieth-century demands for civil rights. In contrast, the South African middle classes—including the rising Black middle classes—were less concerned with fighting concentrated urban poverty. The question of the relation between class and political orientation refers to back to Chatterjee. He distinguishes between civil society, which revolves around equal rights and popular sovereignty for the middle classes, and political society, which revolves around the state taking care of the urban and rural poor. In the United States, the Black Lives Matter movement tapped into middle-class civil society with a broader narrative of racial change. Conversely, in South Africa, the urban poor and local protests for public services remained trapped in the narrow, direct, and contextual political negotiations of political society.

The South African Left

Questions of civil society and the state, and the failure of South Africa's local protests to cohere around a transformative social movement, raise the issue of Left strategy. Indeed, left organizing proceeded alongside widespread local protests, even if the connections between them remained weak. Left strategy took different forms. To illustrate the difference, I briefly consider two left formations that resulted from major splits in the ANC-led Alliance: the United Front (UF) and the Economic Freedom Fighters (EFF). Both formations emerged in the wake of the Marikana massacre, in which police killed thirty-four striking mine workers. Taking place amid an upsurge of worker militancy, the massacre sparked a renewed spirit of resistance in the country.[17] In turn, the major breaks from the ruling party reinvigorated left activists, providing new hope for left alternatives beyond the Alliance. The two left formations came to life during the same political moment, but the UF leaned toward society while the EFF leaned toward the state.

In Gramsci's analysis, the concept of civil society refers to private voluntary associations, such as unions, churches, and political parties. Popular discourse in South Africa revolved around a similar understanding but with a key difference: the exclusion of political parties. Popular references to civil society typically included unions, churches, community groups, and social movements. In contrast, political parties occupied their own distinctive political space defined by the pursuit of state power. For many, civil society rested on higher moral ground. This reflected, on the one hand, its dissociation from corruption and narrow elite maneuvers, and on the other hand, its closer connection to the grassroots and the consciousness of ordinary people. Initiated by the National Union of Metalworkers of South Africa (NUMSA), the UF stood on the civil society side. Seeking to unite workplace and community struggles through opposition to the ANC's neoliberal policies, NUMSA understood the UF as necessarily distinct from political parties.[18] In contrast, the EFF formed in 2013 as a political party with the explicit intention of entering elections and taking over state power. If the EFF's vibrant rallies and marches sometimes approximated a social movement, over time the party's attention shifted increasingly toward the halls of government, including especially standoffs with ANC representatives in parliament.

The contrast came into focus during a July 2015 debate on the possibilities for a "new left" in South Africa.[19] The event featured two prominent activist intellectuals: John Appolis, campaigns coordinator for the UF, and Mbuyiseni Ndlozi, national spokesperson for the EFF. Appolis explained that the UF's primary goal was to overcome current fragmentation by uniting those groups with the closest ties to the working class and the poor, whom he identified as "the heart" of the UF. He criticized the EFF's electoral focus, which he argued limited their ability to build a "unified left mass movement." Ndlozi's political program was the mirror opposite. He noted that social movements were not sustainable and, most crucially, "would not take the ANC toe-to-toe in terms of the state, in terms of the resources, in terms of the spaces where the ANC is dominating." He was very clear about the EFF's goal: "Our ambition is not to go to big protest, win victory, and withdraw. It is to run the country. We can't entrust [the state] to any bourgeois anymore. It's to run it ourselves." [20] Whereas Appolis sought to build solidarity within society, Ndlozi wanted to seize control of the government apparatus.

The two organizations addressed the politics of local protests in different ways. The society-oriented politics of the UF aligned with the dominant emphasis on community within local organizing efforts. It resonated with activists' rejection of political parties. In Tsakane10, for example, some activists wanted the UF to lean even further in this direction, but they appreciated the fact that the UF was not (yet) contesting elections. Conversely, the EFF addressed popular desires to connect with the postapartheid state, and especially to access state resources. Whereas the UF only offered the promise of worker-community solidarity, with the fuzzy possibility of a postneoliberal order in the distant future, the EFF promised to control the levers of government and to improve service delivery more immediately. The latter was more tangible. While the UF appealed to local activists who maintained strong commitments to oppositional struggle and social transformation, the movement failed to capture popular energies, as even Appolis acknowledged. Meanwhile, the EFF continued to ascend. Ndlozi bragged that it was the only left organization with documented support of more than one million people, meaning voters.[21]

Focused on opposition to neoliberalism and the ANC, the politics of the UF resembled those of the Anti-Privatization Forum (APF), which was prominent in the early 2000s. Like the APF, the UF focused on solidarity within society rather than elections. Yet the UF was a decade too late. If NUMSA had broken with the ANC in the early 2000s and joined forces with the APF, the course of history may have been very different.[22] Instead, NUMSA remained loyal to the ANC-aligned COSATU, which rejected the APF. A decade later, the sheer amount of popular resistance was certainly greater, but the political moment was very different. Whereas the APF emerged during a period of fragile national unity and reconciliation, by the time the UF appeared factionalism and division were growing louder. The idea that popular involvement was crucial for directing the country lay in the past. Residents increasingly pressed for their own narrow interests. The UF and NUMSA leadership certainly made important mistakes, such as in failing to allow grassroots activists to drive the process "from below."[23] They arguably placed too much emphasis on building a formal organization and not enough emphasis on mobilizing for disruption.[24] Nevertheless, they also confronted a challenging situation. Within a sea of state-oriented local protests, building a society-oriented movement was an uphill battle.

In a political economy defined by economic insecurity, the state-oriented approach was better suited to capitalize on popular frustration.[25] Given the daily challenges of survival, it is not surprising that residents frequently looked for political alternatives that addressed immediate material needs. Enter the EFF. In contrast to the UF, which focused on longer-term goals, the EFF promised to move immediately within government to enhance welfare provisions, such as houses and social grants. Such promises spoke directly to the interests and desires that lay beneath popular protests. They were precisely what struggles on the terrain of political society were all about. Focused more on winning elections than building solidarity on the ground, however, the EFF remained detached from local organizing efforts. This was the paradox of oppositional politics within political society: the state-oriented approach that garnered the most support also worked against building a coherent left movement within society.

The division reared its head again in April 2017, when frustration with the scandal-ridden ANC leader and president Jacob Zuma briefly exploded into popular resistance.[26] The two biggest anti-Zuma protests took place five days apart at the Union Buildings in Pretoria. Led by Save South Africa, founded by the businessperson Sipho Pityana, commentators labeled the first protest the "civil society" march. Most protesters came from affluent suburbs and held middle-class jobs, though some local activists from impoverished residential areas—including Thembelihle and Tsakane10—participated as well.[27] Propelled by an alliance of opposition political parties, the second protest drew greater support from the working classes and the poor. Within the massive crowd of more than eighty thousand participants—compared to about thirty thousand in the civil society protest—the EFF's signature red attire dominated.[28] The events affirmed both the predominance of political parties over civil society and the separation of political parties from local protests and organizing around service delivery.

The centrality of political parties in South Africa stems from the unfolding of passive revolution, which collapsed civil society into the state and greatly empowered a single political party, the ANC. Within this context, residents frequently turned to political parties as the most effective vehicles for securing change, or at least public resources. At the same time, however, popular frustration with the ANC and narrowly interested political leaders encouraged local activists to reject party politics. Instead, they targeted the state directly, especially the levers of local government. This approach undermined the possibility of using political parties to build solidarity across residential areas and fed into an emphasis on administrative fixes. That emphasis, in turn, enabled the ANC-led state to isolate and manage instances of popular dissent. Such were the contradictory and unstable politics under passive revolution through racial inclusion. These outcomes have important implications for the future of South African capitalism.

From Passive Revolution to Market Hegemony?

The eruption of local protests in South Africa formed part of a global protest wave that followed the onset of the 2008 financial crisis.[29] From the revolutions in Tunisia and Egypt, to antiausterity protests in Spain and Greece, to the

Occupy movement in the United States, to protests for public goods in Turkey and Brazil, protesters challenged political elites and the unequal global capitalism that they represented. In some instances, what began as experiments in direct or participatory democracy gave way to left-leaning political parties, with mixed success. In the United States, for example, the Bernie Sanders campaign, which drew from the energy and slogans of the Occupy movement, lost out to the rightward challenge from Donald Trump. In Spain, the protests spawned the left-leaning party Podemos, which became quickly popular and several years later entered a ruling coalition with the Spanish Socialist Workers Party.

The Spanish example suggests one possible road for the Left in South Africa, though the prospects appear bleak. With the UF limping along on the verge of extinction, NUMSA officially launched the Socialist Revolutionary Workers' Party (SRWP) ahead of the national elections in 2019. The SRWP only secured just under twenty-five thousand votes, demonstrating its weak support among a NUMSA base of more than 350,000 members. The party's future remains incredibly uncertain. For the time being, the EFF represents perhaps the greatest hope for a left-leaning political party. One of the EFF's strengths is its messaging around Black economic empowerment, which speaks to the persistence of extreme and racialized inequality. Yet, as noted above and in contrast to the origins of Podemos, the party remains detached from much local organizing and protest on the ground. Further concerns loom about both the EFF's political character—some point to fascist tendencies—and whether it has the capacity to challenge the ANC in a significant way.

With no sustained left movement on the horizon, where is fractured militancy leading South Africa's postapartheid capitalism? Does it offer the possibility of antisystemic change that the post-2008 global protests appeared at least to put on the table? The case studies presented here suggest a more conservative future. While local mobilizations called on the state to provide social protection, they did not necessarily undermine marketization. This was most evident in Thembelihle, where the Thembelihle Crisis Committee (TCC) connected demands for local development to a socialist politics. Despite claiming opposition to capitalism, however, activists celebrated the installation of prepaid electricity meters as a major victory. The irony, which was certainly not lost on the most experienced activists, was that this victory incorporated residents into the market. Whereas they previously accessed electricity freely, through illegal connections, they now had to pay the corporatized municipal entity City Power. When the money on an individual's account ran out, the city shut off their electricity.

A similar dynamic prevailed in the other cases. In Motsoaledi, residents relocated from shacks to formal houses, which came equipped with the very same prepaid electricity meters that residents received in Thembelihle. Whereas they previously did not have electricity at all, residents began paying for it through City Power. They also had piped water within their homes. Residents expected that they would eventually have to pay for water, whereas previously they accessed it freely through communal taps or illegal connections that extended to their yards. In Tsakane10, most residents remained in the same shacks without access to formal electricity or piped water for individual homes. For those residents who did relocate to formal housing, however, they confronted a similar incorporation into the fee-for-service model. In Bekkersdal, the level of marketization did not change much. Residents in formal housing continued to pay for water and electricity, while residents in the informal settlements continued to experience limited access. In none of the cases did local struggles lead to substantial decommodification. Residents continued to rely heavily on wage labor and household sharing in an economy that did not produce enough jobs and in which, for those with limited skills and education, the few jobs available were often unstable and paid very little.

At the economically insecure margins of the market, therefore, mobilization in defense of social protection often deepened market penetration. Government provision of free houses represented a partial exception, but even decommodified housing enabled the commodification of electricity and water. Residents celebrated these market extensions as victories. Even if they previously accessed similar services freely, they had to do so illegally. Illegal electricity connections were less reliable, and they left residents vulnerable to the persistent possibility of disconnection. Residents welcomed formal electricity, even if they had to pay for it. For some activists in Thembelihle, formal *and* free electricity represented an important goal to pursue in the future. This goal, of course, was central to the APF and the TCC's key ally, the Soweto Electricity Crisis Committee (SECC). There was little evidence, however, that new social movements would emerge to oppose privatization in Thembelihle. In short, the case studies suggest that protests had the unlikely effect of stabilizing postapartheid capitalism.

Broader political dynamics are likely reinforcing the trend. At the ANC's national conference in December 2017, delegates elected the former-union-leader-turned-business-mogul Cyril Ramaphosa as the new party president. Campaigning on an anticorruption platform, Ramaphosa's victory pleased international investors and gave many residents hope that he would restore both the ANC's dignity and the country's democratic structures. With Ramaphosa at the helm, voters returned the ANC to power in the 2019 elections, though with only 57.5 percent support, the ruling party's weakest showing to-date after racial inclusion. Political competition within established institutional frameworks is compatible with capitalist hegemony, and South Africa is moving in this direction.[30] Whether Ramaphosa can reverse the encroachment of patronage and corruption within the ruling party—an outcome that is far from certain, given current factionalism—remains an open question. Political pluralism, however, may help to make the state more efficient, especially if the threat of losing political power contributes to declining corruption within the ruling party. The fact that all major political parties emphasize service delivery also suggests that the state will continue to make material concessions, just as it did in Motsoaledi, Thembelihle, Tsakane10, and Bekkersdal. Ongoing local protests and party competition, therefore, may reinforce each other in constructing popular consent.

Gramsci associates passive revolution with a form of weak leadership that fails to incorporate a large section of the national population. From this perspective, passive revolution represents the absence of hegemony.[31] In South Africa, however, passive revolution through racial inclusion also produced fractured militancy, which revolved around relatively narrow demands for material concessions. To the extent that such livelihood struggles find success, they may help the urban poor to recognize their own interests within the existing system. In doing so, they help dominant groups to secure the hegemony that they were unable to achieve during the democratic transition. This suggests a hypothesis for further exploration: passive revolution eventually leads to capitalist hegemony but only if it also produces fractured militancy. One benefit of this trajectory is that greater bureaucratic efficiency and material concessions—such as free houses or formal electricity—will improve the daily lives of poor residents, even if they do not fundamentally reshape the political economy. For those eking out a living in the impoverished townships and shack settlements, even limited daily improvements are significant.

Nonetheless, without a substantial mass movement in favor of redistribution and social protection, high levels of racialized inequality and Black economic insecurity will persist. What might a possible future defined by capitalist hegemony mean for transformative struggles? In his analysis of early twentieth-century fascism, Dylan Riley suggests that capitalist hegemony is a prerequisite for "counter-hegemonic" struggles.[32] This is because oppositional groups may exploit gaps between the interests of the ruling group and the national interests that they claim to represent. If this is true, then by helping to secure capitalist hegemony, fractured militancy in the present may lay the foundation for transformative social movements in the future. Such movements may cohere, for example, around opposition to the market-driven capitalism that is currently becoming more and more entrenched. While there is only limited evidence of antimarket resistance today, uprisings are difficult to predict. One may appear at any moment.

Methodological Appendix

I visited South Africa for the first time during a short three-month visit in the middle of 2007. Internal battles within the ANC were bubbling, setting the stage for the showdown between Mbeki and Zuma at the ruling party's national conference that December. During this initial exploration, I spent most of my time wandering around the inner-city neighborhoods of Johannesburg, though I also began to visit the more peripheral townships of Soweto and Alexandra. I returned to Johannesburg for a six-month stay in 2010. During this visit, I dug deeper into the life of the city's townships and informal settlements, and I began to immerse myself in social movements. I tagged along with an activist associated with a nongovernmental organization, who was attempting to spark cooperative development projects. Through these travels, I met community activists and trade unionists. I became involved in the Conference of the Democratic Left, which later became the Democratic Left Front (DLF), a social movement that worked to connect various popular struggles. I joined protests and helped to organize them. I also began conducting formal interviews with activists. These first two trips laid a crucial foundation for this book project, even if they contributed little to the data that I eventually drew on. By the time I left in 2010, I had a much greater understanding of the country's political and economic dynamics.

I was initially interested in questions about the linkages between migration, race, and class. The Forced Migration Studies Program (now the African Center for Migration and Society) was my initial institutional host. I had no idea, of course, that shortly after my first visit in 2007, a wave of violent xenophobic attacks would spread across the country. While I remained interested in issues of migration, I grew increasingly focused on local politics and collective organizing by native-born residents. The latter were the protagonists behind both xenophobic attacks and the explosion of local protests. When I returned to Johannesburg for a third, and much longer, visit in 2013–2014, I focused on understanding the protests, their entanglements with xenophobia, and the relationships of both to national politics. A postdoctoral fellowship with the South African Research Chair in Social Change, and the linked Center for Social Change, at the University of Johannesburg provided me with a supportive institutional space in which to work. This opportunity enabled me to live in Johannesburg for eighteen months.

During 2013–2014, I began to develop the four case studies that represent the core of this book. I had already visited Thembelihle in 2010 and met some activists, but I began attending meetings in the area more regularly from April 2013. Following local protest in the respective areas, I began visiting Motsoaledi in July 2013, Bekkersdal in March 2014, and Tsakane10 in April 2014. I explored the residential areas, met with activists, conducted interviews, and attended meetings. During this same period, I was also an active participant in the DLF and later the United Front. This included work organizing the Strike for Youth Jobs in March 2014—the United Front's first public outing, which the DLF supported—and participation in numerous other protests. As part of my research into the United Front, initiated by the National Union of Metalworkers South Africa (NUMSA), I also attended NUMSA meetings at both the union's head office and local offices.

Once I moved back to the United States in August 2014, for the next three years I made shorter trips to South Africa, usually about two weeks at a time. This included one trip in 2015, two trips in 2016, two trips in 2017, and one trip each in 2018 and 2019. During these trips, I returned to the four case study areas to conduct further interviews and gather details about what had happened during my absence. These follow-up visits proved extremely valuable. They provided me with an opportunity to examine how local organizing and activist perspectives were unfolding. Over time, I placed decreasing emphasis on conducting formal interviews. Instead, I spent more time following up with activists for informal discussions about the status of activism in the respective residential areas.

As a white and middle-class academic from the United States, I frequently stood out in the contexts where I was conducting research. This was especially true in the four case study areas, where economic hardship loomed large and most residents were Black. Only very rarely did I see another white person in these places. I suspect that, to a certain extent, my outsider status facilitated the research process. In some instances, individuals seemed more willing to share their views and experiences due to my distance from their situation. Crucially, though, I benefitted greatly from the research assistance of Nhlakanipo Lukhele, a Black activist from Thembelihle. Nhlakanipo assisted me with the research in Bekkersdal and Tsakane10, joining me during most of my visits to these areas and conducting the interviews with me. For interviewees who were more comfortable speaking in languages other than English, Nhlakanipo helped with translation. Yet the significance of his assistance was much broader, as he proved invaluable in terms of making connections and building rapport.

Local and activist connections were also important. For each of the four case study areas, local activists represented my first contacts in the area. Through my involvement in social movement networks around Johannesburg, I was able to secure the contact information of prominent activists in the protest sites. Once I established contact, my association with Nhlakanipo, my involvement in such social movements as the DLF and UF, my affiliation with the University of Johannesburg, and my ties to the activist-oriented Center for Social Change all helped to convince residents—especially the more seasoned activists—to speak with me. I initiated the research through activist connections, therefore, and focused on prominent activists in my interviews. As I grew more familiar with each area, however, I began to extend outward to residents who were more peripheral to local organizing. For instance, I struck up conversations with the neighbors of activists, people walking on the streets, and shop owners, explained the research project, and in some instances asked individuals for interviews.

In addition to extensive ethnographic observation, I gathered 287 interviews with activists and ordinary poor and working-class residents (table 4). This included three broad categories: in-depth interviews, protest interviews, and other short interviews. Of the 105 total in-depth interviews, 71 were with residents in one of the four case study areas, and 34 were with those who lived in other areas. In-depth interviews lasted at least fifteen minutes and typically involved extended discussions about the interviewee's personal experiences and worldviews. The vast majority of these interviews (82 percent) lasted more than thirty minutes, and most were between one and two hours in length. Most of the in-depth interviews included a single interviewee, but 17 percent included two or more interviewees. The analysis in this book focuses primarily on these in-depth interviews.

Conducted on the sidelines of protest events, the protest interviews were shorter, lasting less than fifteen minutes. Research assistants and I gathered the vast majority of these interviews at three different protest events: a Congress of South African Trade Union (COSATU) protest against highway tolls and labor brokers in November 2013, a United Front protest against unemployment in March 2014, and a NUMSA protest associated with a strike in the engineering

TABLE 4. Interview summary

	FOUR CASE STUDY AREAS	OTHER AREAS	TOTAL
In-depth interviews	71	34	105
Protest interviews	5	142	147
Other short interviews	19	16	35
Total	95	192	287

sector in July 2014.[1] While I do not draw directly on much of the interview data from these three protests in this book, the interviews helped to shape my thinking and the project generally. The United Front protest was most relevant to the analysis here, as it featured both union members and community activists. The five protest interviews pertaining to the case study areas included interviews at both these events (two) and local protests (three). In the rare instances when I was able to participate in or witness local protests, I relied primarily on informal conversations to gather information rather than formal interviews.

The third category, other short interviews, included interviews that lasted less than fifteen minutes but did not take place at a protest event. These interviews came almost exclusively from a project on the May 7, 2014, national election, which I designed and executed alongside members of the Center for Social Change at the University of Johannesburg.[2] The study included surveys of voters outside of polling stations, as well as open-ended interviews with both voters and nonvoters beyond the polling stations. Through this project, I collected thirty-three brief interviews that fieldworkers conducted with residents of the West Rand and the south of Johannesburg, including eighteen brief interviews with residents of Motsoaledi, Thembelihle, and Bekkersdal.

In October 2017, I held a workshop with activists from the four different study areas to share the results of my study and solicit their feedback. Including the activists and a handful of other researchers and undergraduate students, about fifty people attended the workshop. It was a remarkable opportunity, not only to discuss my findings but also to participate in a critical dialogue between activists from different areas. Prominent activists from each of the four case study areas attended, and their different approaches and experiences resonated in the discussion. The exchanges that we had over the course of six hours were immensely useful, helping me to clarify and elaborate my arguments. The convergence in the room about the challenge of fragmentation struck me profoundly. Toward the beginning of the workshop, I presented ideas about feelings of betrayal and demands for recognition (chapter 2) and asked participants to discuss them and provide feedback. While verifying and building on my analysis, activists also began to express frustration about their isolation from each other despite the similarities of their struggles. They anticipated where the rest of my presentation was going. The problem of fragmentation and division became a persistent theme throughout the day. My goal in this book is to explain fragmentation by connecting everyday experiences to theory and history. While I take full responsibility for the arguments, I must acknowledge that the core ideas echo the views of local activists.

Uncomfortable Collaborations: Race, Class, and Power in Research on Poor People's Movements

There is a long history of white middle-class involvement in South Africa's working-class Black movements. The former includes professional intellectuals with roots both inside and outside the academy. Under apartheid, for example, middle-class whites played a central role in the burgeoning Black labor movement. Some served as full-time union officials. Others were intellectual supporters with ties to universities, labor-supporting organizations, or periodicals, such as the *South African Labor Bulletin*.[3] An unequal power dynamic evolved within the unions, rooted in the division of labor between the expert/intellectual work performed by white officials and the more menial work performed by Black officials and workers. That middle-class whites dominated public intellectual debates beyond the union only reinforced the racial division of mental versus manual labor. The division created numerous tensions and resentments. The growing prominence of Black intellectuals within the labor movement led to the retreat of white officials, who moved out of unions and into policy-oriented positions within the state, NGOs, consultancy firms, and universities. Today, there is limited white involvement in the predominantly Black unions.

In the postapartheid period, these old dynamics began to resurface with the involvement of predominantly white, activist-oriented, and middle-class academics in community struggles led by the predominantly Black urban poor. This relationship reproduced familiar tensions and unequal power dynamics. In two separate interventions, Shannon Walsh calls for greater attention to these "uncomfortable collaborations" and the problems that they pose for transformative politics.[4] She highlights, in particular, the privileged position of white academics—particularly middle-class white men—and the ways in which they elevate the Black poor as key participants in some future revolution, putting them on a "pedestal of wretchedness." On the one hand, such optimistic attachments constitute the Black poor as objects rather than as thinking subjects with diverse viewpoints and tensions. While failing to sharpen their own critical lens and uncover internal contradictions within movements, she suggests, white academics also exclude the Black poor from discussion and debate. On the other hand, she argues, white academics impose themselves within movements, shaping their internal discussions and presentations to the world.

During my research, I only gradually became aware of South African debates about white intellectuals in Black movements. From the beginning of my fieldwork, however, the unequal power dynamics were so stark that they were difficult to ignore. My whiteness, economic resources, US citizenship, and affiliation with the academy all marked me as substantially privileged in relation to the residents of impoverished, Black, protest-affected communities. For some residents, association with me likely held out the possibility of accessing resources. This may have helped me to secure interviews and access to residential areas, despite my best intentions to counter such expectations. My formal interviews frequently began with uncomfortable conversations about the potential benefits of my research for the interviewee. Amid my own fear of losing the interview, I did my best to communicate to interviewees that the research did not offer any direct benefits. The olive branch in my pitch was my commitment to understand the experiences and views of residents and activists in the particular residential area. I often conveyed this commitment by contrasting myself with journalists. Instead of swooping in quickly to gather bits of information for a short story, I would say, I intended to conduct repeated visits, talk to a variety of people, and develop a deeper understanding. I also had to admit that I was less certain about who would ultimately see or read my work, though I often remarked that I felt it was important to share the experiences of people on the ground.

I remain conflicted about the process, especially because the benefits that I accrue from this research are so much more substantial and direct than those that my research participants will ever experience. My research in South Africa has been crucial to my stable employment and secure livelihood, which are things that most of the residents in Thembelihle, Motsoaledi, Tsakane10, and Bekkersdal do not have. If I am fortunate, the research will also contribute to awards and other forms of professional recognition, as well as pay raises and promotions. For their part, my interviewees will have the limited joy of seeing their stories told, by someone else, in a book that relatively few people will likely ever read. For some, I believe, the interview process itself was affirming, empowering, or cathartic. All of these benefits to my research subjects were intangible. Of course, I have also put substantially greater time and energy into the project. Is this a fair exchange? I feel some regret about not paying my interviewees, even if I am still uncertain about whether it would have been a good idea. When I began the project in 2007 and 2010, as a graduate student with limited funding and steadily depleting savings, the prospect of paying for interviews felt out of reach. This certainly changed when I became an assistant professor, though by this point I had established a pattern. I was also worried about how paying interviewees would influence the interviews and perceptions of me and my research within the study areas. In retrospect, though, paying people for their time and labor may have been more important.

During the uncomfortable conversations about who would benefit from my research, the most frequent request from activists was that I share with them the findings of the research. They wanted to know what I was learning about social movements and how to improve them. The workshop that I held in Johannesburg in October 2017 was my response to this request. It was an amazing day, and I believe that we all learned from each other: I presented preliminary findings and ideas about how to strengthen social movements; activists shared their diverse viewpoints and experiences; and I received considerable amounts of feedback from the people about whom I was writing. While my intention was to give back to those that had helped me, in the end the workshop may have reproduced the unequal benefits of research by furnishing me with further data. I learned a lot. This stemmed partially from the format. Anybody who is familiar with the social movement scene in South Africa is aware of a common practice in which middle-class intellectuals gather community activists, predominantly Black and poor, to disseminate theory and information about how to create social change. I wanted to avoid the trap of assuming that I had the answers. I placed heavy emphasis on small and large group discussions, with the intent of creating space for dialogue and debate about politics and resistance strategies.

Throughout my research, I remained wary of imposing my own views on the movements that I was studying. I did present myself as a supporter of their efforts, and this was not a lie. The entire project grew out of my sympathy with popular protests and my desire to see them lead to broader movements and social change. This desire is precisely what concerns Walsh, who refers to it as a form of "cruel optimism" or fantasy that reinscribes hierarchy and prevents deeper change. In relatively rare instances, I did provide forms of material assistance, such as printing flyers or contributing funds for office furniture. In Thembelihle, on a couple occasions, I made addresses to public mass meetings in support of the Thembelihle Crisis Committee (TCC) and other social movements. Besides these quite rare instances, though, my activism was "relatively autonomous" from my research. It often took place at meetings in the city center, such as at NUMSA offices or the university, geographically removed from the residential areas that I was studying. While I did meet activists from Thembelihle and Tsakane10 at these meetings, helping me to build rapport, when I visited the residential areas, my identity as a researcher was much more prominent. At TCC meetings in Thembelihle (smaller than public mass meetings), for example, I was always a passive observer rather than an active participant. Nor have I done much to promote the movements within the mass media, as became common with the Durban-based movement Abahlali baseMjondolo. This highlights the tension between avoidance of two possible pitfalls: not doing enough to assist movements and not imposing one's own views on them from outside. Dodging the latter pit may have thrust me into the former one.

These issues raise questions about what is now widely known as public sociology. For Michael Burawoy, who popularized the idea during his term as president of the American Sociological Association, public sociology "brings sociology into conversation with publics, understood as people who are themselves involved in conversation."[5] This approach to doing sociology has been the source of much praise, criticism, and debate. In a recent critical intervention from South Africa, Alberto Arribas Lozano condemns public sociology for prioritizing "the unidirectional diffusion of 'expert knowledge' to extra-academic audiences."[6] He calls instead for a "collaborative praxis," which emphasizes negotiation between researchers and research subjects to ensure that the research is beneficial to the community rather than simply extractive. I did not follow such a collaborative process. Over more than a decade of research, I consistently set the agenda, determined the goals, and directed the study. In this sense, my research also falls into another of Walsh's traps: the tendency of white academics to constitute poor Black residents as objects rather than subjects.

At the same time, however, I have also pushed in the other direction. At the Johannesburg workshop, for example, I began by referencing Gramsci's point that everybody is an intellectual, which means having a critical and coherent conception of the world. This idea has underpinned my research throughout, and I hope it shows in the pages of this book. I always approached residents and activists as critical and thinking people whose views are important. This was true even when I disagreed with them, which I often did. The frequent quotes throughout the book attest to my desire to incorporate their views. Further, I have sought to challenge portrayals of the Black poor as passive and undifferentiated foot soldiers in some larger process of social change, about which they have little say. Instead, I have attempted to demonstrate their agency, most importantly by showing the diverse organizing strategies and political orientations that predominated across the four areas. Rather than the traditional public sociology of disseminating research findings in mass media—a practice that conforms closely to Lozano's criticism—my approach was more in line with what Burawoy terms "organic public sociology in which the sociologist works in close connection with a visible, thick, active, local and often counter-public."[7] Nonetheless, it was a much weaker form of engagement than the collaborative coproduction of knowledge that Lozano celebrates.

I support Lozano's project of democratizing knowledge production by bringing nonacademics into the research process and incorporating their views. I also believe, however, that there is room for a variety of research projects, and I place value on the autonomy of researchers. Reflecting on his role as a white intellectual supporter of the Black labor movement under apartheid, which incorporated Black workers in the research process to varied degrees at different moments, Eddie Webster argues for an approach rooted in "critical engagement." Such an approach is "critical in the sense of not being subordinate to any one group or tendency and engaged in the sense that we are committed to give support to the democratic labor movement."[8] For better or worse, I approximated the critical engagement approach in this study. Throughout the research, I sought to balance the priorities of critical autonomy and committed support. I did so partially by shifting my stance depending on the context. I leaned toward critical autonomy when I was in the case study areas and toward committed support when I was engaging with umbrella social movements, such as the Democratic Left Front and the United Front.

The prospects of critical engagement appear greater within a longer-term perspective. In a rejoinder to Walsh's discussion of "uncomfortable collaborations," Ashwin Desai suggests that her critique of power within movements fails to confront broader structures of power. He argues, specifically, "that we need to name the systemic enemy which is capitalism."[9] This is, to a certain extent, what I have attempted to do in this work with the theory of passive revolution. I trace the roots of contemporary protests—and their politics—to the reorganization of South African capitalism during and after the democratic transition. Through close engagement with struggles on the ground, if not necessarily collaboration, and leaning toward the critical side, I emphasize the limits of contemporary resistance for challenging capitalist inequality. I have chosen, therefore, not to present an overly celebratory or glorified account of struggles from below. In an ideal world, within a longer horizon my critical outlook will help contribute to the strengthening of social movements. This would be the supportive side of critical engagement. Such possibilities are probably a pipe dream. But one can always hope, bringing some optimism of the will to balance the pessimism of the intellect.

Notes

PREFACE

1. This includes the Johannesburg, Ekurhuleni (East Rand), and West Rand municipalities.

2. Owen Crankshaw, "Race, Space and the Post-Fordist Spatial Order of Johannesburg," *Urban Studies* 45, no. 8 (2008): 1692–1711.

3. Peter Alexander, Carin Runciman, Trevor Ngwane, Boikanyo Moloto, Kgothatso Mokgele, and Nicole van Staden, "Frequency and Turmoil: South Africa's Community Protests 2005–2017," *South Africa Crime Quarterly* 63 (2018): 35.

4. Mike Davis, "Spring Confronts Winter," *New Left Review* 72 (2011): 5–15.

5. For a comparison of South African and global protest, see Marcel Paret, Carin Runciman, and Luke Sinwell, *Southern Resistance in Critical Perspective: The Politics of Protest in South Africa's Contentious Democracy* (New York: Routledge, 2017); Marcel Paret and Carin Runciman, "The 2009+ South African Protest Wave," *Journal of Labor and Society* 19, no. 3 (2016): 301–319.

6. For more on the contrast, see Marcel Paret, "The Politics of Local Resistance in Urban South Africa: Evidence from Three Informal Settlements," *International Sociology* 33, no. 3 (2018): 337–356.

7. George Reid Andrews, "Comparing the Comparers: White Supremacy in the United States and South Africa," *Journal of Social History* 20, no. 3 (1987): 585–599; John W. Cell, *The Highest Stage of White Supremacy: The Origins of Segregation in South Africa and the American South* (Cambridge: Cambridge University Press, 1982); George M. Fredrickson, *White Supremacy: A Comparative Study in American and South African History* (New York: Oxford University Press, 1981); Anthony Marx, *Making Race and Nation: A Comparison of the United States, South Africa, and Brazil* (Cambridge: Cambridge University Press, 1998); Howard Winant, *The World Is a Ghetto: Race and Democracy Since World War II* (New York: Basic Books, 2000).

8. Taylor, *From #BlackLivesMatter*, 161.

9. Langston Hughes, "Harlem" (1951), accessed September 13, 2018, https://www.poetryfoundation.org/poems/46548/harlem, original emphasis.

10. Ashwin Desai, *We Are the Poors: Community Struggles in Post-Apartheid South Africa* (New York: Monthly Review, 2002); Prishani Naidoo, "Struggles around the Commodification of Daily Life in South Africa," *Review of African Political Economy* 34, no. 111 (2007): 57–66.

11. Larry Buchanan, Quoctrung Bui, and Jugal K. Patel, "Black Lives Matter May Be the Largest Movement in U.S. History," *New York Times*, July 3, 2020; Douglas McAdam, "We've Never Seen Protests like These Before," *Jacobin*, June 20, 2020.

12. This estimate refers to the number of protests by "residents," as calculated by Kate Alexander and Lefa Lenka using the Armed Conflict Location and Event Data (ACLED) database and provided via personal communication. See figure 1 in the introduction for further details.

INTRODUCTION

1. The name Kwatsaduza amalgamates the names of three adjacent Black townships: Kwa-Thema, Tsakane, and Duduza. See Figure 3.

2. I use the term *Black* to describe the group of people in South Africa who the post-apartheid state refers to as *Black African*, and who the apartheid state variously referred to with such terms as *African, Native, Bantu*, and *Black*. This includes descendants of residents who were indigenous to South Africa at the onset of European colonization. Under apartheid, activists frequently sought to challenge racial division by constituting a unified Black identity that included groups classified by the state as *African, Indian/Asian*, and *Coloured*. In the contemporary period, however, popular references to *Black* increasingly refer to the category *Black African*, as distinct from *Indian/Asian* and *Coloured*. In South Africa, *Coloured* represents a distinct ethnic group that is neither Black nor white.

3. "The premier undermines us. He'll see by the smoke we're calling him." Karl von Holdt, Malose Langa, Sepetla Molapo, Nomfundo Mogapi, Kindiza Ngubeni, Jacob Dlamini, and Adele Kirsten, *The Smoke that Calls: Insurgent Citizenship, Collective Violence and the Struggle for a Place in the New South Africa* (Johannesburg: Society, Work and Politics Institute, 2011), 27, 35–36.

4. Hein Marais, *South Africa Pushed to the Limit: The Political Economy of Change* (London: Zed Books, 2011); Patrick Bond, *Elite Transition: From Apartheid to Neoliberalism in South Africa* (London: Pluto, 2014); John Saul and Patrick Bond, *South Africa: The Present as History from Mrs. Ples to Mandela and Marikana* (Johannesburg: Jacana, 2014).

5. Nigel C. Gibson, *Fanonian Practices in South Africa: From Steve Biko to Abahlali baseMjondolo* (Scottsville, South Africa: University of KwaZulu-Natal Press, 2011); Julian Brown, *South Africa's Insurgent Citizens: On Dissent and the Possibility of Politics* (London: Zed Books, 2015); Kerry Chance, *Living Politics in South Africa's Urban Shacklands* (Chicago: University of Chicago Press, 2018); Trevor Ngwane, *Amakomiti: Grassroots Democracy in South African Shack Settlements* (London: Pluto, 2021). For a critique of this perspective, see Shannon Walsh, "The Philosopher and His Poor: The *Poor-Black* as Object for Political Desire in South Africa," *Politikon* 42, no. 1 (2015): 123–127.

6. I am grateful to Erin Hatton for proposing to me the idea of constrained agency.

7. Roger Southall, "Political Change and the Black Middle Class in Democratic South Africa," *Canadian Journal of African Studies* 38, no. 3 (2004): 533.

8. Sidney Tarrow, *Power in Movement: Social Movements and Contentious Politics* (Cambridge: Cambridge University Press, 2011), 190, 204–209. On cycles of protest in contemporary South Africa, see Marcel Paret, "The Persistent Protest Cycle: A Case Study of Contained Political Incorporation," *Current Sociology*, published online, https://journals.sagepub.com/doi/abs/10.1177/0011392120932936.

9. Tarrow, *Power in Movement*, 190, 207–214.

10. Howard Winant, *The World Is a Ghetto: Race and Democracy since World War II* (New York: Basic Books, 2000), 305–308. For Winant, this is a global process. On racial inclusion and demobilization in the United States, see Michael Omi and Howard Winant, *Racial Formation in the United States: From the 1960s to the 1990s*, 3rd ed. (New York: Routledge, 2014), 186–187.

11. Ashwin Desai, *We Are the Poors: Community Struggles in Post-Apartheid South Africa* (New York: Monthly Review Press, 2002); Patrick Bond, "South African People's Power since the Mid-1980s: Two Steps Forward, One Step Back," *Third World Quarterly* 33, no. 2 (2012): 253–257.

12. Peter Alexander, "Rebellion of the Poor: South Africa's Service Delivery Protests—a Preliminary Analysis," *Review of African Political Economy* 37, no. 123 (2010): 25–40.

13. Peter Alexander, Carin Runciman, Trevor Ngwane, Boikanyo Moloto, Kgothatso Mokgele, and Nicole van Staden, "Frequency and Turmoil: South Africa's Community Protests 2005–2017," *South Africa Crime Quarterly* 63 (2018): 35.

14. There were important continuities between popular resistance during and after apartheid. Elke Zuern underscores a parallel emphasis on substantive democracy and resource redistribution. Elke Zuern, *The Politics of Necessity: Community Organizing and Democracy in South Africa* (Madison: University of Wisconsin Press, 2011).

15. Omi and Winant, *Racial Formation*, 151.

16. Eduardo Bonilla-Silva, *Racism without Racists: Color-Blind Racism and the Persistence of Racial Inequality in America* (Lanham, MD: Rowman and Littlefield, 2018); Joe Feagin, *Systemic Racism: A Theory of Oppression* (New York: Routledge, 2006); Shirley Better, *Institutional Racism: A Primer on Theory and Strategies for Social Change* (Lanham, MD: Rowman and Littlefield, 2007); Omi and Winant, *Racial Formation*.

17. Richard Ballard, Adam Habib, and Imraan Valodia, *Voices of Protest: Social Movements in Post-Apartheid South Africa* (Pietermaritzburg, South Africa: University of KwaZulu-Natal Press, 2006).

18. On the United Front, see Sam Ashman, Zachary Levenson, and Trevor Ngwane, "South Africa's ANC: The Beginning of the End?," *Catalyst* 1 (Summer 2017): 75–106; Marcel Paret, "Working-Class Fragmentation, Party Politics, and the Complexities of Solidarity in South Africa's United Front," *Sociological Review* 65, no. 2 (2017): 267–284.

19. AbM activists often claimed a membership of ten to fifty thousand, though such claims are contested. One former AbM activist claimed that actual membership was closer to two thousand and that "we were a minority in almost every settlement we entered." Bandile Mdlalose, "The Rise and Fall of Abahlali baseMjondolo, a South African Social Movement," *Politikon* 41, no. 3 (2014): 345–353.

20. South Africa has long provided fertile ground for pioneering work in this area. For classic accounts, see Harold Wolpe, "Capitalism and Cheap Labor-Power in South Africa: From Segregation to Apartheid," *Economy and Society* 1, no. 4 (1972): 425–456; Harold Wolpe, *Race, Class, and the Apartheid State* (Trenton, NJ: Africa World, 1988); Stuart Hall, "Race, Articulation and Societies Structured in Dominance," in *Sociological Theories: Race and Colonialism* (Paris: UNESCO, 1980), 305–345. For more recent accounts that return to this literature, see Steven Friedman, *Race, Class and Power: Harold Wolpe and the Radical Critique of Apartheid* (Pietermaritzburg, South Africa: University of KwaZulu-Natal Press, 2015), and John Reynolds, Ben Fine, and Robert van Niekerk, *Race, Class, and the Post-Apartheid Democratic State* (Pietermaritzburg, South Africa: University of KwaZulu-Natal Press, 2019).

21. Howard Winant, *Racial Conditions: Politics, Theory, Comparisons* (Minneapolis: University of Minnesota Press, 1994), 126. In the South African context, Michael MacDonald argues that intraracial class differentiation legitimated a highly unequal post-apartheid capitalism. Michael MacDonald, *Why Race Matters in South Africa* (Cambridge, MA: Harvard University Press, 2006). See also Carolyn Bassett, "South Africa: Revisiting Capital's 'Formative Action,'" *Review of African Political Economy* 35, no. 116 (2008): 195–196.

22. Gabriel Hetland and Jeff Goodwin, "The Strange Disappearance of Capitalism from Social Movement Studies," in *Marxism and Social Movements*, ed. Colin Barker, Laurence Cox, John Krinsky, and Alf Gunvald Nilsen (Leiden, Netherlands: Brill, 2013), 91.

23. Gay Seidman, *Manufacturing Militance: Workers' Movements in Brazil and South Africa, 1970–1985* (Berkeley: University of California Press, 1994); Franco Barchiesi, *Precarious Liberation: Workers, the State, and Contested Social Citizenship in Postapartheid South Africa* (Albany: State University of New York Press, 2011).

24. Class differentiation among Black residents was well underway by the late apartheid period. Owen Crankshaw, *Race, Class and the Changing Division of Labor under Apartheid* (London: Routledge, 1997).

25. Bond, *Elite Transition*; Jeremy Seekings and Nicoli Nattrass, *Class, Race, and Inequality in South Africa* (New Haven, CT: Yale University Press, 2005), 6; Owen Crankshaw, "Race, Space, and the Post-Fordist Spatial Order of Johannesburg," *Urban Studies* 45, no. 8 (2008): 1692–1711.

26. Peter D. Thomas, *The Gramscian Moment: Philosophy, Hegemony, and Marxism* (Leiden, Netherlands: Brill, 2009), 156–157.

27. Antonio Gramsci, *Prison Notebooks: Volume III*, ed. and trans. Joseph A. Buttigieg (New York: Columbia University Press, 2007), 252.

28. Alex Callinicos defines passive revolution as "socio-political processes in which revolution-inducing strains are at once displaced and at least partially fulfilled." Alex Callinicos, "The Limits of Passive Revolution," *Capital and Class* 34, no. 3 (2010): 498. Cihan Tugal defines passive revolution as the "incorporation of revolutionary movements in existing systems." Cihan Tugal, *Passive Revolution: Absorbing the Islamic Challenge to Capitalism* (Stanford, CA: Stanford University Press, 2009), 32.

29. Antonio Gramsci, *Selections from the Prison Notebooks*, ed. and trans. by Quintin Hoare and Geoffrey Nowell Smith (New York: International Publishers, 1971), 61–65, 74–75, 80, 97, 100–103.

30. Gramsci, *Selections*, 77–79.

31. Gramsci, 119; Thomas, *Gramscian Moment*, 152, 156–157.

32. Gramsci, 57–59, 109.

33. Dylan Riley and Manali Desai, "The Passive Revolutionary Route to the Modern World: Italy and India in Comparative Perspective," *Comparative Studies in Society and History* 49, no. 4 (2007): 1–2.

34. Riley and Desai, "Passive Revolutionary Route."

35. In Italy, the ongoing passive revolution eventually led to fascism, which enabled a conservative modernization of production. Gramsci, *Selections*, 119–120; Riley and Desai, "Passive Revolutionary Route," 6–14.

36. Gramsci, *Selections*, 104–106. See also Dylan Riley, "Hegemony and Democracy in Gramsci's *Prison Notebooks*," in *Building Blocs: How Parties Organize Society*, ed. Cedric De Leon, Manali Desai, and Cihan Tugal (Stanford, CA: Stanford University Press, 2015), 177–181.

37. Adam David Morton, "The Continuum of Passive Revolution," *Capital and Class* 34, no. 3 (2010): 332; Adam David Morton, *Unravelling Gramsci: Hegemony and Passive Revolution in the Global Economy* (London: Pluto, 2007).

38. Michael Burawoy, "For a Sociological Marxism: The Complementary Convergence of Antonio Gramsci and Karl Polanyi," *Politics and Society* 31, no. 2 (2003): 245.

39. Partha Chatterjee, *Nationalist Thought and the Colonial World: A Derivative Discourse* (London: United Nations University, 1986), 51.

40. Chatterjee, *Nationalist Thought*, 51.

41. Chatterjee, 124–125, original emphasis. See also, Riley and Desai, "Passive Revolutionary Route," 20; Ranajit Guha, *Dominance without Hegemony: History and Power in Colonial India.* (Cambridge, MA: Harvard University Press, 1997), 135–150.

42. "Nationalist discourse at its moment of arrival is passive revolution uttering its own life-history." Chatterjee, 51.

43. Chatterjee, 132–162.

44. Riley and Desai, "Passive Revolutionary Route."

45. Frantz Fanon, *Wretched of the Earth* (New York: Grove, 1963).

46. On the close affinity between Gramsci and Fanon, see Burawoy, "For a Sociological Marxism," 245–248; Gillian Hart, *Rethinking the South African Crisis: Nationalism, Populism, Hegemony* (Athens: University of Georgia Press, 2014); Ato Sekyi-Otu, *Fanon's Dialectic of Experience* (Cambridge, MA: Harvard University Press, 1996). Jean-Francois Bayart's later analysis of African decolonization affirms much of Fanon's analysis and explicitly connects it to Gramsci's notions of passive revolution and trasformismo. Jean-Francois Bayart, *The State in Africa: The Politics of the Belly* (London: Longman, 1993), 21–26, 181–192. For a more recent account of passive revolution during the wave of African democratization in the early 1990s, see Rita Abrahamsen, "The Victory of Popular Forces or Passive Revolution? A Neo-Gramscian Perspective on Democratization," *Journal of Modern African Studies* 35, no. 1 (1997): 129–152.

47. Fanon, *Wretched of the Earth*, 148–158.

48. Fanon, 164–183.

49. Fanon, 179.

50. Fanon, 152–153.

51. Fanon, 61, 129–130, 186–205.

52. Fanon, 164–169, 181–183.

53. Fanon, *Wretched of the Earth*; Burawoy, "For a Sociological Marxism," 246.

54. Fanon, *Wretched of the Earth*, 169.

55. Fanon, 159–160, 169.

56. Vishwas Satgar, "Neoliberalized South Africa: Labor and the Roots of Passive Revolution," *Labor, Capital, and Society* 41, no. 2 (2008): 38–69.

57. Satgar, "Neoliberalized South Africa," 64.

58. Satgar, 53.

59. Gibson, *Fanonian Practices*.

60. Gibson, 68–69.

61. Bassett, "Revisiting Capital's."

62. Bassett, 185–187.

63. Bassett, 187–191.

64. Bassett, 190–195.

65. Bassett.

66. Roger Southall, *The New Black Middle Class in South Africa* (Woodbridge, UK: James Currey, 2016).

67. Barchiesi, *Precarious Liberation*; Edward Webster, "Making a Living, Earning a Living: Work and Employment in Southern Africa," *International Political Science Review* 26, no. 1 (2005): 55–71; Marcel Paret, "Precarious Class Formations in the United States and South Africa," *International Labor and Working-Class History* 89 (Spring 2016): 84–106; Marcel Paret, "The Community Strike: From Precarity to Militant Organizing," *International Journal of Comparative Sociology* 61, no. 2–3 (2020): 164.

68. World Bank, *Overcoming Poverty and Inequality in South Africa: An Assessment of Drivers, Constraints and Opportunities* (Washington, DC: World Bank, 2018); Amory Gethin, *Extreme Inequality and the Structure of Political Cleavages in South Africa, 1994–2019*, WID.world working paper no. 2020/13 (Paris: World Inequality Lab, 2020), 9.

69. Joshua Budlender, Ingrid Woolard, and Murray Leibbrandt, "How Current Measures Underestimate the Level of Poverty in South Africa," *The Conversation*, September 3, 2015.

70. World Bank, *Overcoming Poverty*, 13.

71. Statistics South Africa, *Income Dynamics and Poverty Status of Households in South Africa* (Pretoria: Statistics South Africa, 2015), 41, 43, 47.

72. Among critics, see Marais, *South Africa Pushed*, and Hart, *Rethinking*. For a similar account of elite pacts and marketization that does not emphasize passive revolution, see Bond, *Elite Transition*. Edward Webster and Ben Scully point to the triple shift of globalization, financialization, and informalization, with devastating consequences for many residents. Edward Webster and Ben Scully, "The Countryside and Capitalism: Rethinking the Cheap Labor Thesis in Post-Apartheid South Africa," in *Race, Class, and the Post-Apartheid Democratic State*, ed. John Reynolds, Ben Fine, and Robert van Niekerk (Pietermaritzburg, South Africa: University of KwaZulu-Natal Press, 2019), 31–56.

73. Marais, *South Africa Pushed*, 395–397.

74. Marais, 397–401. Marais' characterization of the ANC and South Africa's bourgeois project as a "hegemonic work-in-progress," resembles Gramsci's analysis of the Moderates in Italy, who established leadership over the ruling bloc but struggled to extend that unity to the entire society.

75. Hart, *Rethinking*, 10–12.

76. Hart, 180.

77. Hart, 197–212.

78. Gramsci, *Selections*, 178.

79. Friedman, *Race, Class, and Power*, 264–275. See also Gibson, *Fanonian Practices*, 94–102, 136–137. Friedman develops this conceptualization through a dialogue with Harold Wolpe, "The Uneven Transformation from Apartheid in South Africa," *Transformation* 27 (1995): 88–101. The state-driven approach undermined participatory mechanisms. Heidi Brooks, *The African National Congress and Participatory Democracy: From People's Power to Public Policy* (Cham, Switzerland: Palgrave Macmillan, 2020).

80. See also Alexander Beresford, "The Politics of Regenerative Nationalism in South Africa," *Journal of Southern African Studies* 38, no. 4 (2012): 863–884.

81. This attachment to the state approximates what Berlant calls "cruel optimism." Lauren Berlant, *Cruel Optimism* (Durham, NC: Duke University Press, 2011).

82. In a kindred account, Francesco Pontarelli similarly underscores the value of Gramsci's passive revolution concept for making sense of popular struggles in South Africa. Francesco Pontarelli, "Gramsci's Passive Revolution and Social Movements in South Africa, 2015–2018: The Student/Worker Rebellion and the National Union of Metalworkers" (PhD diss., University of Johannesburg, 2020).

83. Gibson, *Fanonian Practices*.

84. Gibson, 7.

85. Gibson, 164–173.

86. Gramsci, *Selections*, 181–182.

87. Class formation is the process through which individuals develop a shared sense of belonging based on material conditions of work and livelihood and engage in collective action. Barry Eidlin, "Class Formation and Class Identity: Birth, Death, and Possibilities for Renewal," *Sociology Compass* 8, no. 8 (2014): 1045–1062. Paret, "Precarious Class Formations."

88. Gramsci, *Selections*, 52–55.

89. On fragmentation, see Peter Thomas, "Refiguring the Subaltern," *Political Theory* 46, no. 6 (2018): 870–871.

90. Riley and Desai, "Passive Revolutionary Route," 3.

91. Gramsci, *Selections*, 178.

92. Jeff Goodwin, "Conclusion: Are Protesters Opportunists? Fifty Tests," in *Contention in Context: Political Opportunities and the Emergence of Protest*, ed. Jeff Goodwin and James M. Jasper (Stanford, CA: Stanford University Press, 2012), 277–302. From a less sympathetic angle, Samuel Huntington warns that democratization may generate

instability due to rising expectations and demands. Samuel P. Huntington, *Political Order in Changing Societies* (New Haven, CT: Yale University Press, 1968), 4–5.

93. One estimate suggests that the postapartheid state redistributed about 10 percent of GDP from rich to poor. Jeremy Seekings and Nicoli Nattrass, *Policy, Politics and Poverty in South Africa* (New York: Palgrave Macmillan, 2015), 183. On the limits of the welfare state, see Patrick Bond, "Tokenism in South African Social Policy," *Transformation* 86 (2014): 48–77.

94. On precarious workers, see Arne Kalleberg, "Precarious Work, Insecure Workers: Employment Relations in Transition," *American Sociological Review* 74, no. 1 (2009): 1–22; Guy Standing, *The Precariat: The New Dangerous Class* (London: Bloomsbury Academic, 2011). On surplus populations, see Tania M. Li, "After Development: Surplus Population and the Politics of Entitlement," *Development and Change,* 48, no. 6 (2017): 1247–1261; Mike Davis, *Planet of Slums* (London: Verso, 2007). For a discussion of precarity in South Africa, see Marcel Paret, "Politics of Solidarity and Agency in an Age of Precarity," *Global Labor Journal* 7, no. 2 (2016): 175–176.

95. Peter Alexander and Peter Pfaffe, "Social Relationships to the Means and Ends of Protest in South Africa's Ongoing Rebellion of the Poor: The Balfour Insurrections," *Social Movement Studies* 13, no. 2 (2014): 204–221.

96. Alexander, "Rebellion of the Poor."

97. Fanon, *Wretched of the Earth*, 61, 127–129. Fanon describes the lumpenproletariat as "landless peasants" who "rush toward the towns, crowd into tin-shack settlements," and roam the urban periphery in search of economic opportunities. Gibson draws a parallel between Fanon's peasantry and the poor in South Africa. Gibson, *Fanonian Practices*, 7.

98. Davis, *Planet of Slums*, 201–202; Guy Standing, *A Precariat Charter: From Denizens to Citizens* (London: Bloomsbury, 2014), 28–31, 32–133. For a longer reflection on Standing's view of precariat agency, see Paret, "Politics of Solidarity and Agency."

99. Rina Agarwala, *Informal Labor, Formal Politics, and Dignified Discontent in India* (Cambridge: Cambridge University Press, 2013); Jennifer Chun, *Organizing at the Margins: The Symbolic Politics of Labor in South Korea and the United States* (Ithaca, NY: Cornell University Press / ILR Press, 2009); Federico M. Rossi, *The Poor's Struggle for Political Incorporation: The Piquetero Movement in Argentina* (Cambridge: Cambridge University Press, 2017).

100. Fanon, *Wretched of the Earth*, 108–111, 122.

101. David Harvey, *Rebel Cities* (London: Verso, 2012); Miriam Greenberg and Penny Lewis, *The City Is the Factory: New Solidarities and Spatial Strategies in an Urban Age* (Ithaca, NY: ILR Press, 2017); Ben Scully, "From the Shop Floor to the Kitchen Table: The Shifting Center of Precarious Workers' Politics in South Africa," *Review of African Political Economy* 43, no. 148 (2016): 295–311.

102. Manuel Castells, *The City and the Grassroots* (Berkeley: University of California Press, 1983), xviii.

103. Donatella della Porta, *Social Movements in Times of Austerity* (Cambridge: Polity, 2015); Michael Burawoy, "Facing an Unequal World," *Current Sociology* 63, no. 1 (2015): 5–34; Eduardo Silva, *Challenging Neoliberalism in Latin America* (New York: Cambridge University Press, 2009); Edward Webster, Rob Lambert, and Andries Bezuidenhout, *Grounding Globalization: Labor in the Age of Insecurity* (Malden, MA: Blackwell, 2008).

104. Karl Polanyi, *The Great Transformation: The Political and Economic Origins of Our Time* (Boston: Beacon, 1944), 138–139.

105. Burawoy, "For a Sociological Marxism," 221–223.

106. Partha Chatterjee, *Lineages of Political Society: Studies in Postcolonial Democracy* (New York: Columbia University Press, 2011), 233. An early version of this argument, connecting passive revolution to legitimacy, appears in Partha Chatterjee, *The Nation and Its Fragments: Colonial and Postcolonial Histories* (Princeton, NJ: Princeton University Press, 1993), 211–219. His foundational statement on political society is Partha Chatterjee, *The Politics of the Governed: Reflections on Popular Politics in Most of the World* (New York: Columbia University Press, 2004).

107. Chatterjee, *Lineages of Political Society*, 220–224.

108. Chatterjee, 232.

109. Chatterjee, *Politics of the Governed*, 40–41, 50–51; Chatterjee, *Lineages of Political Society*, 88, 233.

110. On political society in South Africa, see Gillian Hart, "Political Society and Its Discontents: Translating Passive Revolution in India and South Africa Today," *Economic and Political Weekly* 50, no. 43 (2015): 43–51; Thiven Reddy, *South Africa, Settler Colonialism and the Failures of Liberal Democracy* (London: Zed, 2015).

111. Patrick Heller thus describes South African civil society as "deeply bifurcated between an organized civil society that effectively engages with the state and a subaltern civil society that is institutionally disconnected from the state." Patrick Heller, "Democratic Deepening in India and South Africa," *Journal of Asian and African Studies* 44, no. 1 (2009): 123–149.

112. Chatterjee, *Politics of the Governed*, 37; Chatterjee, *Lineages of Political Society*, 232.

113. Chatterjee, *Lineages of Political Society*, 219, 232.

114. Chatterjee, *Politics of the Governed*; Zachary Levenson, "Precarious Welfare States: Urban Struggles over Housing Delivery in Post-Apartheid South Africa," *International Sociology* 32, no. 4 (2017): 474–492.

115. Hannah Dawson, "Youth Politics: Waiting and Envy in a South African Informal Settlement," *Journal of Southern African Studies* 40, no. 4 (2014): 868–869.

116. Edward Webster and Karin Pampallis, *The Unresolved National Question: Left Thought under Apartheid* (Johannesburg: Wits University Press, 2017).

117. Fanon, *Wretched of the Earth*, 158–159.

118. Fanon, 155–164, 183–184.

119. Fanon, 155–158.

120. Riley and Desai, "Passive Revolutionary Route," 29.

121. Chatterjee, *Politics of the Governed*, 41, 47, 64–67; Chatterjee, *Lineages of Political Society*, 220, 225, 234.

122. Cedric De Leon, Manali Desai, and Cihan Tugal, *Building Blocs: How Parties Organize Society* (Stanford, CA: Stanford University Press, 2015), 2–3. On "party dealignment" in South Africa, see Collette Schulz-Herzenberg, "The Decline of Partisan Voting and the Rise in Electoral Uncertainty in South Africa's 2019 General Elections," *Politikon*, 46, no. 4 (2019): 462–480.

123. Susan Booysen, "'The Ballot and the Brick'—Enduring under Duress," in *Local Elections in South Africa: Parties, People and Politics*, ed. Susan Booysen (Bloemfontein, South Africa: Sun Press, 2011), 295–314.

124. Hannah J. Dawson, "Patronage from Below: Political Unrest in an Informal Settlement in South Africa," *African Affairs* 113, no. 453 (2014): 518–539.

125. Karl von Holdt, "On Violent Democracy," *Sociological Review* 62, no. S2 (2014): 135.

126. Peter Alexander, "Barricades, Ballots and Experimentation: Making Sense of the 2011 Local Government Election with a Social Movement Lens," in *Contesting Transformation: Popular Resistance in Twenty-First Century South Africa*, ed. Marcelle C. Dawson and Luke Sinwell (London: Pluto Press, 2012), 63–79; Marcel Paret, "Beyond Post-

Apartheid Politics? Cleavages, Protest, and Elections in South Africa," *Journal of Modern African Studies* 56, no. 3 (2018): 471–496; Carin Runciman, Martin Bekker, and Terri Maggott, "Voting Preferences of Protesters and Non-Protesters in Three South African Elections (2014–2019): Revisiting the 'Ballot and the Brick,'" *Politikon* 46, no. 4 (2019): 390–410; Carin Runciman, "The 'Ballot and the Brick': Protest, Voting and Nonvoting in Post-Apartheid South Africa," *Journal of Contemporary African Studies* 34, no. 4 (2016): 419–436.

1. NATIONAL LIBERATION

1. Mona Younis, *Liberation and Democratization: The South African and Palestinian National Movements* (Minneapolis: University of Minnesota Press, 2000), 40–53.

2. On the rise and fall of the Industrial and Commercial Workers Union, the first major organization for Black workers, see Philip Bonner, "The Decline and Fall of the I.C.U.—a Case of Self-Destruction?," in *Essays in Southern African Labor History*, ed. Eddie Webster (Johannesburg: Ravan Press, 1978), 114–120. On the formation of new industrial Black unions, often with assistance from the Communist Party of South Africa, see Peter Alexander, *Workers, War, and the Origins of Apartheid* (Oxford: James Currey, 2000), 13–15; and Jon Lewis, "'The New Unionism': Industrialization and Industrial Unions in South Africa, 1925–1930," in *Essays in Southern African Labor History*, ed. Edward Webster (Johannesburg: Ravan Press, 1978), 121–142.

3. Alexander, *Workers, War*, 80–85.

4. Alexander, 44–54.

5. Harold Wolpe suggests that, despite these measures, in the 1950s there was still "a space for mass political mobilization." Harold Wolpe, *Race, Class, and the Apartheid State* (London: James Currey, 1988), 67.

6. This stemmed partially from SACTU's explicit political orientation and close ties to the ANC and the SACP. Roger Southall and Edward Webster, "Unions and Parties in South Africa: COSATU and the ANC in the Wake of Polokwane," in *Trade Unions and Party Politics: Labor Movements in Africa*, ed. Bjorn Beckman, Sakhela Buhlungu, and Lloyd Sachikonye (Cape Town: HSRC Press, 2010), 135–137; and Ivor Chipkin, *Do South Africans Exist?* (Johannesburg: Wits University Press, 2007), 82–84. Philip Bonner suggests that restrictions on nonwhite unionism left the organization little other choice. Philip Bonner, "Black Trade Unions in South Africa Since World War II," in *The Apartheid Regime: Political Power and Racial Domination*, ed. Robert M. Price and Carl G. Rosberg (Berkeley, CA: Institute of International Studies, 1980), 174–193.

7. Key legislation included the Sabotage Act of 1962 and the Terrorism Act of 1967. Wolpe concludes that "the terrain of extra-parliamentary mass political struggle was virtually abolished." Wolpe, *Race, Class*, 70.

8. The Black Consciousness Movement did, however, emerge during the 1960s, laying a foundation for popular resistance in the 1970s. Steven Friedman, "The Sounds of Silence: Structural Change and Collective Action in the Fight against Apartheid," *South African Historical Journal* 69, no. 2 (2017): 236–250.

9. Wolpe, *Race, Class*, 71.

10. Owen Crankshaw, *Race, Class and the Changing Division of Labor under Apartheid* (London: Routledge, 1997); Gay Seidman, *Manufacturing Militance: Workers' Movements in Brazil and South Africa, 1970–1985* (Berkeley: University of California Press, 1994), 84–86.

11. Hein Marais, *South Africa Pushed to the Limit: The Political Economy of Change* (London: Zed Books, 2011), 39.

12. Seidman, *Manufacturing Militance*, 173.

13. Ian Macun and Geoffrey Wood, "Comprehending Union Growth and Decline: The Case of the South African Independent Unions," unpublished manuscript (2002), 5.

14. Michelle Friedman, *"The Future Is in the Hands of the Workers": A History of FOSATU* (Houghton, South Africa: Mutloatse Arts Heritage Trust, 2011), 25.

15. "The June 16th Soweto Youth Uprising," South African History Online, accessed February 13, 2016, http://www.sahistory.org.za/topic/june-16-soweto-youth-uprising.

16. Tom Lodge and Bill Nasson, *All Here and Now: Black Politics in South Africa in the 1980s* (New York: Ford Foundation and the Foreign Policy Association, 1991), 25–26.

17. From the middle of the 1970s through the 1980s, South Africa experienced a devastating economic recession. Employer emphasis on capital-intensive production compounded the problem, exacerbating labor surpluses. Unemployment began to tick upward in the late 1960s and took off from the middle of the 1970s. Crankshaw, *Race, Class*, 104–112; Jeremy Seekings and Nicoli Nattrass, *Class, Race, and Inequality in South Africa* (New Haven, CT: Yale University Press, 2005), chap. 5.

18. Jeremy Baskin, "The 1981 East Rand Strike Wave," *South African Labor Bulletin* 7, no. 8 (1982): 21–41; Edward Webster, "The Rise of Social-Movement Unionism: The Two Faces of the Black Trade Union Movement in South Africa," in *State, Resistance, and Change in South Africa*, ed. Philip Frankel, Noam Pines, and Mark Swilling (London: Croom Helm, 1988), 182–183; Mark Swilling, "MAWU and UMMAWSA Fight for the Factories," *Work in Progress* 33 (1984): 9.

19. Matthew Chaskalson, Karen Jochelson, and Jeremy Seekings, "Rent Boycotts, the State, and the Transformation of the Urban Political Economy in South Africa," *Review of African Political Economy* 14, no. 40 (1987): 48–50; Jeremy Seekings, "Political Mobilization in the Black Townships of the Transvaal," in *State, Resistance and Change in South Africa*, ed. Philip Frankel, Noam Pines, and Mark Swilling (London: Croom Helm, 1988), 201–209.

20. Paul Maylam, "The Rise and Decline of Urban Apartheid in South Africa," *African Affairs* 89, no. 354 (1990): 82–83.

21. There is some evidence that the Black-elected councils initially enjoyed some popular legitimacy, particularly "as arbiters of justice and dispensers of patronage." This support did not last. Seekings, "Political Mobilization," 206; Maylam, "Rise and Decline."

22. The ANC referred briefly to the goal of ungovernability in its annual January 8 statements in 1984 and 1985. See African National Congress, "Statement of the National Executive Committee on the Occasion of the 72th Anniversary of the ANC," January 8, 1984, accessed February 21, 2016, http://www.anc.org.za/show.php?id=2632; and African National Congress, "Statement of the National Executive Committee on the Occasion of the 73th Anniversary of the ANC," January 8, 1985, accessed February 21, 2016, http://www.anc.org.za/show.php?id=2631. An April 1985 pamphlet made the intention explicit: "Make Apartheid Unworkable! Make the Country Ungovernable! Forward to People's Power! Long Live the ANC—the Vanguard of Our Revolution!" See African National Congress, "ANC Call to the Nation: The Future Is within Our Grasp," accessed March 16, 2021, https://disa.ukzn.ac.za/sites/default/files/pdf_files/pam19850425.026.021 .000.pdf. Oliver Tambo made a similar call in his July 1985 radio address: "Address by Oliver Tambo to the Nation on Radio Freedom," African National Congress (website), July 22, 1985, accessed February 21, 2016, http://www.anc.org.za/show.php?id=4470.

23. During 1983 and 1984, the UDF mobilized election boycotts in the Black townships, launched the massive Million Signatures petition campaign against the parliamentary reforms, and spearheaded a boycott of the tricameral elections. Lodge and Nasson, *All Here and Now*, 35, 58–61.

24. Lodge and Nasson, 62.

25. Jeremy Seekings, *The UDF: A History of the United Democracy Front in South Africa, 1983–1991* (Cape Town: David Philip, 2000), 23.

26. Of the 565 organizations affiliated with the UDF, close to two-thirds were youth or student organizations. Lodge and Nasson, *All Here and Now*, 51.

27. Murphy Morobe, "Towards a People's View of Democracy: The UDF View," *Review of African Political Economy* 14, no. 40 (1987): 81–87; Heidi Brooks, "Popular Power and Vanguardism: The Democratic Deficit of 1980s 'People's Power,'" *Politikon* 45, no. 3 (2017): 314.

28. Between 1979 and 1986, total union membership skyrocketed from just over 700,000 to 1.7 million. Ian Macun, "Growth, Structure and Power in the South African Union Movement," in *Trade Unions and Democratization in South Africa, 1985–1997*, ed. Glenn Adler and Edward Webster (New York: St. Martin's Press, 2000), 60.

29. "Letter from PTC Du Plessis, Minister of Manpower to Chris Dlamini, President of the Federation of South African Trade Unions," November 8, 1985, University of Witwatersrand Historical Papers, Jane Barrett Papers, A2168, box 3, B3; "Letter from Joe Foster, General Secretary of the Federation of South African Trade Unions to PTC Du Plessis, Minister of Manpower," November 21, 1985, University of Witwatersrand Historical Papers, Jane Barrett Papers, A2168, box 3, B3.

30. Shop steward councils were crucial, as they brought together worker leaders within specific geographic areas to address common problems and coordinate organizing efforts. Jeremy Baskin, "Growth of a New Worker Organ—the Germiston Shop Stewards' Council," *South African Labor Bulletin* 7, no. 8 (1982): 42–53; Mark Swilling, "Workers Divided: A Critical Assessment of the MAWU Split on the East Rand," *South African Labor Bulletin* 10, no. 1 (1984): 99–122; Webster, "Rise of Social-Movement Unionism," 183. Moses Mayekiso, a prominent FOSATU leader from the MAWU, exemplified the growing connection between workplace and community struggles. Kally Forrest, *Metal that Will Not Bend: National Union of Metalworkers of South Africa, 1980–1995* (Johannesburg: Wits University Press, 2011), 333, 338, 359–361.

31. "Paper on 'Worker in the Community': Presented by FOSATU Springs Local Shop Stewards," 1984, University of Witwatersrand Historical Papers, Jane Barrett Papers, A2168, box 3, B4.7, 2–3.

32. Gay Seidman, "Social Movement Unionism: From Description to Exhortation," *South African Review of Sociology* 42, no. 3 (2011): 94–102.

33. Noor Nieftagodien, "Reconstituting and Re-imagining the Left after Marikana," in *New South African Review 5: Beyond Marikana*, ed. Gilbert Khadiagala, Prishani Naidoo, Devan Pillay, and Roger Southall (Johannesburg: Wits University Press, 2015), 30; Forrest, *Metal That Will Not*, 342; Lodge and Nasson, *All Here and Now*, 67.

34. Labor Monitoring Group, "The November Stay-Away," *South African Labor Bulletin* 10, no. 6 (1985): 99.

35. The joint steering committee included workers, students, and residents, and the demands reflected their varied struggles: "democratically elected student representatives; abolition of corporal punishment; withdrawal of soldiers and policemen from the townships; the release of detainees; no increases in bus fares, rents, utilities; and finally, the reinstatement of the Simba strikers." Labor Monitoring Group, "November Stay-Away"; Nieftagodien, "Reconstituting and Re-imagining," 31; Forrest, *Metal That Will Not*, 343–344; Lodge and Nasson, *All Here and Now*, 69; "Minutes of the FOSATU Central Committee Meeting Held at Wilgespruit Fellowship Center Johannesburg on the 20/21st October 1984," October 1984, University of Witwatersrand Historical Papers, Jane Barrett Papers, A2168, box 2, B1.1.2.

36. Lodge and Nasson, *All Here and Now*, 135.

37. Michael Neocosmos, "From People's Politics to State Politics: Aspects of National Liberation in South Africa," in *The Politics of Opposition in Contemporary Africa*, ed. Adebayo O. Olukoshi (Uppsala, Sweden: Nordiska Afrikainstitutet, 1998), 208; Lodge and Nasson, *All Here and Now*, 39.

38. Neocosmos, "From People's Politics," 202–205; Lodge and Nasson, 82–84, 135–139.

39. Lodge and Nasson, 51.

40. Lodge and Nasson, 53.

41. Jeremy Seekings, "'Trailing behind the Masses': The United Democratic Front and Township Politics in the Pretoria-Witwatersrand-Vaal Region, 1983–1984," *Journals of Southern African Studies* 18, no. 1 (1992): 93–114.

42. On the weakness of community organization in general, see Steven Friedman, "A Partly Forgotten Left Critique of ANC Strategy and Its Contemporary Implications," *Journal of Asian and African Studies* 47, no. 1 (2012): 27–28. For example, "people's courts" were notoriously uneven and sometimes devolved into patronage schemes and elite projects of social control. Lodge and Nasson, *All Here and Now*, 135–139; Marais, *South Africa Pushed*, 54.

43. Neocosmos, "From People's Politics," 205.

44. Lodge and Nasson, *All Here and Now*, 84.

45. Brooks, "Popular Power and Vanguardism"; Jonny Steinberg, "A Place for Civics in a Liberal Democratic Polity? The Fate of Local Institutions of Resistance after Apartheid," in *From Comrades to Citizens: The South African Civics Movements and the Transition to Democracy*, ed. Glenn Adler and Jonny Steinberg (New York: Palgrave Macmillan, 2000), 174–204.

46. Morobe, "Towards a People's Democracy," 82.

47. Shop steward councils, which eventually became local union branches, expressed this popular democratic spirit. Swilling, "MAWU and UMMAWSA Fight," 10; Neocosmos, "From People's Politics," 216–220.

48. For an elaboration of this perspective and how it played out within FOSATU, see Sian Byrne, Nicole Ulrich, and Lucien van der Walt, "Red, Black and Gold: FOSATU, South African 'Workerism', Syndicalism and the Nation," in *The Unresolved National Question: Left Thought Under Apartheid*, ed. Edward Webster and Karin Pampallis (Johannesburg: Wits University Press, 2017), 254–273.

49. Forrest, *Metal That Will Not*, 323–324, 361–364.

50. ANC, "First National Consultative Conference: Report on the Strategy and Tactics of the African National Congress," 1969, accessed March 1, 2016, http://anc.org.za/show.php?id=149; Nhlanhla Ndebele and Noor Nieftagodien, "The Morogoro Conference: A Moment of Self-Reflection," in *The Road to Democracy in South Africa, Volume I: 1960–1970*, ed. South African Democracy Trust (Cape Town: Zebra Press, 2004), 595–596; Irina Filatova, "The Lasting Legacy: The Soviet Theory of the National-Democratic Revolution and South Africa," *South African Historical Journal* 64, no. 3 (2012): 530–534.

51. Filatova, "Lasting Legacy," 530–534.

52. Neocosmos, "From People's Politics," 234–235.

53. Under the auspices of a state of emergency, which lasted from July 1985 to March 1986 and June 1986 to June 1990, the National Party government banned meetings and organizations, instituted curfews, and detained and sometimes killed activists. Between June 1986 and June 1987, the police detained about twenty-six thousand people. "States of Emergency in South Africa: the 1960s and 1980s," South African History Online, accessed April 24, 2017, http://www.sahistory.org.za/topic/state-emergency-south-africa-1960-and-1980s.

54. Seekings, *UDF*, 21; Neocosmos, "From People's Politics," 205–210. Lodge and Nasson remark: "In contrast to the mid-1980s, when the insurrectionary movement was being pulled onto uncharted courses by cadres of youth in the streets in the townships, the popular protest in the late 1980s was choreographed and coordinated and seemed much more under the command of its leaders." Lodge and Nasson, *All Here and Now*, 114.

55. Heidi Brooks, "Merging Radical and Liberal Traditions: The Constitution Committee and the Development of Democratic Thought in the African National Congress, 1986–1990," *Journal of Southern African Studies* 44, no. 1 (2018): 167–184.

56. Sampie Terreblanche, *Lost in Transformation: South Africa's Search for a New Future Since 1986* (Sandton, South Africa: KMM Review, 2012); Willie Esterhuyse, *Endgame: Secret Talks and the End of Apartheid* (Cape Town: Tafelberg, 2014); Mark Gevisser, *Thabo Mbeki: The Dream Deferred* (Johannesburg: Jonathan Ball, 2007); Allister Sparks, *Tomorrow Is Another Country: The Inside Story of South Africa's Road to Change* (New York: Hill and Wang, 1995); Vishnu Padayachee and Robert van Niekerk, *Shadow of Liberation: Contestation and Compromise in the Economic and Social Policy of the African National Congress, 1943–1996* (Johannesburg: Wits University Press, 2019).

57. Nelson Mandela, *Long Walk to Freedom* (New York: Little Brown, 1994), 526. Thabo Mbeki, who succeeded Nelson Mandela as president of the ANC and the country, embarked on a similar process of secret talks with Afrikaner elites, producing turmoil within the ANC. Gevisser, *Thabo Mbeki*, 564–591.

58. Brooks, "Popular Power and Vanguardism."

59. Steven Friedman, "Bonaparte at the Barricades," *Theoria* 79 (May 1992): 85.

60. Heidi Brooks, "The Mass Movement and Public Policy: Discourses of Participatory Democracy in Post-1994 South Africa," *Journal of Modern African Studies* 55, no. 1 (2017): 105–127; Heidi Brooks, *The African National Congress and Participatory Democracy: From People's Power to Public Policy* (Cham, Switzerland: Palgrave Macmillan, 2020); Michelle Williams, *The Roots of Participatory Democracy: Democratic Communists in South Africa and Kerala, India* (New York: Palgrave Macmillan, 2008); Devan Pillay, "Fighting the Violence: Mass Action or Mass Struggle?," *Work in Progress* 83 (July–August 1992): 7–9.

61. Friedman, "Partly Forgotten Left Critique," 24–29.

62. Friedman; Nigel C. Gibson, *Fanonian Practices in South Africa: From Steve Biko to Abahlali baseMjondolo* (Pietermaritzburg, South Africa: University of KwaZulu-Natal Press, 2011).

63. Padayachee and Niekerk, *Shadow of Liberation*, 116.

64. This held both within South Africa and internationally, as the ANC developed an impressive knack for diplomacy abroad. Many actors outside of South Africa recognized the ANC as the most important representative of South Africa's oppressed. Marais, *South Africa Pushed*, 64–65, 434–435.

65. Neocosmos, "From People's Politics," 211.

66. Marais, *South Africa Pushed*, 63. Friedman argues that the UDF represented an attempt to ensure that civil society "operated under leadership sympathetic to ANC ideals and willing to accept its leadership." Steven Friedman, "No Easy Stroll to Dominance: Party Dominance Opposition and Civil Society in South Africa," in *The Awkward Embrace: One-Party Domination and Democracy*, ed. Hermann Giliomee and Charles Simkins (New York: Routledge, 1999), 119; Friedman, "Bonaparte at the Barricades."

67. On the civics, see Lodge and Nasson, *All Here and Now*, 40–41. On the absorption of resistance organizations into the ANC, see Marais, *South Africa Pushed*, 63; and Neocosmos, "From People's Politics," 210–216.

68. On insulation from repression, see Lodge and Nasson, 112; Forrest, *Metal That Will Not*, 356–359; Jeremy Baskin, *Striking Back: A History of COSATU* (Johannesburg: Raven Press, 1991), 450; Seidman, *Manufacturing Militance*, 250.

69. Demonstrating their new unity, more than 1.5 million workers joined a stay-away on International Workers Day (May 1) in 1986. With the ANC in exile and the UDF in tatters, by the end of the decade COSATU was arguably the most significant antiapartheid force within the country. Seidman, 250–251.

70. Neocosmos, "From People's Politics," 219–223; Sakhela Buhlungu, *A Paradox of Victory: COSATU and the Democratic Transformation in South Africa* (Pietermaritzburg, South Africa: University of Kwazulu-Natal Press, 2010).

71. ANC, "Communique of the Meeting between COSATU, SACTU and the ANC 5–6 March 1986," accessed February 17, 2016, http://www.anc.org.za/show.php?id=3818.

72. Baskin, *Striking Back*, 432.

73. Southall and Webster, "Unions and Parties"; Chipkin, *Do South Africans Exist?*, 85–97; Friedman, "Partly Forgotten Left Critique," 24–25.

74. Marais, *South Africa Pushed*, 404.

75. ANC, "A Basic Guide to the Reconstruction and Development Program," accessed March 1, 2016, http://www.anc.org.za/show.php?id=234.

76. ANC, "Basic Guide," emphasis added.

77. Michael Neocosmos, *From "Foreign Natives" to "Native Foreigners": Explaining Xenophobia in Post-Apartheid South Africa* (Dakar: CODESRIA, 2010), 62–66.

78. Filatova, "Lasting Legacy," 531.

79. ANC, "ANC Strategy and Tactics: As Amended at the 50th National Conference, December 1997," accessed July 20, 2020, https://www.marxists.org/subject/africa/anc /1997/strategy-tactics.htm. In line with prominent activist usage under apartheid, the term *Black* here encompasses Black African, Indian, and Coloured residents.

80. Gillian Hart, *Rethinking the South African Crisis: Nationalism, Populism, Hegemony* (Athens: University of Georgia Press, 2014), 174–180, 197–212. Neville Alexander suggests that NDR discourse incorporated an unstable and changing mix of nationalist, liberal-democratic, and socialist thought. Neville Alexander, "South Africa—an Unfinished Revolution?," South African History Online, accessed April 12, 2021, https://www .sahistory.org.za/archive/south-africa-unfinished-revolution.

81. Daryl Glaser, "National Democratic Revolution Meets Constitutional Democracy," in *The Unresolved National Question: Left Thought Under Apartheid*, ed. Edward Webster and Karin Pampallis (Johannesburg: Wits University Press, 2017), 276–278.

82. South African Communist Party, *The Road to South African Freedom* (1962), accessed February 20, 2016, http://www.sahistory.org.za/sites/default/files/Programme%20 of%20the%20South%20African%20Communist%20Party%201962-%20The%20 Road%20to%20South%20Africa%20Freedom.pdf.

83. South African Communist Party, *Road to South African*.

84. Edward Webster and Karin Pampallis, *The Unresolved National Question: Left Thought under Apartheid* (Johannesburg: Wits University Press, 2017).

85. Friedman, "Partly Forgotten Left Critique"; Martin Legassick, "The Marxist Workers' Tendency of the African National Congress," in *The Unresolved National Question: Left Thought under Apartheid*, ed. Edward Webster and Karin Pampallis (Johannesburg: Wits University Press, 2017), 149–162; Martin Legassick, "Colonialism of a Special Type and the Approach of the Marxist Workers' Tendency of the African National Congress to the National Question," in *Race, Class, and the Post-Apartheid State*, ed. John Reynolds, Ben Fine, and Robert van Niekerk (Pietermaritzburg, South Africa: University of KwaZulu-Natal Press, 2020), 57–71.

86. Southall and Webster, "Unions and Parties"; Forrest, *Metal That Will Not*, 330-335.

87. Joe Foster, "The Workers' Struggle—Where Does FOSATU Stand?," *South African Labor Bulletin* 7, no. 8 (1982): 67-86.

88. FOSATU, "Summary of FOSATU Central Committee Meeting Held at Wilgerspruit on 15/16 October 1983," October 16, 1983, University of Witwatersrand Historical Papers, Jane Barrett Papers, A2168, box 2, B1.1.1.

89. Southall and Webster, "Unions and Parties," 138.

90. Baskin, *Striking Back*, 463.

91. NUMSA finally broke from the ANC in December 2013 and was subsequently expelled from COSATU. Marcel Paret, "Working Class Fragmentation, Party Politics, and the Complexities of Solidarity in South Africa's United Front," *Sociological Review* 65, no. 2 (2017): 267-284.

92. Brooks notes that by 1992 "all socialist-inspired language had been eradicated." Brooks, "Merging Radical and Liberal," 183. Ivor Chipkin remarks that by the mid-1990s, the NDR had "become unhinged from its traditional object: socialism. Indeed, it is remarkable how rapidly the word has disappeared from the terrain of South African politics." Ivor Chipkin, "Contesting Community: The Limits of Democratic Development," *Urban Forum* 7, no. 2 (1996). After the ANC victory in the 1994 elections, Mandela affirmed that ANC policy did not contain any "things like nationalization." This was "not accidental," he argued, because "there is not a single slogan that will connect us with any Marxist ideology." Marais, *South Africa Pushed*, 97.

93. Marais, 99-109; Padayachee and van Niekerk, *Shadow of Liberation*.

94. Marais *South Africa Pushed*, 106.

95. Bond, *Elite Transition*; Padayachee and Niekerk, *Shadow of Liberation*.

96. Marais, *South Africa Pushed*, 106; Padayachee and Niekerk, 150-151, 228.

97. Bond, *Elite Transition*, 42-66; Padayachee and Niekerk, 153-154.

98. Padayachee and Niekerk, 123-140. There were many steps along the way to the adoption of GEAR in 1996, including the scrapping of the social democratic proposals of the Macro Economic Research Group (MERG) in November 1993; the incorporation of centrist and right-leaning elements into the RDP, which became official ANC policy in January 1994; and the emphasis on privatization and fiscal discipline in the September 1994 RDP White Paper. See also Bond, *Elite Transition*; and William Freund, "Swimming against the Tide: The Macro-Economic Research Group in the South African Transition 1991-94," *Review of African Political Economy* 40, no. 138 (2013): 519-536.

99. ANC, "The State, Property Relations, and Social Transformation," *Umrabulo* 5 (3rd quarter 1998). For an analysis of this transformation of the NDR, see Chipkin, *Do South Africans Exist?*, 106-109.

100. Ashwin Desai, *We Are the Poors: Community Struggles in Post-Apartheid South Africa* (New York: Monthly Review Press, 2002); Marcel Paret, "Labor and Community Struggles, 1994-2014," in *New South African Review 5: Beyond Marikana*, ed. Gilbert M. Khadiagala, Prishani Naidoo, Devan Pillay, and Roger Southall (Johannesburg: Wits University Press, 2015), 34-47.

101. Marais, *South Africa Pushed*, 407-410.

102. Paret, "Labor and Community Struggles"; Hart, *Rethinking the South African*, 31-38, 197-200.

103. Hart, 197-198.

104. Hart, 158, 197-199.

105. Karl von Holdt, *The Political Economy of Corruption: Elite-Formation, Factions and Violence* (Johannesburg: SWOP, 2019), 6-8.

106. Taking the imposition of the market-oriented GEAR policy in 1996 as a key moment, they sometimes referred to this capturing as the "1996 class project."

107. Hart, *Rethinking the South African*, 200–207.

108. von Holdt, *Political Economy of Corruption*, 10.

109. von Holdt. See also Roger Southall, "The Coming Crisis of Zuma's ANC: The Party-State Confronts Fiscal Crisis," *Review of African Political Economy* 43, no. 147 (2016): 73–88; and Tom Lodge, "Neo-Patrimonial Politics in the ANC," *African Affairs* 113, no. 450 (2014): 1–23.

110. For an analysis of debates around Zuma, radical economic transformation, and white monopoly capital, see Ashwin Desai, "The Zuma Moment: Between Tender-Based Capitalists and Radical Economic Transformation," *Journal of Contemporary African Studies* 36, no. 4 (2018): 499–513.

111. The most obvious indicator of continuity was the election of Ace Magashule, a key Zuma supporter who was also accused of corruption, as the new secretary-general. Pieter-Louis Myburgh, *Gangster State: Unravelling Ace Magashule's Web of Capture* (Cape Town: Penguin, 2019).

112. von Holdt, *Political Economy of Corruption*; Patrick Bond, "Who Really 'State Captured' South Africa? Revealing Silences in Poverty, Inequality and Structurally-Corrupt Capitalism," in *Exploring the Link between Poverty and Human Rights in Africa*, ed. Ebenezer Durojaye and Gladys Mirugi-Mukundi (Pretoria: Pretoria Law University Press, 2020), 59–94.

113. Commentators from the Public Affairs Research Institute remarked that "both elite groups claim to be for the poor, but neither is concerned about giving power to the poor." Ryan Brunette, Patronella Nqaba, Joel Pearson, and Mosa Phadi, "Elite Struggle over Zuma Is Making Weapons against the Poor," *Daily Maverick*, June 14, 2017.

114. Susan Booysen highlights the dynamic interaction between internal party dynamics and the party's relationship to other parties and the broader public. Susan Booysen, "The African National Congress and Its Transfer of Power from Zuma to Ramaphosa: The Intraparty-Multiparty Nexus," *Transformation* 98 (2018): 1–26; Susan Booysen, "Hegemonic Struggles of the African National Congress: From Cacophony of Morbid Symptoms to Strained Renewal," *Africa Spectrum* 53, no. 2 (2018): 5–35.

115. Malema famously declared that he would "kill for Zuma." "We Will Kill for Zuma," *IOL News*, June 17, 2008.

116. Hart, *Rethinking the South African*, 208–212.

117. Land expropriation without compensation and nationalization of mines and banks were the first two of the EFF's seven core pillars of economic emancipation. EFF, "Economic Freedom Fighters Founding Manifesto: Radical Movement towards Economic Freedom in Our Lifetime," July 25, 2013, accessed August 29, 2013, http://www.politicsweb.co.za/news-and-analysis/founding-manifesto-of-the-economic-freedom-fighter.

118. Noor Nieftagodien notes that EFF activists tended to swoop into popular struggles for brief moments of solidarity and to impose their own political agendas rather than "becoming part of the rebellion and being shaped by it." Nieftagodien, "Reconstituting and Re-imagining," 26.

119. Peter Alexander, "Marikana: Turning Point in South African History," *Review of African Political Economy* 40, no. 138 (2013): 605–619.

120. NUMSA, "NUMSA Special National Congress, December 17 to 20, 2013: Declaration," accessed January 9, 2018, http://www.numsa.org.za/wp-content/uploads/2013/12/SNC-Declaration-final-copy.pdf.

121. Returning to some of the radical priorities of the 1980s, SAFTU committed to prioritizing militancy, worker control, independence from political parties, and a so-

cialist orientation. SAFTU, "Declaration of the Launching Congress of the South African Federation of Trade Unions, 21–23 April 2017," accessed April 29, 2017, http://www.politicsweb.co.za/documents/this-is-what-we-stand-for—saftu.

122. Paret, "Working Class Fragmentation."

123. Sam Ashman, Zachary Levenson, and Trevor Ngwane note the lack of "an actual base" as "*the* problem of the UF," in "South Africa's ANC: The Beginning of the End?," *Catalyst* 1 (Summer 2017): 95–97, 105–106, original emphasis.

124. Neo Chabane, Andrea Goldstein, and Simon Roberts, "The Changing Face and Strategies of Big Business in South Africa: More than a Decade of Political Democracy," *Industrial and Corporate Change* 15, no. 3 (2006): 553.

125. Major companies increasingly moved their resources out of South Africa, with some relisting on the London Stock Exchange. Sam Ashman, Ben Fine, and Susan Newman, "Amnesty International? The Nature, Scale, and Impact of Capital Flight from South Africa," *Journal of Southern African Studies* 37, no. 1 (2011): 7–25.

126. As of 2013, Black investors accounted for 10 percent of the JSE, compared to 22 percent for white investors and 39 percent for foreign investors. The remaining ownership included indirect Black ownership through institutional investments such as employee-sponsored pension funds (13 percent) and ownership that remained unmeasured (16 percent). Trevor Chandler, "Who Owns the JSE?," in *Tomorrow: Invested As You Are* (Cape Town: Old Mutual Investment Group, 2016), 37–39.

127. Of the top four BEE success stories—Cyril Ramaphosa, Tokyo Sexwale, Saki Macozoma, and Patrice Motsepe—three were major players within the ANC before moving into business, and the fourth was a party adviser and financier. On the evolution of the BEE, see Roger Southall, *The New Black Middle Class in South Africa* (Woodbridge, UK: James Currey, 2016), 87–90.

128. Southall, *New Black Middle Class*, 90–93.

129. The Employment Equity Act of 1998 sought to align the workforce with the country's racial composition. It prohibited unfair discrimination, mandated representation targets for large employers and the reduction of pay differentials, and made compliance a condition for securing government contracts. Southall, 73.

130. Southall traces this lack of transformation to employer resistance, unwelcome workplace environments, and challenges within the country's education system. Southall, 76–84.

131. Southall, 76–81.

132. Justin Visagie and Dorrit Posel, "A Reconsideration of What and Who Is Middle Class in South Africa," *Development Studies* 39, no. 2 (2013): 159.

133. On labor and the democratic transition, see Franco Barchiesi, *Precarious Liberation: Workers, the State, and Contested Social Citizenship in Postapartheid South Africa* (Albany: State University of New York Press, 2011); Edward Webster and Glenn Adler, "Toward a Class Compromise in South Africa's 'Double Transition': Bargained Liberalization and the Consolidation of Democracy," *Politics and Society* 27, no. 3 (1999): 347–385.

134. Jeremy Seekings and Nicoli Nattrass, *Policy, Politics and Poverty in South Africa* (New York: Palgrave Macmillan, 2015), 61. For medium-skill blue-collar workers, average wages declined in the 1990s and then recovered in the 2000s.

135. Seekings and Nattrass, *Policy, Politics and Poverty*, 62.

136. Seekings and Nattrass, 62–63.

137. Christine Bischoff and Malehoko Tshoaedi, "The Experience of Conducting a Longitudinal Study: The COSATU Workers' Survey, 2008," in *COSATU's Contested Legacy*, ed. Sakhela Buhlungu and Malehoko Tshoaedi (Cape Town: HSRC Press, 2012), 52.

138. About half of employees worked in "precarious jobs" that were either unregulated by the state, part-time or temporary, or consisted of "survivalist" casual work or self-employment. Ben Scully, "From the Shop Floor to the Kitchen Table: The Shifting Center of Precarious Workers' Politics in South Africa," *Review of African Political Economy* 43, no. 148 (2016): 303.

139. As of 2012, more than half (54 percent) of households with union members also included somebody who was unemployed, informally employed, or receiving a government cash transfer. Ben Scully, "Precarity North and South: A Southern Critique of Guy Standing," *Global Labor Journal* 7, no. 2 (2016): 167.

140. The ANC promised to deliver one million houses during its first five-year term. It reached this goal within ten years and after fifteen years had provided close to three million homes. Marie Huchzermeyer, "Changing Housing Policy in South Africa," in *Affordable Housing in the Urban Global South: Seeking Sustainable Solutions*, ed. Jan Bredenoord, Paul van Lindert, and Peer Smets (New York: Routledge, 2014), 340.

141. Levenson concludes that "South Africa has distributed more free, formal homes than any other democratic state." Zachary Levenson, "Precarious Welfare States: Urban Struggles over Housing Delivery in Post-Apartheid South Africa," *International Sociology* 32, no. 4 (2017): 474, 476, 480.

142. Statistics South Africa, *General Household Survey: 2019* (Pretoria: Statistics South Africa, 2020), 32–33.

143. Seekings and Nattrass, *Policy, Politics and Poverty*, 136–139. By 2007, 43 percent of households received at least one social grant, and for half of those households, social grants were the primary source of income. Marais, *South Africa Pushed*, 246.

144. The state gradually lifted the age of eligible dependents, which rose from eight years old in 2003 to eighteen years old in 2012. The number of Child Support Grant beneficiaries skyrocketed from less than three million in 2003 to close to twelve million in 2014. Seekings and Nattrass, *Policy, Politics and Poverty*, 136–139.

145. Lasting from 2004 to 2009, the Extended Public Works Program (EPWP) eventually employed about 10 percent of unemployed residents (including discouraged work seekers) in its final year. This was an impressive achievement, though each "work opportunity" only lasted an average of fifty-six days and the program only covered 2 percent of total unemployed workdays. Seekings and Nattrass, 143–145.

146. Gavin Andersson and Peter Alexander, "The Community Work Program: Potentials and Problems," *Transformation: Critical Perspectives on Southern Africa* 91 (2016): 157–177.

147. Bongani M. Mayosi and Solomon R. Benatar, "Health and Health Care in South Africa—20 Years after Mandela," *New England Journal of Medicine* 371, no. 14 (2014): 1344–1353.

148. Seekings and Nattrass, *Policy, Politics and Poverty*, 165–171.

2. BETRAYAL

1. Interview 30; July 22, 2013; Motsoaledi; male.

2. Interview 30; July 22, 2013; Motsoaledi; male.

3. Interview 25; September 19, 2010; Johannesburg; male, forty years old.

4. Interview 99; July 3, 2015; Meadowlands; female, forty years old.

5. Sarah Rich Dorman, "Post-Liberation Politics in Africa: Examining the Political Legacy of Struggle," *Third World Quarterly* 27, no. 6 (2006): 1085–1101.

6. Gillian Hart, *Rethinking the South African Crisis: Nationalism, Populism, Hegemony* (Athens: University of Georgia Press, 2014), 189.

7. Hart, *Rethinking the South African*, 189.

8. Javier Auyero, "The Moral Politics of Argentine Crowds," *Mobilization* 9, no. 3 (2004): 312, original emphasis.

9. Auyero, "Moral Politics," 323.

10. "Protests a Ticking Time Bomb, Warns Vavi," *News24*, May 30, 2013.

11. Ashwin Desai, *We Are the Poors: Community Struggles in Post-Apartheid South Africa* (New York: Monthly Review Press, 2002); Richard Ballard, Adam Habib, and Imraan Valodia, *Voices of Protest: Social Movements in Post-Apartheid South Africa* (Pietermaritzburg, South Africa: University of KwaZulu-Natal Press, 2006).

12. Carin Runciman, "The Decline of the Anti-Privatization Forum in the Midst of South Africa's 'Rebellion of the Poor,'" *Current Sociology* 63, no. 7 (2015): 961–979; Oupa Lehulere, "The New Social Movements, COSATU, and the 'New UDF,'" *Khanya: A Journal for Activists* 11 (2005): 18–40.

13. Dale McKinley, *Transition's Child: The Anti-Privatization Forum* (Braamfontein, South Africa: South African History Archive, 2012), 19.

14. Interview 105; August 5, 2016; Thembelihle; male, twenty-seven years old.

15. Interview 104; May 29, 2016; Tsakane; male, thirty-six years old.

16. An activist from Motsoaledi illustrated the point: "The APF would make sure . . . on the meeting you must eat something. They know that you are not working; they cook something for you and [you] eat. Come back home, they give you money for transport. . . . When they call you tomorrow, you say I am coming because you know you have transport money. You won't struggle and go to your neighbors: 'Please borrow me R10.'" Interview 100; May 22, 2016; Motsoaledi; male, thirty-six years old.

17. Funding also encouraged bureaucratization and narrow struggles over organizational resources. Runciman argues that core activists turned inward, focusing on technical and bureaucratic tasks, such as writing reports and securing funding, to the neglect of "mobilization and political activities." Runciman, "Decline," 972.

18. McKinley, *Transition's Child*, 19, emphasis added.

19. Forces aligned to the ruling party, including the Congress of South African Trade Unions (COSATU), distanced themselves from the oppositional agenda by holding their own ANC-backed event on the very same day. The pro-ANC, progovernment event only managed to secure one-fifth as many participants. Hart recalls: "Of great significance was the contrast between the huge, rollicking March of Movements bedecked in red T-shirts [the APF march], and the embarrassingly meagre turnout for an ANC-sponsored rally in Alexandra addressed by Thabo Mbeki." Hart, *Rethinking the South African*, 32–33. See also Dale McKinley, "Democracy and Social Movements in South Africa," in *The Development Decade? Economic and Social Change in South Africa, 1994–2004*, ed. Vishnu Padayachee (Pretoria: Human Sciences Research Council, 2006), 418; Carl Death, "Troubles at the Top: South African Protests and the 2002 Johannesburg Summit," *African Affairs* 109, no. 437 (2010): 560–562.

20. One activist recalled that they initially planned to have two buses to take people to the march from Thembelihle but had to request more due to popular demand. Even after securing ten buses, some people took their own transportation. Interview 108; May 23, 2017; Thembelihle; female, thirty-eight years old.

21. The WSSD protest drew support from international groups, such as Via Campesina, and represented a key moment within an international global justice movement that extended well beyond South Africa. On South Africa's connection to global protest movements, see Marcel Paret, "Southern Resistance in Critical Perspective," in *Southern Resistance in Critical Perspective: The Politics of Protest in South Africa's Contentious Democracy*, ed. Marcel Paret, Carin Runciman, and Luke Sinwell (New York: Routledge, 2017), 1–17.

22. Interview with John Appolis, March 17, 2010, South African History Archive, collection AL3290, file D2.1.1.

23. The activist academic Ashwin Desai remarked at the time: "If Thabo Mbeki comes around, or Mandela . . . people still see the need to go to the meeting and chant the slogans of the party of liberation: the ANC, the slayer of apartheid. But the next day they are fighting evictions, and denouncing the ANC as a party of neoliberalism." Ashwin Desai and Holly Wren Spaulding, "Between the Broken and the Built: Power to the Neighborhoods," in *We Are Everywhere: The Irresistible Rise of Global Anticapitalism,* ed. Notes from Nowhere (London: Verso, 2003), 486–497.

24. Interview with Johannes Mokonyane, South African History Archive, Anti-Privatization Forum Collection, collection 3290, November 22, 2010, file D2.2.9.

25. The APF's oppositional agenda failed to resonate with many residents. Jakobo recalled, "During the APF times, we were the only group of people that were fighting government. . . . APF started fighting government when no one was thinking of fighting the government. . . . You could not go to a meeting and say, '*Phansi nge ANC*' [down with ANC]." Interview 104; May 29, 2016; Tsakane; male, thirty-six years old. Runciman argues that the APF had difficulty sustaining a layer of committed activists because residents often joined APF activities for practical rather than ideological reasons. She also suggests that Zuma's rise to power facilitated APF decline because it reinforced loyalty to the ruling party. Runciman, "Decline."

26. Paret, "Southern Resistance"; Marcel Paret and Carin Runciman, "The 2009+ South African Protest Wave," *Journal of Labor and Society* 19, no. 3 (2016): 301–319.

27. Hart, *Rethinking the South African.*

28. Field notes, Johannesburg workshop, October 14, 2017.

29. Jennifer Chun, *Organizing at the Margins: The Symbolic Politics of Labor in South Korea and the United States* (Ithaca, NY: ILR Press, 2009).

30. Marcel Paret, "Violence and Democracy in South Africa's Community Protests," *Review of African Political Economy* 42, no. 143 (2015): 107–123.

31. Karl von Holdt, "Insurgent Citizenship and Collective Violence: Analysis of Case Studies," in *The Smoke that Calls: Insurgent Citizenship, Collective Violence and the Struggle for a Place in the New South Africa* (Johannesburg: SWOP, 2011), 26–30.

32. Nancy Fraser, "Rethinking Recognition," *New Left Review* 3 (May–June 2000): 113.

33. Shannon Walsh describes South Africa's local protests as revolving around a "politics of 'demand and recognition' . . . in which being heard and managed is often the end result." Shannon Walsh, "Managing Crisis and Desire in South Africa," in *Contesting Transformation: Popular Resistance in Twenty-First Century South Africa,* ed. Marcelle C. Dawson and Luke Sinwell (London: Pluto Press, 2012), 248.

34. Interview 37; September 4, 2013; Motsoaledi; female.

35. Interview 37; September 4, 2013; Motsoaledi; female.

36. Interview 39; September 28, 2013; Motsoaledi; female, thirty-five years old.

37. Motsoaledi Concerned Residents, "Memorandum," July 28, 2009, author's archive, original emphasis.

38. Motsoaledi Concerned Residents, "Re: Invitation to Attend a People's Inspection of Motsoaledi," 2009, author's archive.

39. Interview 30; July 22, 2013; Motsoaledi; male.

40. Interview 88; August 2, 2014; Thembelihle; male, twenty-five years old.

41. "Thembelihle Residents Respond to MEC by Barricading Roads: 'No One Will Enter or Leave This until We Get a Response,'" February 23, 2015, author's personal archive.

42. Interview 88; August 2, 2014; Thembelihle; male, twenty-five years old.

43. Lebo Malebo and Tebza Mokgope, "Building Protest from Below," *The Socialist: Journal of Keep Left* 4, no. 5 (2014): 5.

44. Interview 93; June 30, 2015; Tsakane; male, forty-four years old.

45. Interview 59; April 14, 2014; Tsakane; male.

46. Interview 66; April 23, 2014; Tsakane; female, thirty-two years old.

47. Interview 67; April 23, 2014; Tsakane; male, thirty-five years old.

48. Emphasizing the importance of local leaders in communicating official decisions, one young activist noted, "The councilor that we have here, we do not know him, so everything they [the municipality] do, they [local leaders] communicate with us." Interview 49; March 12, 2014; Bekkersdal; female.

49. Interview 56; April 2, 2014; Simunye; female.

50. Interview 77; June 12, 2014; Bekkersdal; male, twenty-one years old.

51. Interview 70; May 6, 2014; Bekkersdal; male, thirty-one years old.

52. Interview 65; April 17, 2014; Bekkersdal; male, thirty-one years old; emphasis added.

53. Carien Du Plessis, "The Rainbow's Colors Never Meet," *Mail and Guardian*, December 4, 2020.

54. Peter Alexander, Carin Runciman, and Trevor Ngwane, "Community Protests 2004–2013: Some Research Findings," media briefing, February 12, 2013, accessed July 29, 2020, https://issafrica.s3.amazonaws.com/site/uploads/Public-violence-13March2014-Peter-Alexander.pdf.

55. Interview 110; May 31, 2017; Motsoaledi; male.

56. Interview 41; September 30, 2013; Motsoaledi; three females and two males.

57. Interview 45; January 29, 2014; Motsoaledi; female, fifty-six years old.

58. Interview 32; July 22, 2013; Motsoaledi; two males.

59. The statement explained that residents wanted electricity "for education purposes," for their health, and because "we also want to enjoy the big tournament, the FIFA 2010 World Cup, watching the matches on TV." Motsoaledi Concerned Residents, "Press Statement, Motsoaledi Informal Settlement, Community Protest," author's personal archive.

60. "The irony was evident: while the five thousand dignitaries who attended the formal proceedings were celebrating the freedoms enshrined in the charter, including the right to decent housing, the protesters were demanding a reprieve from their forced relocation from Thembelihle to new plots laid out at Vlakfontein." Martin Murray, *Taming the Disorderly City: The Spatial Landscape of Johannesburg after Apartheid* (Ithaca, NY: Cornell University Press, 2008), 110–111.

61. Marie Huchzermeyer, "The Struggle for In Situ Upgrading of Informal Settlements: A Reflection on Cases in Gauteng," *Development Southern Africa* 26, no. 1 (2009): 59–73.

62. Field notes, May 26, 2013, Thembelihle.

63. Interview 88; August 2, 2014; Thembelihle; male, twenty-five years old.

64. "Thembelihle Residents Threaten Another Round of Protests," *SABC News*, October 28, 2012. Thabo later remarked, "We were told that it is a VIP toilet, but to me it is still the same toilet that people used to dig for themselves." Interview 105; August 5, 2016; Thembelihle; male, twenty-seven years old.

65. Interview 88; August 2, 2014; Thembelihle; male, twenty-five years old.

66. Interview 88; August 2, 2014; Thembelihle; male, twenty-five years old.

67. "Thembelihle Burning: Residents Respond to Electricity Cut-Offs," July 24, 2014, author's personal archive.

68. Operation Khanyisa Movement, "Electricity Is Not a Gift from the ANC—We Fought for It," July 21, 2016, author's personal archive.

69. South African Government (website), "Gauteng Cooperative Governance Registers Thembelihle as a Housing Project," April 28, 2015, accessed April 1, 2016, http://

www.gov.za/speeches/media-statement-special-freedom-day-people-thembelihle
-government-registers-thembelihle.

70. Operation Khanyisa Movement, "Electricity Is Not a Gift."

71. Interview 67; April 23, 2014; Tsakane; male, thirty-five years old.

72. Interview 68; April 23, 2014; Tsakane; male, forty years old.

73. Interview 67; April 23, 2014; Tsakane; male, thirty-five years old.

74. In 1993, just before the transition to democracy, nearly half (46 percent) of the popu-lation lived in freestanding shacks in the informal settlements, one-third lived in backyard shacks behind formal houses, and one-fifth lived in formal houses, the vast majority of which the local town council built. Owen Crankshaw, "Social Differentiation, Conflict and Development in a South African Township," *Urban Forum* 7, no. 1 (1996): 54–56.

75. In 2011, residents opposed their redemarcation from the economic hub of Gauteng Province into the poorer North West Province. Residents expressed concern that such a move would both threaten public provision and require them to travel lon-ger distances to the provincial capital.

76. Interview 47; March 12, 2014; Bekkersdal; male, twenty-eight years old.

77. Interview 80; June 20, 2014; Bekkersdal; female, twenty-three years old.

78. Launched in the early 2000s, the BRP was part of a major national urban renewal program that directed funds to local governments in crucial urban "nodes" for large development projects. South African Government (website), "The State of the Nation Address of the President of South Africa," February 9, 2001, accessed August 27, 2015, http://www.gov.za/node/537670.

79. "Urban Renewal Programs," accessed November 1, 2017, http://www.gdhs.gpg.gov.za/Pages/Urban-Renewal-Programmes.aspx.

80. Interview 53; March 26, 2014; Bekkersdal; male, forty-four years old.

81. Interview 53; March 26, 2014; Bekkersdal; male, forty-four years old.

3. COMMUNITY

1. Gay Seidman, *Manufacturing Militance: Workers' Movements in Brazil and South Africa, 1970–1985* (Berkeley: University of California Press, 1994), 227, 233.

2. Marcel Paret, "Precarious Labor Politics: Unions and the Struggles of the Insecure Working Class in the United States and South Africa," *Critical Sociology* 41, no. 4–5 (2015): 757–784; Marcel Paret, "Labor and Community Struggles, 1994–2014," in *New South African Review 5: Beyond Marikana*, ed. Gilbert M. Khadiagala, Prishani Naidoo, Devan Pillay, and Roger Southall (Johannesburg: Wits University Press, 2015), 34–47; Marcel Paret, "Building Labor Solidarity in Precarious Times: The Danger of Union Paternalism," *Labor Studies Journal* 44, no. 4 (2019): 314–332.

3. Patricia Hill Collins, "The New Politics of Community," *American Sociological Review* 75, no. 1 (2010): 7–30.

4. Collins, "New Politics," 12.

5. Partha Chatterjee, *The Politics of the Governed: Reflections on Popular Politics in Most of the World* (New York: Columbia University Press, 2004), 57, 75.

6. Frances Fox Piven and Richard A. Cloward, *Poor People's Movements: Why They Succeed, How They Fail* (New York: Vintage 1979), 21.

7. Heidi Brooks, "The Mass Movement and Public Policy: Discourses of Participatory Democracy in Post-1994 South Africa," *Journal of Modern African Studies,* 55, no. 1 (2017): 105–127; Ivor Chipkin, "Contesting Community: The Limits of Democratic Development," *Urban Forum* 7, no. 2 (1996): 217–231. The closing of the Reconstruction and Development Office, which had created a national office for participatory development planning, shifted development planning to local government. Philip Harrison, "The Genealogy of South Af-

rica's Integrated Development Plan," *Third World Planning Review* 23, no. 2 (2001): 184–187.

8. Republic of South Africa, "Constitution of the Republic of South Africa No. 108 of 1996," *Statutes of the Republic of South Africa-Constitutional Law* 38 (1996): 1241–1331.

9. Gillian Hart, *Rethinking the South African Crisis: Nationalism, Populism, Hegemony* (Athens: University of Georgia Press, 2014).

10. This partially reflected international norms that prioritized good governance, performance management, fiscal constraint, and efficiency over democracy and empowerment. Brooks, "Mass Movement," 109–113, 123. See also Chipkin, "Contesting Community," 224–226.

11. Patrick Heller, "Moving the State: The Politics of Democratic Decentralization in Kerala, South Africa, and Porto Alegre," *Politics and Society* 29, no. 1 (2001): 144.

12. Brooks, "Mass Movement," 110–111.

13. Jonny Steinberg, "A Place for Civics in a Liberal Democratic Polity? The Fate of Local Institutions of Resistance after Apartheid," in *From Comrades to Citizens: The South African Civics Movements and the Transition to Democracy*, ed. Glenn Adler and Jonny Steinberg (New York: Palgrave Macmillan, 2000), 194; Steven Friedman, *The Elusive "Community": The Dynamics of Negotiated Urban Development* (Johannesburg: Center for Policy Studies, 1993), 28.

14. Heidi Brooks, "Popular Power and Vanguardism: The Democratic Deficit of 1980s 'People's Power,'" *Politikon* 45, no. 3 (2017): 313–334; Steinberg, "Place for Civics"; Steven Friedman, "Bonaparte at the Barricades," *Theoria* 79 (May 1992): 83–95.

15. Brooks, "Mass Movement"; Heidi Brooks, *The African National Congress and Participatory Democracy: From People's Power to Public Policy* (Cham, Switzerland: Palgrave Macmillan, 2020).

16. Laurence Piper and Fiona Anciano, "Party over Outsiders, Center over Branch: How ANC Dominance Works at the Community Level in South Africa," *Transformation* 87 (2015): 72–94.

17. Claire Benit-Gbaffou, "Are Practices of Local Participation Sidelining the Institutional Participatory Channels? Reflections from Johannesburg," *Transformation* 66/67 (2008): 27.

18. Friedman, "Bonaparte at the Barricades," 85; Steinberg, "Place for Civics."

19. Friedman; Steinberg; Chipkin, "Contesting Community."

20. Friedman; Steinberg; Piper and Anciano, "Party over Outsiders." Writing about community-based "civic" organizations, Friedman notes, "Civics, unlike interest-based local pressure groups, relied for their influence on projecting themselves as representatives not of particular interests but of the 'community' as a whole—just as 'liberation' movements rely on claims to represent 'the people' or 'the nation' as a whole." Friedman, *Elusive "Community,"* 5.

21. This process began under apartheid as the state sought out representatives of the community for participation in urban development projects. Not only did state officials view Black residents as an undifferentiated mass with common interests, but they also sought participation to prevent potential resistance. Rather than a commitment to radical democracy, one official described "community participation" as "mobilizing all those who are needed to make the project work." Friedman, 11–16, 35.

22. Piper and Anciano, "Party over Outsiders"; Patrick Heller, "Democratic Deepening in India and South Africa," *Journal of Asian and African Studies* 44, no. 1 (2009): 123–149; Patrick Heller, "Divergent Trajectories of Democratic Deepening: Comparing Brazil, India, and South Africa," *Theory and Society* 48 (2019): 351–382.

23. One antiapartheid activist argued that the predominant organizational form of the era—a single organization representing an entire community—was necessary

under conditions of state exclusion from political participation: "A situation of a liberation movement . . . tends to bring people together—so there can only be one position. . . . The day our people participate through more sophisticated channels of communication . . . that is the day the civic may dovetail into various political formations." Steinberg, "Place for Civics," 201–202.

24. Susan Booysen, *Dominance and Decline: The ANC in the Time of Zuma* (Johannesburg: Wits University Press, 2015), 1–2.

25. This reflected the weakness of the opposition, including both internal divisions within the DA and the instability of the DA-EFF coalition. The former prompted the resignation of the DA-affiliated mayor, Herman Mashaba, and the latter prevented the DA from regaining control of the executive.

26. Interview 47; March 12, 2014; Bekkersdal; male, twenty-eight years old.

27. ANC membership doubled between 2005 and 2012 and then declined between 2012 and 2015, dropping by 37 percent nationally and by 35 percent in Gauteng Province. Ranjeni Munusamy, "ANC NGC: Zuma, Mantashe Ring Alarm Bells as Membership Plunges by 37%," *Daily Maverick*, October 9, 2015.

28. Interview 96; June 30, 2015; Tsakane; male, forty years old.

29. Interview 105; August 5, 2016; Thembelihle; male, twenty-seven years old.

30. He noted, "My childhood life grew inside politics. So you know what, I'm a teenager now, and I don't have a social life. My life is based on politics." Interview 38; September 16, 2013; Motsoaledi; male, twenty years old.

31. Interview 38; September 16, 2013; Motsoaledi; male, twenty years old.

32. Interview 38; September 16, 2013; Motsoaledi; male, twenty years old.

33. Marcel Paret, "Contested ANC Hegemony in the Urban Townships: Evidence from the 2014 South African Election," *African Affairs* 115, no. 460 (2016): 419–442; Marcel Paret, "Beyond Post-Apartheid Politics? Cleavages, Protest, and Elections in South Africa," *Journal of Modern African Studies* 56, no. 3 (2018): 471–496.

34. Jamy Felton, *Increasingly Non-Partisan, South Africans Willing to Trade Elections for Security, Housing, Jobs*, dispatch no. 248 (Cape Town: Afrobarometer, 2018). With respect to the three main parties, 29 percent of residents felt close to the ANC, and only small proportions felt close to either the EFF (6 percent) or DA (4 percent).

35. Collette Shulz-Herzenberg, "The Decline of Partisan Voting and the Rise of Electoral Uncertainty in South Africa's 2019 General Elections," *Politikon* 46, no. 4 (2019): 462–480.

36. Interview 30; July 22, 2013; Motsoaledi; male.

37. Interview 65; April 17, 2014; Bekkersdal; male, thirty-one years old.

38. Interview 66; April 23, 2014; Tsakane; female, thirty-two years old.

39. Interview 66; April 23, 2014; Tsakane; female, thirty-two years old.

40. Interview 95; June 30, 2015; Tsakane; male, thirty-two years old.

41. Ayanda assured me that the ANC members "were so supportive" of the demands of the protest but that they were "limited by their organization not to be part of the march." Interview 68; April 23, 2014; Tsakane; male, forty years old.

42. Rapule Tabane, "Gun-Wielding ANC Man in Bekkersdal a Former Councilor," *City Press*, March 16, 2014.

43. Interview 110; May 31, 2017; Motsoaledi; male.

44. In my research, activists used notions of community to undermine political divisions more often than they did to stoke such divisions. Conversely, though, altruistic claims to community could serve the narrow interests of individuals seeking upward mobility. See Karl von Holdt, "On Violent Democracy," *Sociological Review* 62, no. S2 (2014): 135.

45. "Press Statement: Motsoaledi Informal Settlement Community Protest," 2010, author's archive.

46. Interview 81; July 29, 2014; Tsakane; male.

47. Interview 68; April 23, 2014; Tsakane; male, forty years old.

48. Interview 50; March 12, 2014; Bekkersdal; male, thirty-three years old; emphasis added.

49. Interview 47; March 12, 2014; Bekkersdal; male, twenty-eight years old.

50. Bheki Simelane, "LGE 2016: In Thembelihle, David Takes on Goliath," *Daily Maverick*, August 2, 2016.

51. Field notes, May 27, 2017, Thembelihle.

52. Interview 68; April 23, 2014; Tsakane; male, forty years old.

53. Interview 104; May 29, 2016; Tsakane; male, thirty-six years old.

54. Interview 94; June 30, 2015; Tsakane; male, thirty-seven years old.

55. Election results accessed at http://www.elections.org.za/.

56. James Scott, *Seeing like a State: How Certain Schemes to Improve the Human Condition Have Failed* (New Haven, CT: Yale University Press, 1998), 4–6.

57. Evans and Heller underscore the turn toward Scott's high modernism in post-apartheid South Africa, given the way in which "the dominant party status of the ANC has more or less insulated the state from subordinate civil society" and limited "feedback mechanisms and countervailing democratic power." Peter B. Evans and Patrick Heller, "Human Development, State Transformation, and the Politics of the Developmental State," in *The Oxford Handbook of Transformations of the State*, ed. Stephan Leibfried, Evelyne Huber, Matthew Lange, Jonah D. Levy, Frank Nullmeier, and John D. Stephens (Oxford: Oxford University Press, 2017), 709.

58. Chipkin, "Contesting Community."

59. Chatterjee, *Politics of the Governed*, 57.

60. Interview 45; January 29, 2014; Motsoaledi; female, fifty-six years old.

61. Interview 67; April 23, 2014; Tsakane; male, thirty-five years old.

62. Interview 60; April 14, 2014; Tsakane; male.

63. Interview 50; March 12, 2014; Bekkersdal; male, thirty-three years old.

64. None of these activist-driven efforts managed to secure a ward councilor seat. As a partial exception, the TCC in Thembelihle did secure, through OKM, one proportional representation seat on the Johannesburg council from 2006 to 2016. The ANC still controlled the ward councilor seat and thus the ward executive in the local Ward 8. Further, OKM lost its single proportional representation seat after poor performance in the 2016 election.

65. Human Sciences Research Council, "Rebellion of the Poor 9: Community Responses," August 30, 2016, accessed September 20, 2017, https://www.youtube.com /watch?v=B8ZloGy4soQ.

66. Human Sciences Research Council, "Rebellion of the Poor."

67. Interview 104; May 29, 2016; Tsakane; male, thirty-six years old.

68. Within the Chinese context, Ching Kwan Lee and Yonghong Zhang refer to this process of using concessions to quell protest as "buying stability." Ching Kwan Lee and Yonghong Zhang, "The Power of Instability: Unraveling the Microfoundations of Bargained Authoritarianism in China," *American Journal of Sociology* 118, no. 6 (2013): 1485–1486.

69. Zachary Levenson, "Precarious Welfare States: Urban Struggles over Housing Delivery in Post-Apartheid South Africa," *International Sociology* 32, no. 4 (2017): 474–492; Marcel Paret, "The Politics of Local Resistance in Urban South Africa: Evidence from Three Informal Settlements," *International Sociology* 33, no. 3 (2018): 349–350.

70. "Press Statement: Motsoaledi Informal Settlement Community Protest," 2010, author's archive.

71. Motsoaledi Concerned Residents, "Memorandum," July 28, 2009, author's archive.

72. Interview 66; April 23, 2014; Tsakane; female, thirty-two years old.

73. Interview 38; September 16, 2013; Motsoaledi; male, twenty years old; emphasis added.

74. Interview 65; April 17, 2014; Bekkersdal; male, thirty-one years old.

75. Interview 65; April 17, 2014; Bekkersdal; male, thirty-one years old.

76. Interview 75; May 30, 2014; Bekkersdal; male, forty-one years old.

77. Edward Webster, "The Rise of Social-Movement Unionism: The Two Faces of the Black Trade Union Movement in South Africa," in *State, Resistance, and Change in South Africa*, ed. Philip Frankel, Noam Pines, and Mark Swilling (London: Croom Helm, 1988), 185–187; Edward Webster, "'Stay-Aways' and the Black Working Class: Evaluating a Strategy," *Labor, Capital, and Society* 14, no. 1 (1981): 10–38.

78. Webster notes, "A stay-away is similar to a general strike in that it involves a general withdrawal of labor that does not focus on specific plant-based issues." Webster, "'Stay-Aways,'" 11.

79. Marcel Paret, "The Community Strike: From Precarity to Militant Organizing," *International Journal of Comparative Sociology* 61, no. 2–3 (2020): 159–177.

80. Andrew, a Tsakane10 activist, argued that unemployed residents were "pushing forward" local struggles around service delivery. In contrast to workers who experienced nice facilities at their workplaces—"their factories are well equipped, they have water, they have everything"—unemployed residents had to wrestle with the everyday challenges of living in poverty: "They are always here and are the ones that come across all these problems. . . . If there is a dust here during the day, they would feel the dust. . . . If there is no water, you must go to the nearest communal tap, join a queue, and make sure that there's water for food, there's water for washing, there is water to bath. For those who are unemployed, I think they do all these chores for the employed. . . . So now you encounter problems. So now we are saying we must fight so that we have water here in the yard. We must fight so that we have houses, so that it can be easy for you to clean. . . . In a shack like this, you clean now; in the next four minutes, there is dust; you must clean again." Interview 95; June 30, 2015; Tsakane; male, thirty-two years old.

81. Interview 66; April 23, 2014; Tsakane; female, thirty-two years old.

82. Interview 38; September 16, 2013; Motsoaledi; male, twenty years old.

83. Interview 66; April 23, 2014; Tsakane; female, thirty-two years old.

84. Dawson notes a similar antagonism in Zandspruit. Hannah Dawson, "Youth Politics: Waiting and Envy in a South African Informal Settlement," *Journal of Southern African Studies* 40, no. 4 (2014): 878.

85. Interview 38; September 16, 2013; Motsoaledi; male, twenty years old; emphasis added.

86. Interview 88; August 2, 2014; Thembelihle; male, twenty-five years old.

87. Interview 80; June 20, 2014; Bekkersdal; female, twenty-three years old.

4. NATIONALISM

1. Jean Pierre Misago, Tamlyn Monson, Tara Polzer, and Loren Landau, *May 2008 Violence against Foreign Nationals in South Africa: Understanding Causes and Evaluating Responses* (Johannesburg: Forced Migration Studies Program, 2010).

2. Eric Worby, Shireen Hassim, and Tawana Kupe, "Introduction," in *Go Home or Die Here: Violence, Xenophobia and the Reinvention of Difference in South Africa*, ed. Shireen Hassim, Tawana Kupe, and Eric Worby (Johannesburg: Wits University Press, 2008), 3.

3. Michael Neocosmos, *From "Foreign Natives" to "Native Foreigners": Explaining Xenophobia in Post-Apartheid South Africa* (Dakar: CODESRIA, 2010), 22–59.

4. This distinction resembles what John Lie calls horizontal/political racism and vertical/economic racism. John Lie, *Modern Peoplehood* (Cambridge, MA: Harvard University Press, 2004), 170.

5. Jonathan Crush and Sujata Ramachandran, "Doing Business with Xenophobia," in *Mean Streets: Migration, Xenophobia and Informality in South Africa*, ed. Jonathan Crush, Abel Chikanda, and Caroline Skinner (Waterloo, Canada: Southern African Migration Program, 2015), 25–59. The estimate provided by the authors for 2014 includes reports through August. I multiplied the 2014 estimate by 1.5 to get the annual average for the entire period.

6. Karl von Holdt and Peter Alexander, "Collective Violence, Community Protest, and Xenophobia," *South African Review of Sociology* 43, no. 2 (2012): 104–111; Karl von Holdt, "The Violence of Orders, the Orders of Violence: Between Fanon and Bourdieu," *Current Sociology* 61, no. 2 (2012): 112–131; Marcel Paret, "Violence and Democracy in South Africa's Community Protests," *Review of African Political Economy* 42, no. 143 (2015): 107–123.

7. Neocosmos, *From "Foreign Natives,"* 14.

8. Lie, *Modern Peoplehood*, 144–190; Andreas Wimmer, *Ethnic Boundary Making: Institutions, Power, Networks* (Oxford: Oxford University Press, 2013), 90–92.

9. Nandita Sharma, *Home Rule: National Sovereignty and the Separation of Natives and Migrants* (Durham, NC: Duke University Press, 2020).

10. Marcel Paret, "Migration Politics: Mobilizing Against Economic Insecurity in the United States and South Africa," *International Journal of Comparative Sociology* 59, no. 1 (2018): 3–24.

11. Neocosmos, *From "Foreign Natives."*

12. Sally Peberdy, *Selecting Immigrants: National Identity and South Africa's Immigration Policies, 1910–2008* (Johannesburg: Wits University Press, 2009), 158–169; Michael Neocosmos, "The Politics of Fear and the Fear of Politics: Reflections on Xenophobic Violence in South Africa," *Journal of Asian and African Studies* 43, no. 6 (2008): 586–594.

13. Peberdy, *Selecting Immigrants*, 162–169.

14. Neocosmos, *From "Foreign Natives,"* 71.

15. Southern African Migration Project, *The Perfect Storm: The Realities of Xenophobia in Contemporary South Africa* (Cape Town: Southern African Migration Project, 2008), 44.

16. Dineo Bendile, "Home Affairs Minister: SA Must Tighten Its Immigration Policies," *Mail and Guardian*, June 1, 2017.

17. Savo Heleta, "Xenophobia and Party Politics in South Africa," *Mail and Guardian*, September 3, 2019.

18. Jonathan Crush and Sujata Ramachandran, *Xenophobic Violence in South Africa: Denialism, Minimalism, Realism* (Cape Town: Southern African Migration Program, 2014).

19. Greg Nicolson, "Freedom Day? SANDF Conducts Johannesburg Stop-and-Search Patrols," *Daily Maverick*, April 27, 2015.

20. Qaanita Hunter, "Zuma Says 'Sister Countries' Add to Xenophobia," *Mail and Guardian*, April 27, 2015.

21. Mia Lindeque, "Deputy Police Min Accuses Foreign Nationals in Hillbrow of Economic Sabotage," *Eyewitness News*, July 14, 2017.

22. Loren B. Landau, "Loving the Alien? Citizenship, Law, and the Future in South Africa's Demonic Society," *African Affairs* 109, no. 435 (2010): 221.

23. Landau, "Loving the Alien?," 222–224; Neocosmos, "Politics of Fear," 588–589.

24. Themba Masuku, "Targeting Foreigners: Xenophobia among Johannesburg's Police," *South African Crime Quarterly* 15 (March 2006): 21.

25. Darshan Vigneswaran, "The Complex Sources of Immigration Control," *International Migration Review* 54, no. 1 (2020): 262–288.

26. Nicolson, "Freedom Day?"

27. Christa Kuljian, *Sanctuary: How an Inner-City Church Spilled onto a Sidewalk* (Auckland Park, South Africa: Jacana, 2013).

28. Richard Poplak, "Clean Up the Rubbish: What Happened to the People of Central Methodist Church?," *Daily Maverick*, May 12, 2015.

29. Jonisayi Maromo, "The Numbers behind Operation Fiela," *Mail and Guardian*, September 7, 2015.

30. Trynos Gumbo, "Resilience and Innovation: Migrant Spaza Shop Entrepreneurs in Soweto, Johannesburg," in *Mean Streets: Migration, Xenophobia and Informality in South Africa*, ed. Jonathan Crush, Abel Chikanda, and Caroline Skinner (Waterloo, Canada: Southern African Migration Program, 2015), 100–112.

31. Sally Peberdy, *Informal Sector Enterprise and Employment in Gauteng* (Johannesburg: Gauteng City-Region Observatory, 2015), 8.

32. Christi van der Westhuizen, "Torn between Two Discourses," *The Star*, August 30, 2011.

33. Quinton Mtyala, "Cele's Xenophobic Outburst," *Cape Times*, October 7, 2011.

34. South African Press Association, "Minister's Facebook Post Unrelated to Soweto Unrest," *News24*, January 29, 2015.

35. Kwanele Sosibo, Phillip de Wet, and Thuletho Zwane, "Township Politics Fuel the Attacks on 'Outsiders,'" *Mail and Guardian*, January 29, 2015.

36. Khulekani Magubane, "Reveal Trade Secrets, Minister Tells Foreigners," *Business Day*, January 28, 2015.

37. South Africans were especially hostile to those living in the country illegally. Less than one-quarter of residents believed that undocumented migrants should have access to social services (16 percent) or police protection (22 percent), whereas roughly half (50 percent and 54 percent, respectively) believed that legally residing migrants should have such access. Crush and Ramachandran, *Xenophobic Violence*, 17–18.

38. Crush and Ramachandran, 19.

39. Only a small proportion of respondents interpreted the violence as justifiable (15 percent) or agreed that migrants deserved what happened to them (14 percent), but significant proportions were indifferent on both of these questions (42 percent and 33 percent, respectively). Crush and Ramachandran, 21.

40. Godwin Dube, "Black South Africans' Attitudes toward African Immigrants between 2008 and 2016," *Nationalism and Ethnic Politics* 25, no. 2 (2019): 198.

41. Misago et al., *May 2008 Violence*, 165–167.

42. South African Press Association, "Anatomy of Poverty," *IOL News*, July 17, 2008.

43. Interview 35; August 6, 2013; Motsoaledi; female.

44. David Everatt, *"That Violence Was Just the Beginning": Views on "Foreigners" and the May 2008 Xenophobic Violence as Expressed in Focus Groups Staged at the Time* (Johannesburg: Gauteng City Regional Observatory, 2009), 4.

45. Misago et al., *May 2008 Violence*, 113; Everatt, "That Violence," 22.

46. Xinhua News, "South Africa Politicians Urged to Boost Anti-Xenophobia Service," *Xinhua News*, May 27, 2011.

47. Philippa Kerr, Kevin Durrheim, and John Dixon note the close connection between "anti-foreigner discourses and discourses of liberation and struggle." Philippa Kerr, Kevin Durrheim, and John Dixon, "Xenophobic Violence and Struggle Discourse in South Africa," *Journal of Asian and African Studies* 54, no. 7 (2019): 996. For some residents, xenophobic attacks represented attempts to bolster the state by taking the law into their own hands and shoring up the border. Landau, "Loving the Alien?," 228; Mis-

ago et al., *May 2008 Violence*, 58; Tamlyn Monson, "Making the Law; Breaking the Law; Taking the Law into Our Own Hands: Sovereignty and Territorial Control in Three South African Settlements," in *Exorcising the Demons Within: Xenophobia, Violence, and Statecraft in Contemporary South Africa*, ed. Loren B. Landau (Tokyo: United Nations University Press, 2012), 172–199.

48. Edna Bonacich, "A Theory of Middleman Minorities," *American Sociological Review* 38, no. 5 (1973): 583–594.

49. Bonacich, "Theory of Middleman Minorities," 592.

50. Interview 70; May 6, 2014; Bekkersdal; male, thirty-one years old.

51. Interview 80; June 20, 2014; Bekkersdal; female, twenty-three years old.

52. Interview 77; June 12, 2014; Bekkersdal; male, twenty-one years old.

53. Bonacich, "Theory of Middleman Minorities," 591.

54. "Still, the African Diaspora Forum (ADF) notes that Somali, Bangladeshi, Pakistani and Ethiopian shop owners are targeted during robberies, looting and extortion countrywide." Godfrey Mulaudzi, Lizette Lancaster, and Gabriel Hertis, "Busting South Africa's Xenophobic Myths Starts at Grassroots," Institute for Security Studies, April 12, 2021, https://issafrica.org/iss-today/busting-south-africas-xenophobic-myths-starts-at-grassroots.

55. Jeremy Seekings, "The Continuing Salience of Race: Discrimination and Diversity in South Africa," *Journal of Contemporary African Studies* 26, no. 1 (2008): 1–25.

56. Interview 88; August 2, 2014; Thembelihle; male, twenty-five years old.

57. Interview 88; August 2, 2014; Thembelihle; male, twenty-five years old.

58. Interview 88; August 2, 2014; Thembelihle; male, twenty-five years old.

59. Interview 49; March 12, 2014; Bekkersdal; female.

60. Roger Southall, "The ANC and Black Capitalism in South Africa," *Review of African Political Economy* 31, no. 100 (2004): 313–328.

61. Nadya Bawa, "Family-Owned Business in South Africa: Local Enterprise Responses by South African Indian-Owned Business," *Urban Forum* 17, no. 2 (2006): 167–198; Keith Hart and Vishnu Padayachee, "Indian Business in South Africa after Apartheid: New and Old Trajectories," *Comparative Studies in Society and History* 42, no. 4 (2000): 683–712.

62. Bonacich, "Theory of Middleman Minorities," 589–590.

63. Gary Baines, "Racist Hate Speech in South Africa's Fragile Democracy: The Case of Ngema's 'AmaNdiya,'" in *Popular Music Censorship in Africa*, ed. Michael Drewett and Martin Cloonan (Abingdon, UK: Ashgate, 2006), 55.

64. Nandi was not overly enthusiastic about Zimbabweans, but she noted that they "can stay" because the country "is already messed up there is nothing they can do." Interview 31; July 22, 2013; Motsoaledi; one female and one male.

65. Interview 81; July 29, 2014; Tsakane; male. Often translated as "coolie," some critics understand the term *amakula* as a derogatory slur. While general usage of the term may reflect or promote unequal power or discrimination, many individuals used it without any apparent malicious intent. Robert, for example, seemed to use the term descriptively, not disparagingly. Debate surged in 2011 when Julius Malema, then president of the ANC Youth League, used the term in a speech to Thembelihle residents. Sipho Hlongwane, "Malema May Face Court over the 'Makula' Slur," *Daily Maverick*, November 7, 2011.

66. Dube, "Black South Africans' Attitudes," 199.

67. Bonacich suggests that "middleman minorities" prioritize "law and order" to protect their businesses and therefore "tend to oppose disruptive political movements." In the South African case, the antimigrant environment that protests often produced was at least as important as law and order. Bonacich, "Theory of Middleman Minorities," 591.

68. Interview 90; June 27, 2015; Thembelihle; male, thirty-five years old.

69. Crush and Ramachandran, "Doing Business with Xenophobia," 48–49; Crush and Ramachandran, *Xenophobic Violence.*

70. Interview 89; June 27, 2015; Thembelihle; male, thirty-eight years old.

71. Interview 89; June 27, 2015; Thembelihle; male, thirty-eight years old.

72. Misago et al., *May 2008 Violence,* 167.

73. Interview 37; September 4, 2013; Motsoaledi; female.

74. Interview 49; March 12, 2014; Bekkersdal; female.

75. Interview 75; May 30, 2014; Bekkersdal; male, forty-one years old.

76. Interview 41; September 30, 2013; three female, two male.

77. Interview 31; July 22, 2013; Motsoaledi; one female and one male.

78. Interview 97; July 2, 2015; Bekkersdal; female, twenty-three years old.

79. Interview 94; June 30, 2015; Tsakane; male, thirty-seven years old.

80. Author's archive.

81. Interview 94; June 30, 2015; Tsakane; male, thirty-seven years old.

82. Trevor Ngwane and Nonhlanhla Vilakazi, *Social Movement Responses to Xenophobia: A Case Study of the Soweto Electricity Crisis Committee; The Anti-Privatization Forum, and the Coalition Against Xenophobia* (Bermuda: Atlantic Philanthropies, 2010), 13.

83. Ngwane and Vilakazi, *Social Movement Responses,* 29.

84. Department of Home Affairs, "The Winners of the 2016 Mkhaya Migrants Awards," December 12, 2016, accessed November 2, 2017, http://www.dha.gov.za/index .php/statements-speeches/920-the-winners-of-the-2016-mkhaya-migrants-awards; Planact, "Thembelihle Community Cohesion against Xenophobia," YouTube video, July 25, 2016, accessed November 2, 2017, https://www.youtube.com/watch?v=E3XEOLgdA-I&fea ture=youtu.be.

5. CLASS POLITICS

1. Ira Katznelson, *City Trenches: Urban Planning and the Patterning of Class in the United States* (New York: Pantheon, 1981).

2. Antonio Gramsci, *Selections from the Prison Notebooks,* ed. and trans. Quintin Hoare and Geoffrey Nowell Smith (New York: International Publishers, 1971), 181. In a similar analysis, Patrick Heller distinguishes between the horizontal and vertical dimensions of civil society. Patrick Heller, "Democracy, Participatory Politics and Development: Some Comparative Lessons from Brazil, India, and South Africa," *Polity* 44, no. 4 (2012): 646–648; Patrick Heller, "Divergent Trajectories of Democratic Deepening: Comparing Brazil, India, and South Africa," *Theory and Society* 48 (2019): 358–359.

3. Gramsci, *Selections,* 181.

4. Gramsci, *Selections,* 181.

5. The quote refers to Booysen's description of her "ballot-and-brick" theory. Susan Booysen, "'The Ballot and the Brick'—Enduring under Duress," in *Local Elections in South Africa: Parties, People and Politics,* ed. Susan Booysen, (Bloemfontein, South Africa: Sun Press, 2011), 295–314. For the interpretation of local protest as stemming from internal ANC factionalism, see Karl von Holdt, "On Violent Democracy," *Sociological Review* 62, no. S2 (2014): 135; Karl von Holdt, "South Africa: The Transition to Violent Democracy," *Review of African Political Economy* 40, no. 138 (2013): 589–604; and Karl von Holdt, Malose Langa, Sepetla Molapo, Nomfundo Mogapi, Kindiza Ngubeni, Jacob Dlamini, and Adele Kirsten, *The Smoke that Calls: Insurgent Citizenship, Collective Violence and the Struggle for a Place in the New South Africa* (Johannesburg: SWOP, 2011).

6. Partha Chatterjee, *Lineages of Political Society: Studies in Postcolonial Democracy* (New York: Columbia University Press, 2011), 219.

7. Patrick Heller, "Democratic Deepening in India and South Africa," *Journal of Asian and African Studies* 44, no. 1 (2009): 134–137; Heller, "Democracy, Participatory Politics," 651, 654–655, 658, 664; Heller, "Divergent Trajectories," 364; Heidi Brooks, "The Mass Movement and Public Policy: Discourses of Participatory Democracy in Post-1994 South Africa," *Journal of Modern African Studies* 55, no. 1 (2017): 105–127.

8. Local elections in South Africa have two ballots, one to determine local ward councilors and the other to determine the proportional representation of political parties on the city council. Independent candidates only stand on the ward councilor ballot.

9. As of the 2019 national government elections, for example, the big three of the ANC, DA, and EFF secured 85 percent of the vote in Bekkersdal, 93 percent in Motsoaledi, and 95 percent in Tsakane10 and Thembelihle.

10. Prior to the EFF, the three main breakaways from the ANC included the Pan Africanist Congress of Azania (PAC, founded 1959), the United Democratic Movement (UDM, founded 1997), and the Congress of the People (COPE, founded 2008). Between 2006 and 2019, these three parties never reached higher than 10 percent in the focal voting stations of the case study areas, and in 2016 and 2019 they remained below 5 percent.

11. The EFF also had to compete with the Azanian People's Organization (AZAPO), founded in 1978–1979 as a continuation of the BC movement. Within Bekkersdal (voting station 33030515), AZAPO performed slightly better during local government elections (19 percent, 22 percent, and 14 percent in 2006, 2011, and 2016, respectively) than it did during national government elections (6–12 percent between 2004 and 2019).

12. Interview 110; May 31, 2017; Motsoaledi; male.

13. On anarchist organizing in Motsoaledi and Gauteng Province, see Leroy Maisiri, Philip Nyalungu and Lucien van der Walt, "Anarchist/Syndicalist and Independent Marxist Intersections in Post-Apartheid Struggles, South Africa: The WSF/ZACF Current in Gauteng, 1990s–2010s," *Globalizations* 17, no. 5 (2020): 797–819.

14. Interview 111; June 14, 2017; phone; male, forty-three years old.

15. Interview 111; June 14, 2017; phone; male, forty-three years old.

16. Interview 111; June 14, 2017; phone; male, forty-three years old.

17. The OKM held its public launch in Motsoaledi. Field notes, Johannesburg, May 19, 2017, informal discussion with OKM activist.

18. "A major blow was the capture of MCR by ANC supporters." Maisiri, Nyalungu, and van der Walt, "Anarchist/Syndicalist," 813.

19. Within Motsoaledi (voting station 32862719), the OKM secured 7 percent support on the proportional representation ballot in 2006 but disappeared afterward, securing less than 1 percent in 2011 and 2016.

20. Interview 111; June 14, 2017; phone; male, forty-three years old.

21. Interview 100; May 22, 2016; Motsoaledi; male, thirty-six years old.

22. Interview 41; September 30, 2013; three females and two males.

23. Mark Olalde, "Protesters Demand Services and Housing," *The Star*, April 18, 2013.

24. Interview 110; May 31, 2017; Motsoaledi; male.

25. Field notes, Motsoaledi, July 30, 2013.

26. Interview 110; May 31, 2017; Motsoaledi; male.

27. Interview 100; May 22, 2016; Motsoaledi; three males, twenty-six years old, twenty-eight years old, and thirty-six years old.

28. Graeme Gotz and Mark Shaw, "The Election on the Reef: Choice and First-Time Voters in Gauteng (the PWV)," in *Launching Democracy in South Africa: The First Open Election, April 1994*, ed. R. W. Johnson and Lawrence Schlemmer (New Haven, CT: Yale University Press, 1996), 220. Like many Black townships, Bekkersdal experienced bloody "internal" conflict during the early 1990s. The conflict ensued in different configurations.

AZAPO first aligned with the IFP against the ANC and second with the ANC against the IFP.

29. Thapelo Lekgowa and Greg Nicolson, "Bekkersdal Protests: 'Dirty Votes' and the ANC in the Eye of the Storm," *Daily Maverick*, October 30, 2013.

30. Interview 75; May 30, 2014; Bekkersdal; male, forty-one years old.

31. Interview 74; May 14, 2014; male, forty-one years old.

32. Field notes, Johannesburg workshop, October 14, 2017.

33. Amanda Watson, "Bekkersdal Makes Its Own Peace," *Citizen*, April 28, 2014.

34. Interview 53; March 26, 2014; Bekkersdal; male, forty-four years old.

35. Field notes, Westonaria, June 5, 2014.

36. Interview 109; May 24, 2017; Bekkersdal; two females.

37. Interview 109; May 24, 2017; Bekkersdal; two females.

38. The People's Movement, "Draft Guiding Document," 2014, author's archive.

39. Interview 104; May 29, 2016; Tsakane; two males, thirty-six years old and unknown age.

40. On the United Front mobilization, see Marcel Paret, "Working-Class Fragmentation, Party Politics, and the Complexities of Solidarity in South Africa's United Front," *Sociological Review* 65, no. 2 (2017): 267–284; Marcel Paret, "NUMSA Strike and the United Front," *South African Labor Bulletin* 38 (May/June 2014): 23–26.

41. Interview 68; April 23, 2014; Tsakane; male, forty years old.

42. Interview 87; August 1, 2014; Nigel; male, thirty-eight years old; emphasis added.

43. Interview 95; June 30, 2015; Tsakane; male, thirty-two years old.

44. Interview 104; May 29, 2016; Tsakane; two males, thirty-six years old and unknown age.

45. Interview 95; June 30, 2015; Tsakane; male, thirty-two years old.

46. The NUMSA Secretariat Report to the December 2013 Special National Congress raised concern that unemployed youth were "a less reliable class force" that was susceptible to "populist" politics, which could be "dangerous to the interests of workers." It concluded that workers might be able to win over unemployed youth to the "socialist struggle" but that "they need the leadership of the organized working class." National Union of Metalworkers South Africa, "NUMSA Special National Congress, December 17 to 20, 2013: Secretariat Report," accessed April 26, 2016, http://www.numsa.org.za/wp-content/uploads/2013/12/Secretariat-Report-as-in-.pdf.

47. National Union of Metalworkers South Africa, "NUMSA Special National Congress."

48. Samantha Ashman and Nicolas Pons-Vignon, "South Africa's Troubled Alliance and the Road Ahead: An Interview with Karl Cloete," *The Bullet: Socialist Project E-Bulletin* 1092 (2015), https://socialistproject.ca/2015/03/b1092/. These political positions regenerated concerns that were central to previous debates between "workerists" and "populists" (see chap. 2).

49. Interview 87; August 1, 2014; Nigel; male, thirty-eight years old.

50. Interview 94; June 30, 2015; Tsakane; male, thirty-seven years old.

51. Field notes, Johannesburg workshop; October 14, 2017.

52. Interview 95; June 30, 2015; Tsakane; male, thirty-two years old.

53. Interview 104; May 29, 2016; Tsakane; two males, thirty-six years old and unknown age.

54. Paret, "Working-Class Fragmentation."

55. Interview 95; June 30, 2015; Tsakane; male, thirty-two years old.

56. The United Front's weak performance and its emphasis on formal organization echoed the criticisms of Frances Fox Piven and Richard A. Cloward, *Poor People's Movements: Why They Succeed, How They Fail* (New York: Vintage 1979).

57. Political Coordination Committee of the United Front, "At the Crossroads . . . a Political Assessment of the United Front," December 2015, author's archives.

58. Tido, a KCWF activist who also took up a formal position within the local United Front structure, explained: "In Kwatsaduza Community Forum we discuss the issues of the community and their needs. Here at the United Front, we discuss political issues and building the political party." Interview 96; June 30, 2015; Tsakane; male, forty years old.

59. Interview 82; July 29, 2014; Tsakane; male.

60. Interview 104; May 29, 2016; Tsakane; two males, thirty-six years old and unknown age.

61. This was not an aberration, as the United Front fared poorly across the country. The United Front's national secretary Mazibuko Jara posted a critical public comment on Facebook about their mistakes and the absence of a left-wing force in the country. He concluded, "It is not failure that we should lament about; but the lessons learnt from the experience. . . . A revolutionary movement . . . cannot emerge from the Unions. Nor can they lead it. That was the mistake and fallacy of the now collapsed Numsa moment." Mazibuko Jara, untitled Facebook post, accessed August 14, 2016, https://www.facebook.com/mazibuko.jara/posts/10210264352188330.

62. Interview 95; June 30, 2015; Tsakane; male, thirty-two years old.

63. On the antieviction campaign, see Michael Clark, *An Anatomy of Dissent and Repression: The Criminal Justice System and the 2011 Thembelihle Protest* (Johannesburg: Socio-Economic Rights Institute of South Africa, 2014); and Socio-Economic Rights Institute of South Africa, *Thembelihle: Engaging an Unresponsive State* (Johannesburg: Socio-Economic Rights Institute of South Africa, 2014), 11–16.

64. Interview 105; August 5, 2016; Thembelihle; male, twenty-seven years old.

65. Interview 108; Thembelihle; May 23, 2017; female, thirty-eight years old.

66. Operation Khanyisa Movement, "The Voter's Pledge," 2016, author's archive.

67. Interview 108; May 23, 2017; Thembelihle; female, thirty-eight years old.

68. In Zwane's view, politicians were usually "politically deployed there not because of what to do with the challenges or changing people's lives but just giving the opportunity that your father was in the struggle long ago and now we [are] putting you here as a candidate." In contrast, OKM representatives forfeited their salary to the organization, which in turn paid them a "living wage" that amounted to less than half of the original salary. Interview 108; May 23, 2017; Thembelihle; female, thirty-eight years old.

69. Operation Khanyisa Movement, "Electricity Is Not a Gift from the ANC—We Fought for It," July 2016, author's archive. *Emarobhothini* translates roughly into English as "at the robots," signaling the key way in which Thembelihle residents protested: by blocking the road at the nearby traffic light or robot.

70. Bheki Simelane, "LGE 2016: In Thembelihle, David Takes On Goliath," *Daily Maverick*, August 2, 2016, emphasis added.

71. Simelane, "LGE 2016."

72. This included debates over who controlled the organization and how they made decisions. At least partially due to internal divisions, the TCC failed to retain its single seat on the local ten-person ward committee. On the relationship between the TCC and the ward committee, see Anneke Le Roux, "Contesting Invited Spaces: Where a Ward Committee and a Social Movement Meet," *Transformation* 89 (2015): 87–111.

73. Field notes, Thembelihle, May 20, 2017.

CONCLUSION

1. Doug McAdam, John D. McCarthy, and Mayer N. Zald, eds, *Comparative Perspectives on Social Movements: Political Opportunities, Mobilizing Structures, and Cultural Framings* (Cambridge: Cambridge University Press, 1996).

2. Donatella della Porta, "Political Economy and Social Movement Studies: The Class Basis of Anti-Austerity Protest," *Anthropological Theory* 17, no. 4 (2017): 453–473; Donatella della Porta, *Social Movements in Times of Austerity* (Cambridge: Polity, 2015); Colin Barker, Laurence Cox, John Krinsky, and Alf Gunvald Nilsen, *Marxism and Social Movements* (Leiden, Netherlands: Brill, 2013); Laurence Cox and Alf Gunvald Nilsen, *We Make Our Own History: Marxism and Social Movements in the Twilight of Neoliberalism* (London: Pluto Press, 2014).

3. John D. McCarthy and Mayer Zald, "Resource Mobilization and Social Movements: A Partial Theory," *American Journal of Sociology* 82, no. 6 (1977): 1212–1241.

4. On the idea of economic threats, see Paul Almeida, *Mobilizing Democracy: Globalization and Citizen Protest* (Baltimore: Johns Hopkins University Press, 2014). This approach is consistent with Aldon Morris's recent call for a Du Boisian approach to social movements, which emphasizes the lived experiences, grievances, and political orientations of subaltern groups, as well as their relationships to broader forces of racism, colonialism, slavery, empire, and capitalism. Aldon Morris, "Social Movement Theory: Lessons from the Sociology of W. E. B. Du Bois," *Mobilization* 24, no. 2 (2019): 125–136.

5. James M. Jasper and Jan Willem Duyvendak, *Players and Arenas: The Interactive Dynamics of Protest* (Amsterdam: Amsterdam University Press, 2015); James M. Jasper and Brayden G. King, *Protesters and Their Targets* (Philadelphia: Temple University Press, 2020).

6. Doug McAdam, "Conceptual Origins, Current Problems, and Future Directions," in *Comparative Perspectives on Social Movements: Political Opportunities, Mobilizing Structures, and Cultural Framings*, ed. Doug McAdam, John D. McCarthy, and Mayer N. Zald (Cambridge: Cambridge University Press, 1996), 23–40.

7. On postapartheid repression, see Jane Duncan, *Protest Nation: The Right to Protest in South Africa* (Pietermaritzburg, South Africa: University of KwaZulu-Natal Press, 2016); Marcel Paret, "Violence and Democracy in South Africa's Community Protests," *Review of African Political Economy* 42, no. 143 (2015): 107–123.

8. Gillian Hart, *Rethinking the South African Crisis: Nationalism, Populism, Hegemony* (Athens: University of Georgia Press, 2014), chap. 5.

9. Tianna Paschel, *Becoming Black Political Subjects: Movements and Ethno-Racial Rights in Colombia and Brazil* (Princeton, NJ: Princeton University Press, 2016), 227–229.

10. Howard Winant, *Racial Conditions: Politics, Theory, Comparisons* (Minneapolis: University of Minnesota Press, 1994), 111–129; Howard Winant, *The World Is a Ghetto: Race and Democracy Since World War II* (New York: Basic Books, 2001), 305–308; Howard Winant, *The New Politics of Race: Globalism, Difference, Justice* (Minneapolis: University of Minnesota Press, 2004), 108–121; Michael Omi and Howard Winant, *Racial Formation in the United States: From the 1960s to the 1990s*, 3rd ed. (New York: Routledge, 2014).

11. Winant, *Racial Conditions*, 125–126.

12. Winant, *The World Is a Ghetto*.

13. For a critique of Winant that similarly emphasizes capitalism, among other dynamics, see Jodi Melamed, *Represent and Destroy: Rationalizing Violence in the New Racial Capitalism* (Minneapolis: University of Minnesota Press, 2011).

14. The difference may partially reflect my focus on South Africa. Indeed, in a comparative analysis of the United States and South Africa that deviates slightly from *The World Is a Ghetto*, Winant suggests that in the case of South Africa, the central "dilemma" is not so much racial hegemony but the way that global capital influences and constrains the ANC. Winant, *New Politics of Race*, 118–121.

15. Keeanga-Yamahtta Taylor, *From #BlackLivesMatter to Black Liberation* (Chicago: Haymarket, 2016); Cedric Johnson, *Revolutionaries to Race Leaders: Black Power and the Making of African American Politics* (Minneapolis: University of Minnesota Press, 2007).

16. Omi and Winant, *Racial Formation*, 161–190.

17. On the spirit of resistance following Marikana, see Luke Sinwell and Siphiwe Mbatha, *The Spirit of Marikana: The Rise of Insurgent Trade Unionism within South Africa* (London: Pluto Press, 2016); Peter Alexander, "Marikana: Turning Point in South African History," *Review of African Political Economy* 40, no. 138 (2013): 605–619; Marcel Paret and Carin Runciman, "The 2009+ South African Protest Wave," *Journal of Labor and Society* 19, no. 3 (2016): 301–319.

18. This separation was difficult to maintain. Many observers, including local activists, understood the UF as a precursor to a future political party, and some believed that NUMSA would abandon the UF once the new party came to fruition. NUMSA officials countered this interpretation. At the 2014 National Preparatory Assembly for the United Front, the NUMSA deputy general secretary Karl Cloete remarked, "Even as the Workers' Party is established, this United Front must be non-aligned to that Workers' Party, and must continue to be an independent formation." "United Front Established a 25 Member National Working Committee," *SABC Digital News*, December 14, 2014, accessed January 23, 2015, https://www.youtube.com/watch?v=pH5NOWdO4II.

19. The debate took place at the University of Johannesburg. Fieldwork, Johannesburg, July 1, 2015. The discussion and quotes in this paragraph derive from my own field notes and recording of the debate.

20. Field notes, Johannesburg, July 1, 2015.

21. Field notes, Johannesburg, July 1, 2015. The EFF secured 1.17 million votes (6.4 percent) in the 2014 national government elections, 1.23 million votes (8.2 percent) on the proportional representation ballot in the 2016 local government elections, and 1.88 million votes (10.8 percent) in the 2019 national government elections.

22. Like the UF, initiated by NUMSA, the APF also drew support from organized labor. The latter emerged out of union-supported struggles against privatization at the city of Johannesburg and the University of the Witwatersrand. The opposing unions, the South African Municipal Workers Union (SAMWU) and the National Education Health and Allied Workers Union (NEHAWU), were affiliates of the Congress of South African Trade Unions (COSATU), which initially supported the APF but later withdrew support as the ANC cracked down on oppositional movements. Some within the APF remained committed to union-community alliances, but these efforts did not get very far. Marcel Paret, "Labor and Community Struggles, 1994–2014," in *New South African Review 5: Beyond Marikana*, ed. Gilbert M. Khadiagala, Prishani Naidoo, Devan Pillay, and Roger Southall (Johannesburg: Wits University Press, 2015), 34–47.

23. Sam Ashman, Zachary Levenson, and Trevor Ngwane, "South Africa's ANC: The Beginning of the End?," *Catalyst* 1 (Summer 2017): 95–97, 105–106.

24. Frances Fox Piven and Richard A. Cloward, *Poor People's Movements: Why They Succeed, How They Fail* (New York: Vintage 1979).

25. In defense of an election-oriented left strategy in South Africa, Benjamin Fogel writes: "For better or worse, elections are the political arena that South Africans participate in the most." Benjamin Fogel, "It's Not Right for SA's Left to Reject Elections," *Mail and Guardian*, June 6, 2019.

26. Zuma's manipulation of the Ministry of Finance, including his sacking of Pravin Gordhan in March 2017, helped to galvanize popular resistance. On the extent of corruption under the Zuma administration, see Ivor Chipkin and Mark Swilling, *Shadow State: The Politics of State Capture* (Johannesburg: Wits University Press, 2018).

27. Carin Runciman, Linah Nkuna, and Pier Paolo Frassinelli, "Survey Sheds Light on Who Marched against President Zuma and Why," *The Conversation*, April 20, 2017. Save South Africa and left activists associated with the Democratic Left Front (DLF) occupied Church Square, located in central Pretoria, in the week before the anti-Zuma

protest. It was a strange pairing, given the DLF's anticapitalist politics and Save South Africa's roots within the business community.

28. The political commentator Richard Poplak recounted, "This could not have been confused for anything other than an EFF event." Richard Poplak, "At the Day of National Action, Malema Makes Friends—100,000 of Them," *Daily Maverick*, April 13, 2017.

29. Marcel Paret, Carin Runciman, and Luke Sinwell, *Southern Resistance in Critical Perspective: The Politics of Protest in South Africa's Contentious Democracy* (New York: Routledge, 2017); Paret and Runciman, "2009+ South African Protest."

30. Riley notes: "When a social class is truly hegemonic, it does not require organization into a party. As Gramsci himself was aware, the most well-established capitalist classes never ruled through a single party but rather through a system of alternating political parties." Dylan Riley, "Hegemony and Democracy in Gramsci's *Prison Notebooks*," in *Building Blocs: How Parties Organize Society*, ed. Cedric de Leon, Manali Desai, and Cihan Tugal (Stanford, CA: Stanford University Press, 2015), 185.

31. This is a matter of debate. Some scholars suggest that passive revolution is a pathway to or synonymous with capitalist hegemony. See Hart, *Rethinking the South African*; Cihan Tugal, *Passive Revolution: Absorbing the Islamic Challenge to Capitalism* (Stanford, CA: Stanford University Press, 2009), 32.

32. Dylan Riley, *The Civic Foundations of Fascism in Europe: Italy, Spain, and Romania* (Baltimore: Johns Hopkins University Press, 2010).

METHODOLOGICAL APPENDIX

1. For further details about these protest interviews, see Marcel Paret, "Working-Class Fragmentation, Party Politics, and the Complexities of Solidarity in South Africa's United Front," *Sociological Review* 65, no. 2 (2017): 267–284; Marcel Paret, "COSATU and Community Struggles: Assessing the Prospects for Solidarity," in *COSATU in Crisis: The Fragmentation of an African Trade Union Federation*, ed. Vishwas Satgar and Roger Southall (Sandton, South Africa: KMM Review, 2015), 54–82; Marcel Paret, "Building Labor Solidarity in Precarious Times: The Danger of Union Paternalism." *Labor Studies Journal* 44, no. 4 (2019): 314–332.

2. For further details on the election study, see Marcel Paret, "Contested ANC Hegemony in the Urban Townships: Evidence from the 2014 South African Election," *African Affairs* 115, no. 460 (2016): 419–442.

3. Sakhela Buhlungu, "Rebels without a Cause of Their Own? The Contradictory Location of White Officials in Black Unions in South Africa, 1973–94," *Current Sociology* 54, no. 3 (2006): 427–451.

4. Shannon Walsh, "'Uncomfortable Collaborations': Contesting Constructions of the 'Poor' in South Africa," *Review of African Political Economy* 35, no. 116 (2008): 255–270; Shannon Walsh, "The Philosopher and His Poor: The *Poor-Black* as Object for Political Desire in South Africa," *Politikon* 42, no. 1 (2015): 123–127.

5. Michael Burawoy, "For Public Sociology," *American Sociological Review* 70 (February 2005): 7.

6. Alberto Arribas Lozano, "Reframing the Public Sociology Debate: Towards Collaborative and Decolonial Praxis," *Current Sociology* 66, no. 1 (2018): 92.

7. Burawoy, "For Public Sociology," 7.

8. Edward Webster, "Choosing Sides: The Promise and Pitfalls of Public Sociology in Apartheid South Africa," in *Public Sociology: Science in Dialogue with Society*, ed. Brigitte Aulenbacher, Johanna Sittel, Michael Burawoy and Klaus Dörre (Frankfurt am Main: Campus, 2017), 273–287.

9. Ashwin Desai, "Rejoinder: The Propagandists, the Professors and *Their* 'Poors,'" *Review of African Political Economy* 35, no. 116 (2008): 275–277.

Index

Note: *Figures, notes, and tables are indicated by f, n, and t following page numbers. Organizations and political parties are indexed by their acronyms, not the spelled-out form of their names.*

AbM (Abahlali baseMjondolo), 8, 17, 158, 163n19
ADF (African Diaspora Forum), 189n54
administrative fixes, 24, 73, 84–89, 91, 112, 115, 123, 126, 141, 147, 185n68
Afrobarometer Survey (2015), 52, 53t
AGANG, 123
agency: of Black poor and working class, 4, 17, 24, 158; from opposition to apartheid, 48; precarious nature of, 5
Alexander, Kate, 18, 161n12
Alexander, Neville, 174n80
Alliance (ANC, COSATU, and SACP), 20, 36, 39–40, 42, 43, 55, 124, 143
"amakula" (derogatory slur), 105, 189n65
ANC (African National Congress): abandonment of socialist leanings and detachment from working class, 13, 14–15, 43, 115; Alliance partnership with COSATU and SACP, 20, 36, 39–40, 42, 43, 55, 124, 143, 195n22; banned and in exile, 29, 30–31, 37, 174n69; classes composing, 13; considered as harbinger of national liberation, 16, 73; considered to represent the interests of the people, 64, 74; Constitution Committee, formation of (1986), 34; co-optation efforts and responses to protests and resistance, 2, 19, 43, 54, 72, 75, 78–81, 114–118, 121–122, 125, 126, 129, 136–137, 141, 145–147; economic policy of, 36–37, 39, 41–42; election results, 76, 116, 149; elites and, 11, 13, 19, 35, 53, 74, 140, 142; fluid party affiliation and, 78–80; Freedom Charter, 38, 63, 181n60; IFP vs., 118, 122–123; loyalty of people to, 35, 55, 74, 78–80, 112, 119, 121, 122, 180n23, 180n25, 184n34; migrant labor, negativity toward, 96–97; MK as military wing of, 29, 30; National Conference (2017), 42; National Executive Committee's corporate ownerships, 45, 177n126; NDR capitalism and, 28, 37–41; passive revolution and, 21, 22, 72; people's power and, 35, 184n41; promises of better life for all, 18, 22, 36–37, 56, 101; rise to power and as dominant party, xiii, 6, 21, 28–29, 34–36, 50–51, 75–76, 137, 138, 173n64; secret talks with Afrikaner elites, 35, 45, 173n57; "Strategy and Tactics" document (1969), 33; structure of central control in, 35, 42–43, 73–74; UDF and, 31; waning of support for (1994–2019), 16, 75, 76f, 149, 184n27; waning of support for (2004–2019), 115–118, 116f; Women's League, 36; Youth League (ANCYL), 36, 43, 116, 119–120, 123. *See also* governance and the state; RDP (Reconstruction and Development Program)
Anglo American Corporation, 39
anticolonial nationalism, 11–13, 20, 27, 37, 113
Anti-Eviction Campaign (Cape Town), 8
antimigrant attacks (2008 and later), 24, 93, 97–102, 106–110, 151–152, 188n39, 188n47
apartheid: Black and racial identity, definition during, 93–94, 103–104, 162n2; economic inequality and insecurity associated with, 8, 27–30; illegitimacy of state and, 32; Jim Crow compared to, xiii; legacy of, xii, 27, 58, 143; Mandela's private meetings with apartheid state representatives, 34–35; mass mobilization and resistance to, 5, 16, 22, 28–30, 48, 169n5; middle-class whites' role in Black labor movement, 155; new apartheid, form of, 9, 49–50; NUMSA's role in antiapartheid resistance, 126; pass laws, 29, 31; popular participation weakened by, 34; Progressive Party in opposition to, 115; renationalization invoking struggles against, 15–16; urbanization and, 28. *See also* ANC (African National Congress); democratic transition (end of apartheid)
APF (Anti-Privatization Forum), 8, 41, 52–55, 126–127, 139, 149, 179n16, 180n25, 195n22; affiliation with MCR, 119; compared to UF, 146

Appolis, John, 54, 145–146
Arab Spring, xii
Argentina, 51
Armed Conflict Location and Event Data (ACLED) database, 6, 161n12
Auyero, Javier, 51
AZAPO (Azanian People's Organization), 30, 38, 79, 123, 126

Baltimore protests, xiii, xiv
Bangladeshi migrants, 98, 103, 189n54
Baskin, Jeremy, 39
Bassett, Carolyn, 14–15
Bayart, Jean-Francois, 165n46
BEE (Black Economic Empowerment) programs, 13, 40, 41, 45, 177n127
Bekkersdal, xi, xvi; administrative fixes and, 86–88; ANC co-optation of activists, 125, 137; ANC support declining in (2004–2019), 82, 115–118, 116f, 126; anti-ANC sentiment in, 82, 123; AZAPO support in, 123, 126; as case study area, 21–22, 23f; characteristics of, 24t, 66; community activism in, 82; competition with other areas for scarce resources, 88; DA electoral performance in (2004–2019), 116; EFF support in, 79–80, 117, 117f, 123, 126; as formal township, 22; gravesites fees, 66; housing and services demands in, 66–68, 149, 150; larger than other three case study areas, 22; local solidarity operating through people's parliament, 113–114, 114t, 122–126; mix of formal and informal housing in, 22, 66, 68, 182n74; PAC support in, 126; removal of mayor in, 86, 125; resentment toward migrant traders in, 101–102, 107; sewage infrastructure in, 87; state neglect and feelings of betrayal in, 59–60; workers at odds with protesters in, 90; xenophobia opposition in, 108–110
Bekkersdal Black Consciousness Philosophy Academy, 123
Berlant, Lauren, 166n81
Bernstein, Rusty, 38
betrayal, feelings of: Afrobarometer Survey (2015), 52, 53t; community activism in reaction to, xiv, 4–5, 16, 18, 22, 48, 49–68, 80, 138, 139, 143; inferior treatment compared to peer residential areas and, 88; new social movements of late 1990s and early 2000s in reaction to, 6–7, 51–55, 127, 140–141; parallels among communities and, 141; political parties experiencing effect of,

81, 125, 143; workers going to their jobs instead of joining protests, 90. *See also* housing and service delivery; recognition, protesters' demand for
Biko, Steve, 30
Black, use of term, 162n2, 174n79
Black Consciousness movement (BCM), 30, 38, 79, 117, 123, 169n8
Black Lives Matter (BLM) movement, xiv–xv, 142–144
Black Local Authorities Act (1982), 30, 31
Black middle class: BEE programs to generate, 13, 41; growth of, 14, 45; Mbeki programs to encourage, 41; outnumbering white middle class, xv
Black poverty and the poor, xiv, 3; capacity to develop and exercise agency, 17; case studies of, 21–24, 152–155; concentration in peripheral areas of Johannesburg, 22; exclusion from centers of power and decision making, 19, 35, 138; households living in poverty, 14; reliance on welfare state, 37, 46–47; resistance protests and, xii, 139. *See also* Bekkersdal; Motsoaledi informal settlement; Thembelihle informal settlement; Tsakane10
Black Power movement (United States), 143
Bonacich, Edna, 101, 103, 104, 189n67
Bond, Patrick, 9
Bonner, Philip, 169n6
Booysen, Susan, 75, 176n114
Brazil, xii, 148
Brooks, Heidi, 175n92
Brown, Michael, xiii
BRP (Bekkersdal Renewal Project), 67–68, 182n78
Burawoy, Michael, 158
Buthelezi, Mangosutho, 97

Callinicos, Alex, 164n28
capitalism, xv; ANC's catering to, 35, 39, 44; Black investors, 40, 45, 177n126; economic inequality and insecurity and, 14, 45; GEAR (Growth, Employment and Redistribution) program and, 40; integration into social movement studies, 19; local protests and fractured militancy reinforcing capitalist hegemony, 24, 148–150; NDR capitalism adopted by ANC, 28, 37–41, 50, 174n80, 175n92; passive revolution in connection with fractured militancy and, 150, 159; post-global financial crisis (2008) challenges to, 148; racial inclusion and, 8,

13, 40, 45, 140; as systemic enemy, 159; US Black elites, racial inclusion, and, 143–144; white capital, role in postapartheid transition, 13–14; Zuma and, 42

case studies (overview). *See* methodology of study

case study participants and places of residence: Alice (Motsoaledi), 56; Andile (NUMSA organizer), 127, 129; Andrew (Tsakane10), 79–80, 128–132, 186n80; Ayanda (Tsakane10), 66, 82, 83, 127, 184n41; Bobo (Tsakane10), 59, 65; Charles (Bekkersdal), 66–67, 76–77; Daniel (Ethiopian shop owner in Thembelihle), 106; Dumisani (Bekkers-dal), 60, 102; George (Tsakane10), 84, 109; interview summary, 154*t*; Jakobo (Tsakane10), 54, 83, 87, 128, 130, 131, 180n25; Kabelo (Motsoaledi), 108; Kaya (Tsakane10), 59, 79, 87, 89–90; Laurence (Ivory Park), 49–50; Lindiwe (Bekkersdal), 104, 107; Mandla (Motsoaledi), 49, 57, 79; Matsobane (Bekkersdal), 60, 79, 88; Moeletsi (Bekkersdal), 101–102; Moloetsi (Bekkers-dal), 60; Mpho (Motsoaledi), 77, 88, 89–90; Nandi (Motsoaledi), 105, 108, 189n64; Nonkonzo (EFF activist), 125; Norma (Motsoaledi), 56, 107; Nyeleti (Motsoaledi), 100–101; Rejoice (Motsoaledi), 62, 85; Robert (Tsakane10), 105, 189n65; Sello (Bekkersdal), 82, 86; Sizwe (Bekkersdal), 67–68, 124, 126; Tebogo (Bekkersdal), 80; Thabo (Thembelihle), 54, 58, 64, 77, 85–86, 90, 103–104, 133; Thapelo (Motsoaledi), 61–62, 80–81, 118; Thato (Tsakane10), 131; Themba (Bekkersdal), 89, 107, 123; Thuli (Bekkersdal), 125; Tido (Tsakane10), 77; Tumelo (Bekkersdal), 67, 90, 102, 109; Vuyo (Bekkersdal), 124; Xolani (PMCP activist), 118–120; Zinhle (Soweto), 50

cash transfers, xii, 46–47, 78, 178n143

Castells, Manuel, 19

CAX (Coalition against Xenophobia), 110

Cele, Bheki, 99

Center for Social Change (University of Johannesburg), 6, 152

Chamber of Mines, 43

Chatterjee, Partha: on community's collective identity, 72, 84–85; on direct political negotiations within political society, 51, 114; on government administration associated with political society, 74; linking passive revolution to anticolonial nationalism, 9, 11–13, 14, 16, 140, 164n42; linking passive revolution to legitimacy, 168n106; on political society's ability to rejuvenate democracy with popular participation, 113; on political society vs. civil society, 19–20, 144; on state's obligation to care for the poor, 60

Chikane, Frank, 61

Chinese use of concessions to quell protest, 185n68

Ching Kwan Lee, 185n68

Chipkin, Ivor, 175n92

Chun, Jennifer, 55–56

citizenship, 95, 96, 101

City Power, 86, 148–49

civic organizations: community-based, 183n20; merging into ANC, 36; SANCO (South African National Civic Organ-ization), 36, 108, 122

civil rights movement in United States. *See* United States

civil service: bourgeoisie of, 12; transition in racial composition of, 45. *See also* patronage

civil society: ANC domination of, 74, 147; community and, 74; connection to grassroots and disassociation from corruption, 145; elites as, 19; Fanon on, 12; Heller on, 168n111; independent candidates and, 120, 125; Land Development Objectives and Integrated Development Plans (IDPs), role in, 73; Marais on, 15; political society vs., 19–20, 144; SANCO and, 122; Save South Africa and, 147; UDF ensuring adherence to ANC ideals and leadership, 173n66

class differences and class struggle, xiv, xv; anti-trader attacks and, 106; class formation, 17, 72, 141, 166n87; among the colonized, 27; fractured militancy and, 4; growing consciousness of activists and class solidarity, 113; between Indian residents and Black shack dwellers, 63; intraracial class differentiation, 163n21, 164n24; in national liberation movement, 13; passive revolution and, 10; racial inclusion and, 8–9, 142; shift of struggle from workplace to cities and communities, 18–19; unions bringing class struggles into antiapartheid resistance, 72. *See also* middle class; working class

Cloete, Karl, 129, 195n18

Cloward, Richard A., 73

CNETU (Council of Non-European Trade Unions), 28

collective action. *See* solidarity and collective action
collective consumption, 19, 140. *See also* housing and service delivery
Collins, Patricia Hill, 72
Colonialism of a Special Type (CST) thesis, 38
Coloured: in apartheid era, 104; South African parliament admitting, 31; use of term, 162n2
Communist International (Comintern) 1927–1928 declaration on South Africa, 38
Communist Party of South Africa. *See* SACP (South African Communist Party)
community activism, 3, 6, 7f, 71–92; administrative fixes to quell, 24, 73, 84–89, 112, 115, 123, 126, 141, 147, 185n68; amorphous nature of protests, 55; ANC creating hostile environment for, 74–78, 83–84, 183n21; apolitical nature of, 82–83; community discourse, 81–84, 124; competition over scarce resources and, 4, 19, 20, 24, 68, 85, 87–89; construct of community, 72, 81; cross-community coordination, attempts of, 83–84, 137; division and isolation of each community, 2–3, 19–20, 55, 71, 72, 91–92, 126, 136–137, 140, 141, 144, 147; economic-corporate phase of, 112, 113; fluid party allegiances and, 78–81, 129; individual exploiting altruism to community for personal gain, 184n44; participation and, 73–75; passive revolution and, 16–17, 72; patronage used to quell, 87; political power not goal of, 82; public goods, community-based delivery of, 20, 74–75; speed of locals to organize a protest vs. slow bureaucracy of union organization, 128, 130; as vehicle for protest in postapartheid era, 52, 55, 91; weakness of organizations, 114, 129, 131, 137; workers vs. protesters, 18, 89–91; xenophobia's overlap with, 95, 108, 110; under Zuma government, 42. *See also* betrayal, feelings of; *specific movements and parties by acronyms*
Community Councils Act (1977), 30
competition for scarce resources. *See* fragmentation
Concerned Citizens Forum (Durban), 8
Conference of the Democratic Left, 151
Congressional Black Caucus (US), xiv
Consolidated Goldfields, 34
conspicuous consumption, 12
COPE (Congress of the People), 43, 123
corruption, 3, 27, 41–43, 48, 50–52, 67–68, 75, 79, 85, 86, 100, 122, 125, 150, 176n111. *See also* patronage

COSAS (Congress of South African Students), 30, 32
COSATU (Congress of South African Trade Unions): Alliance partner of ANC, 20, 36, 39–40, 124, 143, 195n22; APF and, 146, 195n22; challenging ANC's policies, 41–42, 179n19; Marikana massacre and, 43, 144; NUMSA and, 43, 130, 146, 175n91; significant role in antiapartheid resistance linking workplace and residential struggles, 71–72, 174n69; top-down decision making in, 36; wage increases of union members, 46; workerism and, 39
COVID-19 pandemic, xv
Crush, Jonathan, 94
CSG (Child Support Grant), 47, 178n144
CWP (Community Work Program), 47

DA (Democratic Alliance), 75–76, 78–81, 82, 127, 184n25; electoral performance (2014–2019), 115–116
Dawson, Hannah, 186n84
Defiance Campaign (1952), 29
deindustrialization, 1, 45
De Klerk, F. W., 5
demobilization: elite-led, 11, 13, 19, 53, 74, 140; loss of fervor once some concessions obtained and, 87; of national social movement, 6, 11, 36, 53, 141; passive revolution and, 4, 10, 72; patronage as method to achieve, 87; state politics at democratic transition, 34–37
democracy: exclusion based on class in, 9; instability due to rising expectations and demands, 166–167n92; national liberation and, 27; participatory, 33, 73–74; passive revolution and, 19; plurality needed for radical democracy, 35; political society and, 19; Ramaphosa on, 42; resource redistribution and, 163n14; skepticism of representative democracy, 32, 74, 76; top-down decision making and, 34–35, 73–74; working class's central role in, 33. *See also* democratic transition (end of apartheid)
democratic transition (end of apartheid): ANC/NP negotiations leading to, 35, 45; combining racial inclusion with politics of precarity, 5, 13, 138; constraining popular initiative, 13, 35–36; elite struggles within NDR, 41–44; hopes attached to, 5–6, 16, 48, 54, 166n81; NDR capitalism adopted by ANC, 37–41; non-hegemonic form of class rule in, 13; remobilization after, 6–7, 51–55,

127, 140–141; shift from society-driven to state-driven politics under ANC, 37; social movements, decline of, 8. *See also* ANC (African National Congress); demobilization

Department of Home Affairs, 2016 Mkhaya Migrants Awards, 110

Department of Trade and Industry, 99

Desai, Ashwin, 159, 180n23

Desai, Manali, 10, 11

Desai, Rehad: *Miners Shot Down* (documentary), 43

Development Bank South Africa, 40

dictatorship, emergence from nationalist movement, 12, 24, 41, 77

dignity sought by protesters, 49, 50, 52, 55

Dixon, John, 188n47

DLF (Democratic Left Front), 8, 127, 151, 159, 195n27

double movement theory, 19. *See also* Polanyi, Karl

Duduza township, 128

Durrheim, Kevin, 188n47

East Africans, treatment of, 94, 98, 103–104. *See also* Ethiopian migrants; Somalian migrants

East Rand, 1; stay-away (1984), 32. *See also* Tsakane10

economic development: during 1960s, 29; foreign direct investment and, 29, 39, 42; global economy, connection to, 11, 13–14, 42–43, 45, 140, 142, 166n72; global financial crisis (2008) and, 51, 147; national independence as precondition of, 11; radical economic transformation and, 42; recession (1970s through 1980s), 170n17

economic inequality and insecurity: capitalism's role in, 14, 45; continuation in postapartheid era, 4, 7–8, 9, 18, 47, 50, 140–141, 150; leading to popular resistance, 17–19; passive revolution and, 14, 50, 140; racial inclusion limited by, 48, 50, 52, 53*t*; resentment of foreign-born residents and, 95, 100–103; resistance to apartheid due to, 30; state-oriented approach to, 146. *See also* systemic racism

education: Afrikaans language education required, 30; educated youth, declining fortune of, xii; people's education efforts, 32; protesters' demands for, 67; public education in postapartheid state, 47; secondary education for Blacks under apartheid, 30

EFF (Economic Freedom Fighters): as ANC's opposition, 137, 145; anti-Zuma protests (2017) and, 147; Black economic empowerment as focus of, 78, 123, 148; compared to UF, 44, 145–146; criticism of, 137, 176n118; DA in alliance with, 75–76, 79, 184n25; detached from local organizing and protest, 43, 147, 148; electoral performance (2014–2019), 115–118, 117*f*, 195n21; fluid support for, 80, 126; formed as political party, 2, 43, 116, 123, 145; future of South African Left and, 144–147; goals of, 145–146; OKM and, 117–118; protests by, 2–3; rise of and support for, 79–80, 117, 117*f*, 123, 126, 146; state-oriented approach of, 146–147; younger voters and, 78–79, 116

Egypt, xii, 147

Ekurhuleni municipality, 21–22, 23*f*, 65, 75–76, 76*f*. *See also* Tsakane10

elections. *See* voting; *specific political parties*

electricity, demand for dependable service, 1, 50, 52, 57, 62–63, 64–65, 85–86, 120, 135, 148–149, 181n59. *See also* housing and service delivery issues; *specific informal settlements*

Elias Motsoaledi informal shack settlement. *See* Motsoaledi informal settlement

elites: ANC and, 35, 142; anticolonial nationalism and, 11, 140; as civil society, 19; coalition of old and new elites, 13; conspicuous consumption of, 12; demobilization and, 11, 13, 19, 53, 74, 140; failure to deliver on promises of racial inclusion, 18, 22, 51, 56–57; Fanon on organized working class's alignment with, 40; Gramsci on weakness of, 142; growth of Black elites, 13, 14, 41, 45, 48; nationalist elites, 11–12, 16, 24, 40, 96; NDR and resulting factionalism among, 16, 41–44; passive revolution and, 4, 9, 35, 81, 84, 95; privileging of, xii, 3, 4, 10, 35, 48; racial inclusion and, 8, 140; reliance on the state, 10, 12

employment: Blacks in semiskilled jobs during apartheid, 29; community-based activism and, 72; job opportunities for youth, 49–50; local protests and, 89–91; precarious nature of, 18, 55, 149, 178n138; public employment programs, 47. *See also* trade unions; unemployment

Employment Equity Act (1998), 177n129

empowerment: EFF focus on Black economic empowerment, 78, 123, 148. *See also* BEE (Black Economic Empowerment) programs

entitlement, feelings of, 60
Erwin, Alec, 40
Ethiopian migrants, 98, 103, 107–108, 189n54
Evans, Peter B., 185n57
expropriation of land, 43, 176n117
Extended Public Works Program, 47, 178n145

Fanon, Frantz: on anticolonial nationalism, 27, 140; on Black elite's creation, 40; on competition within political society, 20; on demographics of revolutionaries, 18; on devolution of nationalist party into dictatorship, 24, 41, 77; Gibson and, 16; Gramsci and, 140, 165n46; on group solidarity and negative effects of elite pursuit of narrow interests, 113; lumpen-proletariat view and skepticism of organized working class, 18, 40–41, 167n97; on passive revolution, 9, 15, 16; on revolutionary potential of economically excluded groups, 139; South African transition mirroring, 14; warnings about pitfalls of national consciousness, 11–13, 50; on xenophobia, 95
Far East Rand March against Xenophobia (2015), 109
Federation of South African Women, 29
Ferguson protests, xiii, xiv
Floyd, George, xv
Fogel, Benjamin, 195n25
Forced Migration Studies Program (now the African Center for Migration and Society), 151
FOSATU (Federation of South African Trade Unions), 29, 31–32, 38–39
fractured militancy, xv, 3–5; community trenches of, 114; defined, 3; explanation of and factors contributing to, 4, 8, 19, 141, 150; extrapolating to United States, 142–143; passive revolution and, 138, 150; path forward for, 148, 150; precarious resistance and, 4–5
fragmentation, xv; administrative fixes and, 85; in antimigrant antagonism, 111; competition over scarce resources and, 4, 19, 20, 24, 68, 85, 87–89, 97, 100, 138, 141; divergence among community groups and, 113; ethnic, generating exclusion, 20, 94–95; explanation of and factors contributing to, 155; social movements fracturing in late 2000s, 55, 71; spatial, creating regionalism, 20; UF's goal to overcome, 145
framing, 139–141. See also social movements

Fraser, Nancy, 56
Freedom Charter, 38, 63, 181n60
French Revolution, 9–11
Friedman, Steven, 16, 166n79, 173n66, 183n20

Gandhi, Mohandas, 11
Gauteng Province, 8, 21, 32, 52, 65, 75, 98, 135, 182n75, 184n27
GEAR (Growth, Employment and Re-distribution) program, 40, 175n98, 176n106
Gibson, Nigel, 13–14, 16–17, 167n97
Goldman Sachs, 39
Goodwin, Jeff, 8, 18
governance and the state: community protests aimed at, 140, 147; continuous engagement and communication of local communities with, 124; racial hegemony and, 142; self-governance of GWCRA in Bekkersdal, 123–124, 126; state as key vehicle of transformation, 140, 146–147; state politics at democratic transition, 34–37; struggles to supplement through popular governance, 113. See also ANC (African National Congress); betrayal, feelings of; housing and service delivery; state neglect
government cash transfers. See cash transfers
Gramsci, Antonio: on civil society as private voluntary associations, 145; on class struggle and group solidarity, 113; on crisis continuation due to status quo's preserva-tion, 18; on economic-corporate struggles, 112–113; on elite class formation, 142; Fanon and, 140, 165n46; Gibson and, 16; on limits for class formation, 139–140; Marais and, 15, 166n74; passive revolution theory, 4, 9–12, 140, 144, 166n82; political society and, 19, 196n30; on restoration/revolution dichotomy of passive revolution, 13, 17, 144; on stages of development for social change, 17; on universal intellect, 158; on weak leadership resulting from passive revolu-tion, 150; Winant and, 141–142
Gray, Freddie, xiii
Greece, xii, 147
Gupta business family, 42
GWCRA (Greater Westonaria Concerned Residents Association), 82, 86, 108–109, 123–126, 137

Hart, Gillian, 15–16, 41–42, 50–51, 55, 179n19
health care offered by postapartheid state, 47
Heller, Patrick, 73, 168n111, 185n57
Hetland, Gabriel, 8

housing and service delivery, xi, xiv; ANC (state) provision of, 46–47, 78, 80–81, 149, 150, 178n140; antitrader nationalism and, 107, 110; under apartheid state, 30; in case study areas, 22; desire to make system work better, 79, 85, 121, 132, 146, 150; EFF focus on improving, 146; fluid party allegiance and, 80–81; KCWF meeting about, 1–2; local protests focused on, 19, 58, 63–68, 71, 82, 121, 138, 139, 146, 186n80; parallel activism among communities and, 141; political society seeking from the state, 20, 51, 125; "right to the city" demands, 140; scope of services, 61. *See also* administrative fixes; Bekkersdal; Motsoaledi informal settlement; RDP (Reconstruction and Development Program); Thembelihle informal settlement; Tsakane10; *specific types of services*
Hughes, Langston: "Harlem," xiii
human rights violations, 5
Huntington, Samuel, 166n92

IFP (Inkatha Freedom Party), 118, 122–123
India, anticolonial movement and passive revolution in, 11, 16, 28
Indian residents of South Africa: in apartheid era, 104; South African parliament admitting, 31; in Thembelihle, 63, 64, 116; as traders, 101–105
informal shack settlements. *See* Bekkersdal; Motsoaledi informal settlement; Thembelihle informal settlement; Tsakane10
institutional racism. *See* systemic racism
intraracial relations: anti-African nationalism and, 94–98; antitrader nationalism and, 94, 98–102; class differentiation, 163n21, 164n24; foreign-born Blacks in South Africa, 93
invisibility, feelings of, 56. *See also* recognition
Italian unification and passive revolution, 9–10, 164n35, 166n74

Jackson, Jesse, xiv
Jim Crow, xiii
Johannesburg, 21–22, 23f; antimigrant attacks in (2008), 110; author's workshop (2017), 157, 158; construction in Motsoaledi promised by, 120; history of, xi–xiii; migrant population in, 97; waning support for ANC in, 75–76, 76f. *See also* Motsoaledi informal settlement; Thembelihle informal settlement

Johannesburg Stock Exchange, 43, 45, 177nn125–126
JP Morgan, 39

Katznelson, Ira, 112
KCWF (Kwatsaduza Community and Workers Forum), 1–2, 109, 128, 130–132, 162n1
Kerr, Philippa, 188n47
Keys, Derek, 40
King, Martin Luther: "I Have a Dream" speech, xiii
kinship networks, xii
Kobese, Major, 99
Kwa-Thema township, 128

Landau, Loren, 98
Land Development Objectives and Integrated Development Plans (IDPs), 73
Lehae (new housing settlement), 64, 88
Lenasia, 22, 58, 63. *See also* Thembelihle informal settlement
Lenka, Lefa, 161n12
Levenson, Zachary, 178n141
Lie, John, 187n4
Lindela migrant detention center, 110
Local Government Transition Act (1993), 73
localization of popular resistance. *See* community activism
Lodge, Tom, 173n54
Lozano, Alberto Arribas, 158–159
Lusaka, Zambia, as ANC base in exile, 31

MacDonald, Michael, 163n21
Magashule, Ace, 176n111
Maimane, Mmusi, 78
Malema, Julius, 43, 78, 176n115, 189n65
Mamabolo, Jacob, 135
Mandela, Nelson, 5, 34–35, 39–41, 79, 121, 138, 175n92
Marais, Hein, 14–15, 16, 36, 39, 166n74
March for Economic Freedom (2011), 43
March of Movements (2002), 179n19
Marikana massacre (2012), 43–44, 140, 144
Marxism, 37–38, 175n92
Mashaba, Herman, 184n25
MAWU (Metal and Allied Workers' Union), 33, 39
Mayekiso, Moses, 171n30
Mbeki, Thabo, 41–43, 119–120, 151, 173n57
McCarthy, John, 139
McKinley, Dale, 53–54

MCR (Motsoaledi Concerned Residents), 82, 108, 119–122, 126; affiliation with APF, 119; merger into Motsoaledi Activists, 122

MERG (Macro Economic Research Group), 175n98

methodology of study, 151–159; case studies of resistance after racial inclusion, 21–24, 152–155; critical engagement approach and, 159; map of case study areas and Johannesburg, Ekurhuleni, and West Rand municipalities, 23f; passive revolution and, 159; public sociology and, 158–159. *See also* Bekkersdal; case study participants and places of residence; Motsoaledi informal settlement; Thembelihle informal settlement; Tsakane10

middle class: declining fortune of, xii; FOSATU wanting to prioritize worker struggles over, 39; US middle class, 143, 144. *See also* Black middle class

Middle East and North Africa uprisings (2010s), xii, 147

"middleman minorities," 101, 103, 104, 189n67

migrants. *See* nationalism

Million Signatures petition campaign (1984), 170n23

mines: Marikana massacre of striking workers (2012), 43–44, 140, 144; nationalization, calls for, 43, 176n117; workers' strikes (1920 & 1922), 28

misrecognition, 56, 58, 60

Mkhize, Hlengiwe, 97

Mkongi, Bongani, 97

MK (*Umkhonto we Sizwe*), 29, 30

Modise, Wonder, 124, 125

Mohlakeng township vs. Bekkersdal development, 88

Mokgope, Tebogo, 86

Mokonyane, Nomvula, 99, 123

Morobe, Murphy, 33

Morris, Aldon, 194n4

Motsoaledi Activists, 122

Motsoaledi informal settlement, xi, xv; administrative fixes and, 86–87; anarchists in, 118–119; ANC loyalty in, 121, 137; ANC's early history in, 118; ANC support declining in (2004–2019), 115–116, 116f, 118; as case study area, 21–22, 23f; characteristics of, 24t, 61; competition with other areas for scarce resources, 87; DA electoral performance in (2004–2019), 116; division and isolation from other communities, 136–137; EFF support in, 117f; fluid party affiliation and, 81–82; formal housing construction in, 87, 148; Freedom Park vs. Motsoaledi development, 87–88; housing and services demands in, 61–63, 118–120, 137, 150; illegal land occupation of, 22, 61, 118; independent candidate in, 120–121; local solidarity as focus of community activists in, 113–114, 114t, 118–122, 137; migrant attacks to gain government attention, 107; migrants, attitude toward, 100–101, 105; OKM support in, 119, 120; recognition of existence of, 62; redistricting of, 119; SANCO and, 122; state neglect and feelings of betrayal in, 56–57; workers at odds with protesters in, 89–90; xenophobia, opposition to, 108–110; youth activism in, 119. *See also* MCR (Motsoaledi Concerned Residents)

Movement for Socialism, 131

"movements beyond movements," 55

Mozambicans, 103–104, 107

MWT (Marxist Workers Tendency), 38

Nasson, Bill, 173n54

nationalism, 93–111; anti-African nationalism, 94; anticolonial, 11–13, 20, 27, 37, 113; antimigrant attacks (2008 and later), 24, 93, 97–102, 106–110, 151–152, 188n39, 188n47; antitrader nationalism, 94, 98–102; antixenophobia march (2015), 109; citizenship and, 95, 96, 101; denialism associated with antimigrant attacks, 106; equality of foreign-born residents, 105; fragmentation in antimigrant antagonism, 111; liberation discourse and, 50; official nationalisms, 96–100; overlap of liberation discourse and anti-foreigner discourse, 95, 101, 106, 188n47; passive revolution enabled by, 9, 11–13, 14, 16, 140, 164n42; privileging native-born South Africans over foreign-born residents, 99, 100–101; resentment of foreign-born residents, 95, 100–103, 105–106, 112; resistance and, 106–110; silencing of dissent, 12, 112; threat, foreign residents viewed as, 96–97, 102–103; ultra-nationalism, 20; undocumented migrants, deportation of, 98, 100; undocumented migrants, hostility toward, 188n37. *See also* elites, *for* nationalist elites

national liberation, 27–48; ANC's governance and, 37, 50–51, 68; politics of, reinforcing top-down decision making, 73; radical transformation as possibility, 30–34.

See also ANC (African National Congress); democratic transition

national liberation movement, 27–30; abandonment of socialist leanings of, 13; conflict between populists and workerists in, 38; migrant exclusion and, 96; single organization as best option in, 183n23; working-class leadership as possible alternative to ANC, 38–40, 114, 144. *See also* ANC (African National Congress)

National Prosecuting Authority, 42

Native Labor (Settlement of Disputes) Act (1953), 28–29

Ndlozi, Mbuyiseni, 145–146

NDR (national democratic revolution): Alliance's goal of, 36; ANC's adoption of NDR capitalism, 22, 37–41, 50, 174n80, 175n92; elite struggles within, 41–44; renationalization discourse and, 15–16; significance in South Africa, 28, 37; triumph over workerism, 39

Nedcor/Old Mutual, 39

Nehru, Jawaharlal, 11

Neocosmos, Michael, 34, 95

neoliberalism, 42, 44, 54–55, 126, 146, 180n23

New Unity Movement, 38

Ngema, Mbongeni: "AmaNdiya" (song), 105

Ngobeni, Lucky, 101, 120, 121

Nieftagodien, Noor, 176n118

Niekerk, Robert van, 35–36, 40

Nkandla estate, 122

nonviolence, 11

NP (National Party), 28, 34, 35, 172n53

NUM (National Union of Mineworkers), 43

NUMSA (National Union of Metalworkers of South Africa), 39, 43–44, 126–132, 145, 146, 148, 157, 175n91, 195n18. *See also* UF (United Front)

Occupy movement (US), xii–xiii, 148

OKM (Operation Khanyisa Movement), 83–84, 115, 117, 119–120, 132, 133–137, 185n64; not considered a political party, 134–35; voters' pledge developed by, 134

Omi, Michael, 7

Operation Fiela (2015), 98

Oppenheimer, Harry, 39

PAC (Pan Africanist Congress), 29, 123, 126

Padayachee, Vishnu, 35–36, 40

Pakistani migrants, 98, 99, 103–105, 189n54

Parliament concept on the local level. *See* Bekkersdal

Paschel, Tianna, 140

passive revolution, 4–5, 9–12; ANC and, 21, 22, 72; capitalism produced by, in connection with fractured militancy, 150, 159; civil society and, 19; definitions of, 164n28; demobilization and, 4, 10, 72; economic inequality and insecurity and, 14, 50, 140; electoral and party politics as context for, 114–118; elite-led state power and, 4, 9, 35, 81, 84, 95; emergence of, 34; factors contributing to, 74, 112, 140; legitimacy and, 168n106; NDR and, 40, 44; political parties' centrality and, 147; "politics of waiting" generated by, 20, 121; racial inclusion's role in, 9, 12–17, 150; resistance produced by, 17–19, 51, 68, 138; trench warfare and, 112; undermining solidarity and favoring community-focused action, 16–17, 72; US compared to South Africa, 143

patronage, 42–43, 45, 51, 74, 75, 77, 87, 125, 126, 149, 172n42

PEMO (People's Movement), 125–126

People's courts, 32, 172n42

People's power, 32–35, 40, 65, 73

Piedmont-type function, 10. *See also* Gramsci, Antonio

Pityana, Sipho, 147

Piven, Frances Fox, 73

PMCP (Phambili Motsoaledi Community Project), 118–119

Podemos (Spanish party), 148

Polanyi, Karl, 19

police: arrests and detention of protesters, 77, 135; blockades of protesters, 59–60; brutality against antiapartheid activists, 29; brutality in United States, xiv–xv, 143; deportation practices, 98; surveillance and detention of antiapartheid activists, 29, 96, 173n53; Zuma and, 42. *See also* repression of protests

political opportunities, 139–140. *See also* social movements

political parties, xii; activists' fluid attachment to and separation from, 78–81, 118, 131; betrayal's effect on, 81, 147; competition increasing for ANC, 149; excluded from South African civil society, 145; passive revolution and, 10, 20, 147; political society and, 20–21. *See also specific parties by acronym*

political society: civil society vs., 19–20, 144; community identification and, 72; Left politics and, 147; obligation to care for the poor, 60, 146; political parties and, 20–21; reinvigorating democracy, 113; role of, 22; as site of local protests, 51; South African protesters within, 144, 146; strategic politics, 72, 74, 84, 95, 114, 144; US Blacks and, 143; xenophobia and, 95

Pontarelli, Francesco, 166n82

poor people's movements, 73, 139. *See also* Black poverty and the poor

Poplak, Richard, 196n28

popular resistance. *See* protests and popular resistance

Portugal, xii

precarity of resistance, 4–5, 19–21

precarity to popular resistance, 17–19. *See also* economic inequality and insecurity

privatization, 41, 45, 148–149, 175n98

Progressive Party, 115

property destruction as protest strategy, 56, 59–60, 64, 107, 121, 138

protests and popular resistance: anti-Zuma protests (2017), 147; against apartheid, 5, 16, 28–30; continuities during and after apartheid, 163n14; demographics of revolutionaries, 18–19; from economic precarity to, 17–19, 139; foreign-born residents' failure to participate in, ramifications of, 107; fragmented nature of, xvi; goals, strategies, and tactics, xi, 21, 55–56, 128; increase of, xii, xiv–xv, 6, 7f; as mobilization without resources, 139; NUMSA's view of local protests, 129; passive revolution's role in shaping, 16–17; as rebellion of the poor, 18, 138; reemergence (late 1990s and early 2000s), 52–55, 138; shift from popular nationalism to state nationalism, 34; UF's view of local protests, 145–146; uncomfortable collaborations in, 155–159. *See also* betrayal, feelings of; community activism; people's power; repression of protests; *specific areas of case studies*

Public Affairs Research Institute, 176n113

public sector. *See* civil service

public service delivery. *See* housing and service delivery

public sociology, 158–159

racial exclusion: racial categorization in postapartheid era and, 95; racial identity, definition of, 103–104; as result of fragmentation, 20; xenophobia and, 93–95. *See also* nationalism

racial inclusion, xiii–xiv; ANC discourse of, 50; BCM legacy and, 123; betrayal from unfulfilled promises of, 55–68; capitalism and, xv, 8, 14, 40, 45, 140; case studies and, 21–24, 152–155; definition of, 5; elites enriched by and limiting potential of, 142; Employment Equity Act (1998) and, 177n129; formalization of, 6, 48, 138, 142; limited by economic insecurity, 48, 50, 52, 138; migrant exclusion and, 95–96; NDR preserving capitalism in language of, 40; passive revolution and, 4–5, 9, 12–17, 142; political society and, 19, 140; precarious resistance and, 4–5; racial hegemony and, 141–142; "rainbow nation" label applied to South Africa, 3, 41, 93; in South Africa, limits of, xiii–xv, 3, 5, 9; in South Africa compared to United States, 143–144; in United States, limits on, xiii, xv, 143–144

racism, 5–8; horizontal/political vs. vertical/economic racism, 187n4. *See also* apartheid; nationalism; racial exclusion; systemic racism

rainbow nation, South Africa considered as, 3, 41, 93

Ramachandran, Sujata, 94

Ramaphosa, Cyril, 42–43, 149–150

Rand Merchant Bank, 39

Rand West City municipality, 66, 75–76, 76f. *See also* Bekkersdal

RDP (Reconstruction and Development Program), 1, 36–37, 40, 46, 62, 85, 97, 175n98

recognition, protesters' demand for, 20, 22, 51, 55–60, 68, 72, 107, 138, 141–142, 180n33

redistribution of resources, 12, 35, 39–40, 42, 48, 163n14, 167n93; elite empowerment prioritized over, 43; postapartheid state's programs and obligations, 46–47, 60; South African focus on, 144. *See also* fragmentation *for* competition over scarce resources; political society

renationalization, 15–16

repression of protests and resistance, 2–3, 6, 11, 29–30, 36, 41, 60, 78, 119, 140. *See also* ANC *for* co-optation efforts; apartheid; police

resentment. *See* betrayal, feelings of; nationalism

resistance politics: countering xenophobia through solidarity discourse, 95; of gap between elite and the masses, 35. *See also* community activism; protests and popular resistance resource mobilization, 139. *See also* social movements

"right to the city" demands, 140

Riley, Dylan, 10, 11, 150, 196n30

road barricades as protest strategy, 2, 56–59, 63, 90, 107, 138

Runciman, Carin, 179n17, 180n25

Sabotage Act (1962), 169n7

SACP (South African Communist Party), 28, 29, 33, 36–38, 42, 44, 124, 126, 143, 169n2; *The Road to South African Freedom*, 38

SACTU (South African Congress of Trade Unions), 29, 38, 169n6

SAFTU (South African Federation of Trade Unions), 44, 176n121

SAIC (South African Indian Congress), 29

SANCO (South African National Civic Organisation), 36, 108, 122

Sanders, Bernie, 148

Sandton, 23f, 50

Sanlam, 39

SARS (South African Revenue Service), 42

Satgar, Vishwas, 13–15

Save South Africa, 147, 195n27

Scott, James, 51, 84

Scully, Ben, 166n72

SECC (Soweto Electricity Crisis Committee), 133, 136, 137, 149

Seekings, Jeremy, 31

Seidman, Gay, 72

Sharpeville protest (1960), 29

Sharpton, Al, xiv

Shiceka, Sicelo, 62

Simba factory strike (1984), 32

Sisulu, Zwelakhe, 33

Slabbert, Frederik van Zyl, 34

SMMEs (small, medium, and micro enterprises) summit (2013), 99

social grants. *See* cash transfers

socialism, 13, 33–35, 38, 39, 79, 85, 91, 126, 131, 143, 175n92; Thembelihle activists pursuing class solidarity with socialist party politics, 114, 114t, 132–137, 148. *See also* SRWP

social movements: conditions conducive to, 140; cross-community coordination, attempts of, 83–84, 137; decline of, 8, 53, 179n17; Du Boisian approach to, 194n4; failure of local protests to cohere around larger movement, 71, 140, 144; framing, 141; "long march" view of, 140; Ndlozi's criticism of instability of, 145; remobiliza-

tion at community level, 6–7, 51–55, 127, 140–141; studies and theories of, 19, 138–141. *See also* betrayal, feelings of; community activism; demobilization; solidarity and collective action

solidarity and collective action: of antiapartheid movement, 5, 16, 28, 30–31, 34, 71; APF as example of, 53–54; class solidarity with socialist party politics, 114, 114t, 132–137, 148; class solidarity with union alliance politics, 114, 114t, 126–132, 137; of economically insecure groups, 18; EFF social policies for, 43; foreign-born residents, efforts to create solidarity with, 109–110; growing consciousness of activists and, 12, 113, 145; independent candidates prioritized over, 120; intraracial antagonism and, 93–94, 141; lack of, across communities, 3, 19–20, 71, 140, 141, 144, 147; limited class formation and, 141; local solidarity operating through people's parliament, 113–114, 114t, 122–126; local solidarity with community focus, 113–114, 114t, 118–122, 137; passive revolution and racial solidarity, 13; of place-based community, 83, 139, 141; political orientations required for, 141; squandered by nationalist leaders, 12; of students and workers in stay-aways (1984), 32; UF working for, 145–146

Somalian migrants, 98, 99, 102–105, 107, 189n54

SOPA (Socialist Party of Azania), 123

South African Chamber of Business, 39–40

South African constitution, 6, 34, 73, 96

South African Left, 38, 42–44, 112, 130, 137, 144–147

South African National Civic Organization, 108

South African National Defense Force, 98

South African Native National Congress, 28

South African Research Chair in Social Change, 152

Southall, Roger, 177n130

South Asians, treatment of, 94, 98, 103–104. *See also* Pakistani migrants

Southern African Migration Project survey (2010), 100

Soweto: attacks on migrants in (2015 & 2018), 94, 99, 109; stay-away (1984), 32; students' uprising (1976), 30, 119. *See also* Motsoaledi informal settlement; SECC (Soweto Electricity Crisis Committee)

Spain, xii, 147, 148

SRWP (Socialist Revolutionary Workers' Party), 44, 148

state neglect, 49–50, 54, 56–60, 66, 80, 88. *See also* betrayal, feelings of

stay-aways. *See* strikes

strikes: compared to stay-aways, 186n78; dockworkers and textile industry (1972–1973), 29; mine workers (1920 & 1922), 28; NUMSA engineering sector (2014), 127; Simba factory strike (1984), 32; stay-aways (mid-1980s), 32, 174n69; stay-aways (postapartheid), 89–91. *See also* Marikana massacre

subaltern groups, 10, 17, 168n111, 194n4

Suppression of Communism Act (1950), 28

systemic racism, 7–8, 14, 85

Tambo, Oliver, 33, 121

Tarrow, Sidney, 6

Tau, Parks, 62

taxis, effort of stay-aways to get support from, 90

Taylor, Keeanga-Yamahtta, xi, xiii

TCC (Thembelihle Crisis Committee), 58, 83, 109–110, 132–137, 148–149, 157–158, 185n64

Terrorism Act (1967), 169n7

Thembelihle informal settlement, xii, xvi; administrative fixes and, 86–88, 91; ANC support declining in (2004–2019), 115–118, 116*f*, 133; anti-Zuma protests (2017), 147; attempt to coordinate with other communities, 83–84, 137; as case study area, 21–22, 23*f*; characteristics of, 24*t*, 63; class solidarity with socialist party politics, 114, 114*t*, 132–137, 148; community apolitical protests in, 83–84; competition with other areas for scarce resources, 87–88; DA electoral performance in (2004–2019), 116; division and isolation from other communities, 136–137; EFF support in, 117, 117*f*; electricity, provision of, 87, 135, 148, 149; formal registration as housing project, 65, 87, 135; geotechnical reports on safety of area for human settlement, 63–65, 133; housing and services demands in, 63–65, 85–88, 133, 137, 150; illegal land occupation of, 22, 63; OKM support in, 84, 115, 120, 137; state neglect and feelings of betrayal in, 57–58; threat of eviction and relocation, 22, 63–64, 133, 181n60; workers at odds with protesters in, 90; xenophobia, opposition to, 109–111. *See also* TCC (Thembelihle Crisis Committee)

Thompson, E. P., 51

tire burnings, 2, 56, 59

top-down decision making, 13, 34–36, 43, 73–75, 146

trade unions, xii; ANC coopting, 72; Black membership banned by law, 28–29; Black workers organizing in 1970s, 29; conflict between populists and workerists in national liberation struggle, 38; federations, formations and splits of, 44; history of, 169n2; middle-class whites' involvement in, 155; in opposition to apartheid, 5, 31–32; postapartheid noninvolvement in local resistance movement, 89; power after transition to democracy, 36; proliferation of and membership increase, 28, 171n28; shop stewards and floor organizing, 33, 36, 171n30, 172n48; Tsakane10 activists pursuing class solidarity with union alliance politics, 114, 114*t*, 126–132, 137; unemployment in households with union members, 46, 178n139; wage increases and gains for members, 46; worker control as demand of, 33. *See also* strikes; *specific union or federation by acronym*

transportation disruption, 90

trasformismo (gradual but continuous absorption of oppositional forces), 10, 165n46

Tripartite Alliance. *See* Alliance

Trump, Donald, 148

Truth and Reconciliation Commission, 5

Tsakane10 (Tsakane Extension 10), xi, xvi; administrative fixes and, 86–87, 91; ANC creating hostile environment for activists in, 77; ANC support declining in (2004–2019), 115–116, 116*f*; anti-Zuma protests (2017), 147; apartheid history of, 1; attempt to coordinate with other communities, 83, 137; as case study area, 21–22, 23*f*; characteristics of, 24*t*; class solidarity with union alliance politics, 114, 114*t*, 126–132, 137; community aspect of protests in, 82–84; compared to Tsakane 17 activism, 3; DA support in, 82, 116, 127; dedensification demands in, 66; dissension between NUMSA and UF in, 127; economic conditions in, 1; EFF protests and, 2–3; fluid party affiliation and, 127; housing and services demands in, 65–66, 128, 137, 149, 150; independent candidate in, 131; informal settlements of, 1, 65, 149; KCWF formation and role in, 128, 132; municipal budget's inadequacy for Ward 84, 2; new formal housing settlement, relocation of residents to, 87; NUMSA and, 126–132; political discussion forums (PDFs) to implement United Front in, 128; removal of local ward councilor as priority in, 86; state neglect and feelings of betrayal in, 58–59; state relocation of residents to, 22, 65; UF in, 126–128, 146; unemployment in, 1, 186n80; workers at odds with protesters in, 89; xenophobia, opposition to, 109–111

Tsakane17 (Tsakane Extension 17), 2–3

Tsakane Community Forum, 128

Tugal, Cihan, 164n28

Tunisia, xii, 147

Turkey, xii, 148

"ubuntu" (common humanity), 109

UDF (United Democratic Front), 31–33, 35, 36, 39, 71–72, 170n23, 171n26, 173n66

UF (United Front), 8, 44, 126–128, 130–132, 144–146, 148, 159, 177n123, 195n18; compared to APF, 146; compared to EFF, 44, 145–146; Political Coordination Committee, 130

Ukraine, xii

unemployment, xii–xiii, 3, 45, 47; under apartheid state, 30; in Black urban peripheral areas, 22; Extended Public Works Program, 47, 178n145; local protests and, 55, 67, 89–91, 186n80; NUMSA's view of, 129; under postapartheid state, 50; rise (1960s and mid-1970s), 170n17; rise (2000–2020), 14, 15f; in Tsakane10, 1, 186n80; UF protest over, 127

United Nations' goal of cities without slums, 46

United States: Black Lives Matter (BLM) movement, xiv–xv, 142–144; Black population in, xiii; Black Power movement, 143; civil rights movement, xiii, xv, 143; civil society and narrative of racial change in, 144; clash of young Black activists with older generation, xiv; compared to South Africa, xii–xv, 141–144; Occupy movement, xii–xiii, 148; police brutality in, xiv, xiv–xv; racial hegemony and, 142; racial inclusion, limits on, xiii, xv, 143–144; right-wing winning out over leftists in, 148

Unlawful Organizations Act (1960), 29

urbanization and urban renewal programs, 28, 182n78

Vaal townships, stay-away in (1984), 32

Vavi, Zwelinzima, 52

violence: ANC threats and violence against activists, 77, 119; antimigrant attacks (2008 and later), 24, 93, 97–102, 106–110, 151–152, 188n39, 188n47; looting of migrant traders, 94, 97, 102, 107–108, 110, 189n54; of protesters, 56, 129; United States, anti-Black state violence in, xiv–xv, 143; workers trying to go to job subject to attack, 90–92

Vlakfontein, 133, 181n60

Von Holdt, Karl, 41–42

voting: abstention rates, increase in, 78; ANC's opposition securing council seats in local elections, 185n64; ANC's waning popularity (1994–2019), 75, 76f; boycotts, 170n23; OKM support in elections, 84, 120; removal of local officials through elections, 86; universal suffrage, 6, 10

Walsh, Shannon, 155, 157–159, 180n33

Ward 84, 2. See also Tsakane10

ward councilors: ANC and, 74, 76, 121, 133, 185n64; election ballots for, 191n8; frustration and protest directed toward, 88, 134; independent candidate elected as, 120–121, 125; OKM's failure to secure in Motsoaledi, 115; removal of, 85–86, 120; residents' desire for involvement of, 57, 181n48

War on Want (UK-based), 54

water and sewage services, 64–65, 67–68, 87, 133, 149. See also housing and service delivery; specific informal settlements

Webster, Edward, 159, 166n72, 186n78

Wesi, Thabang, 123–125

Western Cape Province, 78, 79

Westonaria municipality, 21–22, 66, 76. See also Bekkersdal

West Rand, 21–22, 23f. See also Bekkersdal

white academics as collaborators in social movements of the Black poor, 155–159

"white elephant" projects, 67

White Paper on International Migration (2017), 97

whites: ANC protection of wealth of, 48; capital, role in postapartheid transition, 13–14, 142; domination of private sector, 45; involvement in working-class Black movements, 155; in middle and upper classes, 45; racial hegemony and, 142; white migrants not included in nationalist exclusion, 94. See also apartheid

Winant, Howard, 6–9, 141–142, 194nn13–14

Witwatersrand gold mining industry, xii

Wolpe, Harold, 169n5, 169n7

women: ANC Women's League, 36; anti-pass-law march (1956), 29; delegation sent to police station, 3; UDF and women's organizations, 31

working class: ANC detachment from, 43; Fanon's criticism of, 18, 40; in NDR evaluation, 46; OKM engagement with, 134; socialist/Marxist approaches to end of apartheid and, 38; UF and, 131, 145; wage increases promised by national liberation movement, 46. *See also* betrayal, feelings of; people's power; socialism

workplace resistance: demands of, 30; local protests and, 89–91, 132, 140; NP measures to crush, 28; in opposition to apartheid, 28–29. *See also* strikes; trade unions

World Bank, 13, 39

WSSD (World Summit on Sustainable Development) protest (2002), 54, 179nn20–21

xenophobia, 93–113. *See also* nationalism

Xhosa, 104

Yonghong Zhang, 185n68

youth: ANC Youth League (ANCYL), 36, 43, 116, 119–120, 123; antiapartheid militancy of, 30, 173n54; clash of young US Black activists with older generation, xiv; COSAS (Congress of South African Students), 30, 32; EFF's appeal to, 78–79, 116; lack of job opportunities for, xii, 49–50, 67, 102; Motsoaledi informal settlement and, 119, 121; UDF and, 31, 171n26; Youth Day commemorating Soweto students' uprising (1976), 119

Zabalaza Anarchist Community Foundation, 118

Zald, Mayer, 139

Zimbabweans, 103–105, 107, 189n64

Zuern, Elke, 163n14

Zulu, Lindiwe, 99–100

Zuma, Jacob, 42–43, 48, 97, 120, 122, 135, 147, 151, 180n25, 195n26

Zwane, Simphiwe, 83, 133, 134–135

CPSIA information can be obtained
at www.ICGtesting.com
Printed in the USA
LVHW040153110522
718417LV00009B/1645